Our Man In Scotland

Our Man In Scotland

Sir Ralph Sadleir, 1507–1587

by

Humphrey Drummond

LESLIE FREWIN : LONDON

© Humphrey Drummond, 1969

First published in 1969 by Leslie Frewin Publishers Limited,
15 Hay's Mews, Berkeley Square, London W1

Set in Garamond
Printed by Anchor Press
and bound by William Brendon
both of Tiptree, Essex

WORLD RIGHTS RESERVED

09 096510 8

Contents

ACKNOWLEDGEMENTS

Among the many people to whom I am indebted for much helpful information in the preparation of this study of Sir Ralph Sadleir, I would like particularly to thank the Reverend Ralph Sadleir, Mrs Thomas Sadleir, Captain Michael C S Sadler, Miss Millicent Hayes-Sadler, Sir Francis Astley, Mrs May Langham, Brigadier E F E Stoney, and other of Sir Ralph's descendants and connexions who have so kindly assisted me and given me access to unpublished family letters and documents.

I am also most grateful to Mr Kingsley Adams, former Director of the National Portrait Gallery, the Staff of the British Museum and of the Public Record Office, the Staff of the Research Department of the Library of the House of Commons, Mr Bates, Director of the Scottish Record Office, and his staff, Lieutenant-Commander D W Waters, RN, Director of Navigation at the Maritime Museum at Greenwich, Le Capitaine de Vaisseau Vichot, Directeur des Musées de la Marine at Paris, as well as to Directors and Secretaries of other Museums and of Historical Societies in other parts of the country: they have all given me unstinted assistance in research which has been invaluable.

To my wife Cherry for her constant help, for typing and indexing my longhand manuscript, and especially for giving it priority over her own manuscripts, I am more than grateful.

H D

I
'I'll tak' the low road . . .'

THE FALL OF the famous Cardinal Wolsey was a catastrophe
for the great man himself, and also for most of those who had
worked with him. But, for one of them, it was the chance of a
lifetime. This was Thomas Cromwell, son of a disreputable
Putney blacksmith.

Thomas had run away from the dubious surroundings and
unhappy influence created by his father. For some years he lived
abroad on his wits. He was hard and clever. By the time he returned to England about 1513, he was known as an astute
moneylender. Such a man could be useful to the Cardinal;
Wolsey promptly engaged him as rent and debt collector.

From these beginnings, Thomas Cromwell soon became a
man of importance in his own right, himself in need of assist-
ants and young trainees. At his home in fashionable Hackney,
he took pupils into his household. This was an accepted practice. A father who could get his young son placed on the personal staff of a man of growing importance could be sure the boy
would accompany his patron on the upward journey of his
career. The pupil would hope to launch out in due course with
a powerful recommendation. A bad choice of patron could bring
disaster for the son, and trouble from which he might never
recover.

In the opinion of most people in London, Thomas Cromwell
was bound to go far. One of these was Henry Sadleir, who
rented a house for £40 a year in the more modest part of Hack-

ney. He had managed to get his seven-year-old son Ralph taken on by Cromwell in 1514. For Henry Sadleir, life was becoming increasingly difficult. For many years he had been accountant and man of business to Sir Edward Belknap, who held the lucrative appointment of Chief Butler to the King. But Sir Edward had died, leaving Henry without patron or employer. Eventually, he had managed to get an appointment with the Marquis of Dorset, a connexion of the Belknaps. This was not as good as it sounded, since the fortunes of the Marquis were waning rapidly.

Henry was installed at Tiltey in Essex, the country head-quarters and last stronghold of the Dorsets. Lack of money was becoming a serious problem for Henry as well as for his Marquis. Ralph, on the other hand, had been making great progress with Thomas Cromwell. He became his private secretary and confidential agent, and was now considerably more prosperous and secure than his father Henry. Soon, Henry Sadleir was writing urgently and plaintively to his son saying that the Marquis was cutting his staff rapidly, and that after the coming Christmas he intended to dismiss more. He could not even get paid the little amount he was due . . . 'Whereas I should have had of my Lord at this time 20 marks, I can get never a penny but fair words, with which I cannot live.'[1] He wrote to Cromwell himself, seeking his good offices in getting repayment of £28 he was due from a man called Shelley, an acquaintance of Cromwell's. Shelley had gone off to Sussex leaving his debt behind him. Henry Sadleir badly needed it towards his £40 rent: Shelley, although expected back shortly from Sussex, had not reappeared.

Increasingly desperate, Henry next implored his son to put in a good word with Cromwell to get him some office in the Tower of London for which he had evidently been lobbying. 'Good son,' he wrote hopefully, 'do the best you can for me.'

Ralph was certainly making the most of his opportunities. He had a keenly receptive brain and quick wits. At an early age he had full command of Latin, essential for an educated person of the time, and also of Greek, which was exceptional. The fluency of his writing, and the clarity and style of his prose, all point to the advanced education he received. Of any brothers and sisters, no record survives except that of one brother, John, who joined the army. He rose to command a company at the Siege of Boulogne in 1544. Apart from this brief appearance, there is no trace of him.

Ralph proved not only to be a young man of intellect. He combined scholarship and brains with great feats of horsemanship. His exploits at vaulting and galloping about on horseback were the admiration of all who saw him. Surpassing even this was his gentle skill at falconry which developed in later years to become his ruling passion and chief pastime. He learnt this from his patron Cromwell, a master of the art. Ralph was eventually appointed Grand Falconer to Queen Elizabeth in recognition of this knowledge and enthusiasm.[2]

The closer Thomas Cromwell came to the heart of affairs, and the more he enjoyed the trust and confidence of King Henry VIII, the more Ralph Sadleir saw of Court circles and of the inner workings of the State. He studied closely all the papers and memoranda to which he could get access, and was constantly assessing the motives and inclinations of the statesmen and politicians who revolved in fitful orbit round the throne. To his classical languages he soon added a fluent French; it was not surprising therefore that the King himself took a liking to this intelligent, resourceful young man, whom he frequently saw in Cromwell's company or going about Cromwell's business.

By 1530, Ralph was firmly established at Court, although not yet on the strength of the King's household. Three years later Ralph married. Unlike so many others at the time, it must have been for love. It is uncharitable and out of character to suggest there could have been any element of necessity: such matters were easily arranged. The woman upon whom his affections fastened was Helen Mitchell: her name also appears as Ellen and Margaret. A certain mystery surrounds her, more particularly as Ralph must have known how helpful a wife of some social standing could become to him in his future career. For Helen's father John Mitchell was little more than a rag-and-bone man from Great Hadham in Essex, and Helen herself a laundress in Cromwell's household.³ Ralph is recorded as selling John Mitchell a small plot of land in London, apart from which there is no mention of him or his wife. It is not clear whether Helen's association with Cromwell as laundrymaid stemmed from a closer relationship to the great man than her position suggested, or whether she was an ordinary employee. She was evidently fully accepted in the household, since Cromwell consented to be godfather to their first-born son, who died, and then to their second son Thomas. This child was named after Cromwell, as can be seen from the letter written by Ralph to Cromwell asking him to 'vouchsafe once again to be gossip'⁴ – as godfathers were then called.

It was not until twelve years later that something astonishing occurred in connexion with the marriage. It was divulged that Helen had been married before, had never been divorced, had two children living by this marriage, and that her husband was still alive. This was made public in a dramatic manner.

Sir Ralph – since he had now received the honour of knighthood – was in Scotland in 1545. In a tavern in London, a man called Matthew Barre was celebrating his recent return from Ireland. To the undoubted astonishment of everyone present, Barre declared that he was the lawful husband of Lady Ralph Sadleir, and that he had come back to put matters right with Sir Ralph. It happened that an official of the Lord Chancellor, then Sir Ralph's friend Thomas Wriothesley, overheard this scandalous remark, and had Barre detained until Sir Ralph returned from Scotland. On examination, Barre maintained the truth of his apparently outrageous claim, and announced his intention of taking his wife back.

This was such an important matter involving a man of such stature as Sir Ralph that a Commission was appointed to look into it. Sir Ralph's friend Thomas Cranmer, made Archbishop of Canterbury in 1533, presided over the inquiry, in company with four other bishops. They found that according to local records, and the fact that two children were generally recognised to be those of Barre's marriage with Helen, Matthew and Helen Barre had indeed contracted a lawful marriage that was still binding. The bishops declared themselves in a quandary as to what to do, eventually deciding that further investigation was necessary.

It is curious that Sir Ralph, before he married Helen Barre, apparently knew nothing of the existence of her marriage contract with Barre, nor of her two children. She was a local girl, and the local records were local for Sir Ralph as well. No one will know whether Helen disclosed her alliance to Barre before accepting Ralph, nor whether Ralph did have any knowledge of it. One cannot believe that Ralph would not have heard some whisper about his fiancée. It is probable that he was deeply in love with her, and knew all about her previous history. They may both have thought that Barre was dead, or had permanently deserted her, which Helen herself believed. It was reported that she had not seen very much of him even when she was married, since 'living riotously and consuming his time at unlawful games, led with the spirit of the devil', he took himself off and 'did not send to her any knowledge of his state'.[5]

She spent some years searching for him, finally, in despair, deciding to enter a convent. She was only dissuaded from this by a friend of Thomas Cromwell's, who obtained for her the humble post in Cromwell's household. At that time it is recorded that 'a man of Sarum' came forward and 'affirmed certainly' that Matthew Barre was dead. Ralph must have known of all this, since he had been in that same household himself from the age of seven. With his legal training and respect for the law, he would never have contracted a marriage to which he thought any taint might attach, especially such a serious one as bigamy.

If, as seems clear, Barre had abandoned Helen and their two children, he presumably had no intention of returning. It was only when word reached him of the grand status now enjoyed by his wife that he thought he could turn the situation to his advantage. A man of wealth and position such as Sir Ralph Sadleir would surely pay handsomely to suppress such an awkward revelation.

But Sir Ralph was not the man to buy himself out. He was anyway forced to take some official action, since he had seven children with Helen, all of whom were now illegitimate. He at once obtained and accelerated the passage of a Private Bill through both Houses of Parliament. There was a certain amount of delay in the Commons. But the Bill finally unravelled Helen's relationship with Mr Barre, set the marriage aside and declared Sir Ralph's a true and proper union. He managed to prevent publication of the Bill, and its details never appeared with the statutes of the period. The only reference to the whole procedure appears in a document entitled 'The Unprecedented Case of Sir Ralph Sadleir' unearthed among obscure parliamentary manuscripts still preserved in the Public Record Office. Matthew Barre was not heard of again. He was presumably paid off or removed in some other way.

Many attempts were made by enemies of Sir Ralph to discredit him through the awkward facts of his marriage and of his wife's lowly origin. It is commonly suggested that this was the reason for Lady Sadleir never once appearing at Court, nor apparently ever being received in the aristocratic company kept by Sir Ralph. She does not seem ever to have ventured out at all. This is put forward to explain why Sir Ralph never succeeded to the highest offices in the land and was never ennobled.

But this picture is one painted by his detractors. A man could not have reached his position without arousing enmity. The suggestion that Lady Sadleir was no more than an uncouth wench, not fit to be produced in company, does not accord with Sir Ralph's known tastes and way of life. He was devoted to his wife and all his children. 'One day away from them,' he wrote to John ap Rice on 28th September 1535, 'is like a year to me.' He loved his home, his hawks, his horses and hounds. He took every opportunity of getting away to them whenever he could, and of enjoying the quiet library and garden at his great house of Standon Lordship.

It is far more likely that he made the most of his wife's disinclination to mingle in Court society. This would strengthen his excuses for going home. There would have been many fewer opportunities had Lady Sadleir wished to be present at every party and social occasion to which her husband was invited.

She made no claim to gentility even after her marriage to Sir Ralph. She either made no effort, or was incapable of adapting herself and her manners to grand circles. It is possible she knew well enough the hazardous uncertainties of public life, and thought she could best serve her husband's interests by maintaining a comfortable home, devoting herself to the children and well-being of the family. In this she was evidently very successful. She bore Ralph three sons – in addition to the one who died in infancy – and four daughters; all of them reflected nothing but credit on their parents.[6] She ran the household of the man who was to become the richest commoner in England. In spite of the vicissitudes and separations of his busy life, they stayed happily and devotedly married until death duly parted them over fifty years later.

*   *   *

The year of 1530 was a momentous one for Cromwell and Ralph, as well as for the rest of the country. For on 4th November, the great Cardinal Wolsey, betrayed and disgraced, died at Leicester, on what would anyway have been his last journey to London.

Cromwell, his ear astutely to the ground, had heard well in advance the ominous crumbling of his patron's power and glory. He did not, as his critics unworthily suggest, immediately seek to secure his own position. He was not himself influential enough to stem the decay of Wolsey's authority : had he not judiciously disengaged from the Cardinal in adequate time, he would merely have been swept into oblivion. That would have been a triple tragedy, for it would also have meant the end of Ralph Sadleir.

As it was, Cromwell did what he could for the Cardinal until well after the time when lesser men would have made themselves scarce. The way was then clear for Cromwell, whom the King took into his personal service.

Meanwhile Ralph Sadleir occupied himself busily with his

newly-important master's affairs. His religion became a delicate blend of Roman Catholicism tempered with an adequate amount of anti-Papism. He continued to impress the King with his penetrating mind and his agility on horseback, both qualities well calculated to endear him to the monarch. By 1533 he was of sufficient importance to start drafting copies of state papers.

By 1536 matters had progressed so well that he was invited to leave Cromwell's employ and join the King's service. This was a useful if perilous step, but Ralph delightedly accepted the office of Gentleman of the King's Privy Chamber. Shrewd, courageous and confident, he seized without hesitation this opportunity for advancement.

Cromwell himself had now become an eminent figure. In this year he was created Baron Cromwell and made Lord Keeper of the Privy Seal. Another appointment gained shortly before, by which he set even greater store, was that of Vicar-General. This gave him the chairmanship over all the bishops in convocation, and an even freer hand with which to harass the priesthood. The harshness with which he pursued the dissolution of the smaller monasteries and disposed of their possessions is one of the few blemishes on his career.

His position at Court gradually appeared unassailable. In 1535 the head of Anne Boleyn had rolled on Tower Hill: the following day Jane Seymour had married the King. This latter event established Cromwell even more firmly in the hierarchy, for his slow-witted son Gregory was married to Jane Seymour's sister.

Before Anne Boleyn's downfall, Catherine of Aragon had died at Kimbolton on Friday, 7th January, a little before 2 pm. Her death deeply affected the King, but not Anne Boleyn, who put on a dress of bright yellow for the court mourning. 'I *am* sorry,' she said, 'not because she is dead, but because her death has been so honourable.'[7] It was with just irony that the spiteful woman was herself hurried to a dishonourable death within a matter of months. Had her prematurely-born son been granted life, her character might have improved, but it is doubtful.[7]

Henry and Catherine had probably truly loved each other, and their squalid divorce was no measure of the affection Henry bore for her. He wept on reading the little note she had written him from her deathbed. Had one of their sons reached manhood, their marriage might well have endured. Henry was fortunately spared the knowledge that it was their sour-faced offspring, Mary, who would one day sit on his throne.

For the next eighteen months Ralph Sadleir, now free from the whirlpool of Cromwell's increasingly numerous activities, devoted himself to the study of internal affairs, and to learning the art of courtier and diplomat.

By the beginning of 1537 King Henry had made great progress in freeing England and Wales from their ties with the Vatican and was turning his attention northwards to Scotland.

Here the general situation was not at all clear to Henry. It was difficult to get reliable news from north of the Border. Such information as did percolate down was usually adjusted so as to be sure of being acceptable to the hearer.

Henry knew that European sympathisers of the Pope were most anxious to maintain the power of the Catholic Church in Scotland. They suspected that Henry would soon bring pressure upon his nephew James V, King of Scotland, to follow suit and relinquish his country's traditional links with the Pope. King Francis I of France plied James regularly with lavish gifts, sending countless boxes of gold chains, enamels, damascened armour, rapiers of Toledo steel with jewelled hilts, furs, bundles of taffetas, silks and embroideries, diamonds and sapphires, stallions and ships, the like of which had never been seen in Scotland.[8] It was natural that James should go to some lengths to keep in with Francis. Any attempt at unorthodox Catholicism, however tentative, would soon have halted this flow of largesse. King James therefore saw no reason to emulate his scheming uncle.

But Henry was not content to take no action. Apart from a secret fear that the French in conjunction with Spain and the rest of Catholic Europe might amass an army in Scotland, for an invasion of England, Henry was keen to know how far his nephew was committed to France. He also wanted to find out how much sympathy there might be for an anti-Vatican party in Scotland, if he could by devious means stir one up.

In addition to these weighty matters, he was constantly receiving letters from his sister Margaret, widow of James IV of Scotland and mother of the present King James V, complaining of her treatment by the Scots. She was Queen Dowager, expecting deferential service and attention to all her wants, wishes and opinions. It had possibly never occurred to her that she had, in the eyes of the Scottish people, forfeited a certain amount of respect by marrying Archibald Douglas, Earl of Angus, less than twelve months after the noble death of her first husband, the revered King James IV, on the field of Flodden. Divorcing Angus in 1527, she married yet again. This time it was Henry Stuart, the louche Lord Methven. He abandoned her almost at once.

Even her son, the present King, was finding her increasingly tiresome and, at times, a positive nuisance. Margaret's plaintive letters gave Henry a reasonable excuse to send an investigator to Scotland. Who could be more suitable for such a delicate mission than Ralph Sadleir? Thirty years old, five foot eight, with his honest, open face, wide blue eyes and neat little beard,[9] he was just the man to disarm the sturdy suspicous Scots and wheedle their secrets out of them. Combined with this, his learning would surely earn their awe and his knowledge of hunting and horsemanship their ready respect. So thought the subtle King Henry, and he proceeded to brief Ralph most carefully.

His wife and family were at this time living quietly and comfortably at Lesnes, Ralph's small manorial farm in Kent. This was a place of great beauty, formerly part of Bruton Abbey, and was the Sadleirs' favourite country retreat in the early years. Ralph had been allowed to acquire this and neighbouring Fauntes as a reward for loyal service to the King. The previous occupant had been William Brereton, who had become too closely acquainted with Anne Boleyn for survival.

On 15th January 1537, Ralph clattered out of Hackney on his first really important mission, the personal envoy of the King of England to Queen Margaret, Queen Dowager of Scotland. Riding from London to Edinburgh and back in a month in mid-winter was no mean achievement, but Ralph made light of it. He wrote copious descriptions of his journey to Lord Cromwell, for whom, although no longer employed by him, he had a great affection. These letters and descriptions nearly all survive. Ralph took a copy of many of the letters or reports of importance that he wrote, and kept many of those he received.[10]

This first journey was uneventful. With a small mounted bodyguard, changing horses at the regular posting-stations some twenty miles apart on the great northern route, Ralph travelled about thirty miles a day in all weathers, reaching York on 23rd January. From here he addressed his first letter to Cromwell.

The King's religious policies had not been accepted without protest in many parts of the country. There were serious risings in Yorkshire and Lancashire, and considerable bitterness at the peremptory way the ancient manner of worship had been officially swept away. To travel through such a disgruntled countryside as a state official so far from the seat of authority required some nerve, but Ralph was never short of pluck. He cheerfully observed and recorded any signs of discontent or danger likely to threaten his royal master and reported in detail all he saw. His ability to sum up a local situation and the clarity of his reports were astonishing.

The riots and disturbances in the northern counties had died down, although there was constant rumour of new risings under this or that important local figure. Most of the people whom Ralph questioned about the insurrections seemed inclined to blame the hotheads of Lincolnshire, saying that the ordinary folk had merely done what their neighbours were doing, resentful at new scales of fines and taxes on their traditional religious activities. Ralph came to the conclusion that the gentry as well as the workers all shared this bitterness, and that there was more than a yokels' revolt to contend with. If he felt any apprehension at striking out into such disturbed territory, he gave no hint of it in his dispatches and trotted bravely northwards evidently enjoying the whole situation.

At Darlington, where he spent one night, an incident occurred which must have unnerved him a little.[11] On arrival, about six o'clock in the evening, at the lodging allotted him by the Mayor, whose duty it was to provide accommodation, transport, and, if necessary, an escort, for government officials, he noticed three or four people standing round the door of the inn. These customers had evidently been expecting him, and at once gave rapid signals to lurking colleagues. By the time Ralph had clambered up the stairs to his room, an ugly band of some thirty or forty ruffians had issued out of the dark cobbled streets. They started milling about beneath his window, armed with 'clubs and bats . . . and stood together on a plompe whispering and rounding together'.[12] Hurriedly shutting the casement window, Ralph called the innkeeper and asked the meaning of such a menacing assembly.

To the innkeeper, this scene was evidently no novelty. He explained that anyone arriving from the South was the object of much interest at the moment, since he could be expected to have the latest news about any fresh revolts or other goings on. If he turned out to be a government official, he was of even greater interest, since he might be coming either to spy out the land or to produce some new proclamation. This particular gathering was not, however, composed of a few curious citizens anxious to keep abreast of events, as the innkeeper sought to assure Ralph. For when Ralph protested that they were behaving in a very unruly way, and should be dispersed at once, the publican threw up his hands in horror.

'Even the heads of the town cannot rule them,' he exclaimed, 'nor durst for their lives speak a foul word to them.'

And when Ralph suggested catching up the gang-leaders and puttings them in the stocks for a while, the innkeeper was even more vehement.

'God defend,' he said, 'for [if we did that] we might bring a thousand men on our tops within an hour.'

The situation certainly seemed rather grim. It is doubtful whether Darlington in January has ever been a very cheerful place, and for Ralph the prospect was not reassuring. He looked like having to spend a night in a room whose window gave on to a crowd of hooligans of uncertain purpose, rampaging up and down the ill-lit streets.

But they proved to be a more subtle band, for when the brave innkeeper went out and 'prayed them to leave their whispering and every man to go home', a spokesman at once started asking questions about Ralph and his business. On being told that Ralph was envoy of the King travelling to Scotland, the well-informed leader at once suspiciously disbelieved, saying that the King of Scotland was in France. This happened to be true, and it began to sound very much as if Ralph had made up a good story on the spur of the moment.

However, by some wile or other, the crowd was persuaded to disperse peaceably and the rest of the night passed uneventfully for Ralph.

On 28th January he arrived at Newcastle, where he was well entertained by the Mayor and Aldermen. From this it is apparent that he normally sent one of his company on ahead to find out the best lodgings, and to make contact with the officials of each town. He formed a high opinion of the city fathers of Newcastle, a city which looked at the beginning of all the insurrections as if it might go over entirely to the rebels. The Mayor was at pains to explain to Ralph how diligent the administration had been in keeping the people in check and how they had gradually won over all the dissenters in the city to the side of the King. They had spent large sums in preparing the city for defence against any assault. The Mayor even took Ralph round the walls of the town for him to inspect their armament, all of which was proudly displayed by James Lawson, a loyal Alderman 'interested in military affairs'.

As a result of what he saw, and doubtless gratified by the extent of the civic entertainment focused upon him, Ralph suggested in his dispatches that a letter of thanks from the King for all that they had done would 'greatly encourage them'. It is to be hoped that such a letter was duly sent, but a search of the city records has not revealed it.

The next day he got to Berwick-on-Tweed, expecting to find waiting for him his safe conduct into Scotland.

To his annoyance, there had been some delay and he had to wait a couple of days for it to arrive. The cautious Scots, their King abroad in France, were chary about issuing safe conducts at such a time, but it eventually came. Ralph then set off on the last lap to Edinburgh, which he reached on 3rd February.

He has left no written record of what he did during his few days in Scotland, other than commenting on his interview with the Queen Dowager. She gave him a long description of her ill treatment and general complaints, and a letter to take back to her brother King Henry.

Ralph took mental note of all that he saw and heard and, his limited mission fulfilled, left Edinburgh inside the week. He made a speedy return along the same route by which he had come up, and reached London again on 16th February.

He must have been very fit to make such a long double journey on horseback in that time, and then be able to hurry at once to the King and his Council to give a lengthy verbal report.

He had not discovered anything very significant, but he had accomplished his mission completely and promptly. It was his first important assignment, and even if the results were not important he had now established himself as a reliable man on whom the King could depend for confidential reports.

This was the modest beginning of a great career.

2

The Three Queens

HENRY VIII'S PEREMPTORY treatment of the Pope's agents in England and Wales had, not unnaturally, built up resentment against him in the European stronghold of Catholicism. There was more incentive now than ever before to attempt some sort of invasion of England : apart from the huge material profit gained, any such expedition could now be given the flavour of a Holy Crusade. Henry knew this was an attractive proposition to Francis of France and the Hapsburgs of Austria and Spain. He also knew that as soon as any or all of them could disengage from their own entanglements and individual wars, they would turn their eyes on Britain.

It gave him no pleasure to learn that his nephew James V of Scotland was at that moment in France, not only getting married, but being subjected to all manner of flattery, cajolement and pressure to tie Scotland closer to France, both in religion and in politics. Henry also had taken to heart the catalogue of complaints from his sister Margaret, the Queen Dowager of Scotland, which Ralph Sadleir had delivered to him.[1]

He was determined to keep as close a watch as possible on his nephew. He decided to send Ralph this time to France, ostensibly to invite James to make better provision for his mother ensconced in draughty unfurnished Methven Castle, near Perth. The furniture had been sold from under her to pay Lord Methven's 8,000-mark debts.[2]

Ralph, while trying to assess how far James was being enmeshed by the French, was also to see Doctor Gardiner, Bishop of Winchester, who was Henry's Ambassador to the French Court. To the learned Doctor, Ralph brought a special assignment. This was to persuade King Francis I to deliver up to Henry one of Henry's most influential critics, thirty-seven-year-old Reginald Pole. Pole was a distant cousin of Henry's and reputedly genuinely fond of him. But he found himself unable to approve of Henry's divorce of Catherine of Aragon nor of his assumption of leadership of the Church. From being a close friend he had become a dangerous opponent, even a claimant to the throne itself. Created Cardinal in 1536, and only missing election as Pope by a handful of votes, Pole was at this moment in France. Under an extradition treaty between the two countries, Henry might have obliged Francis to hand Pole over: Ralph was to get Doctor Gardiner to set this in motion. But, by the time it was brought up, Pole had taken himself off to Liège, which was not subject to the treaty.

Entrusted once more with an important mission, barely a month after his return from Scotland, Ralph set off for France. Embarking in a diminutive vessel at five o'clock in the morning, he spent the next twelve hours being buffeted by the March winds and Channel seas, unable to make landfall on the French coast.[3] More by accident than design, he eventually blew into the tiny port of St John's Road, Picardy, six miles away from Boulogne, at which he was doubtless aiming.

Staggering ashore after this uncomfortable crossing, he made at once for Amiens, where he found Doctor Gardiner, the Ambassadorial Bishop, on 28th March. To him Ralph divulged his errand and handed over his diplomatic bag of letters.

He then tracked down King James at Rouen, where he arrived the very next day. Ralph was not one for losing time on a mission.

King James of Scotland had been enjoying a lengthy stay in France combining marriage and a honeymoon with sightseeing and shopping expeditions. He had arrived in France the previous September with the original intention of marrying Marie, daughter of the Duc de Vendôme. But when he got to Paris he discovered, as others discovered before and since, that Paris abounds in pretty girls. One of these was Madeleine de Valois, daughter of the King. Accordingly a marriage with Madeleine was quickly arranged and shortly took place.[4] Marie de Vendôme pined away and died very soon after the wedding, a tragic jilted figure.

With his little navy of fifty assorted ships, including two French men of war, the *Salamander* and the *Merisher*,[5] wedding gifts from the King of France, James was waiting at Rouen for a fair wind to Scotland.[6] He had originally proposed crossing the Channel and travelling up through England, which would have made a less fatiguing journey for his glamorous but consumptive bride. Henry's advisers counselled against granting permission for various reasons, chief of which may have been the fact that Henry had received no invitation to the Paris wedding. James waited until May before putting to sea, but the beautiful Madeleine, now pregnant, died in July.

Ralph Sadleir needed only a day at Rouen to acquaint the King of his business. The day was apparently long enough, for during the following month, Henry heard from his sister to say that her son James had sent instructions by letter for a more seemly respect to be paid to his fractious mother.[7]

Ralph then returned home. By way of reward he received from the King the first of a series of properties of which his ultimately vast estates were chiefly composed. These were the abbey lands of the former Monastery of St Thomas the Martyr, at Lesnes in Kent. They were not very much, and Ralph soon traded them in for something better, but at least the gift established him on the roll of recipients of confiscated Church lands. Some of them were very lucrative.

*   *   *

It had become increasingly urgent to get information about what was going on in Scotland. In April an agent was sent to Scotland, a cloak-and-dagger figure called Henry Ray. Holding the heraldic office of Berwick Pursuivant, now discontinued, Ray was described as 'an envoy more obscure than Ralph and better able to perform the office of spy'.

But, before the following month of May was out, Ralph was again trekking north to the Court of King James for a brief visit. This time he had three specific tasks : first, to counter the goodwill towards France which James was undoubtedly feeling strongly at that moment, and to assure him that his uncle was most kindly disposed towards his 'gentle nephew'. Ralph was to assure the King that the many defensive preparations which James might have heard were being made the length and breadth of England were by no means, of course, directed against his 'dearest nephew'. He wished for nothing better than a harmonious and peaceful co-existence with his 'good nephew'.

Second, the King was to be informed that his uncle, whose only thought was for the well-being and prosperity of his 'kind nephew', was apprehensive lest he should be taken in by the 'fair painted words of the priests and monks' who were working throughout Scotland in the pay of the Bishop of Rome, the Pope, and not in the true interests of King James and his realm of Scotland.[8]

'The practices of the prelates and clerks,' declared Henry, 'be wondrous, and their juggling so crafty as unless a man beware of it, and as occulate as Argus, he may be lightly led by the nose and bear the yoke of it, yea, and yet for blindness not know what he doeth.'[9]

Third, Ralph was to get James to agree to a meeting with Henry somewhere in the North. Henry intended to hold the coronation of his new Queen, Jane Seymour, at York that summer, so would anyway be in the vicinity of the Borders, easily reached by James. Such a meeting, stated Henry, 'would tend to strengthen the amity and increase the love between his Highness and his nephew'.

Ralph's missions were becoming progressively more difficult. This was the most exacting so far, and it is not easy to assess the outcome of his negotiations. He certainly obtained a half-promise from James to meet Henry at York. Nothing eventually came of it, but Ralph was not to blame for that. James was made amply aware of Henry's feelings towards Papism in general, and Cardinal Pole in particular ('the King's rebel'), although there cannot have been much doubt by that time.

James was probably glad to know of Henry's professedly tender affection and general solicitude for his nephew. Ralph would have put this most charmingly.

As an additional mark of goodwill, Ralph took up with him some modest but now unidentifiable little gift, typical of Henry's tight-fisted parsimony.

'Present him,' said Henry, 'with this small present and token, requiring him to accept the same in good part, considering the good heart and will, rather than the smallness of the thing.'[10]

Here was surely some faulty diplomacy. James was accustomed to splendid gifts of all descriptions from those who wanted something out of him. And the mighty Henry VIII, his very uncle, sends up such a paltry little present that there is not even a record of what it was. It was probably a rather indifferent pony, which doubtless looked even more indifferent by the time it had walked all the way from London to Edinburgh. But no splendid cast of falcons with golden bells and jewelled hoods, calculated to delight the heart of the sportsman King, and no gem to vie with the treasures of France.

However, Ralph delivered his messages as best he could, and returned at once to London, where he continued to rise in the esteem of the King and his counsellors and to increase his knowledge of diplomatic affairs.

*   *   *

The King's marriage to Jane Seymour within twenty-four hours of the execution of her predecessor, triple-breasted Anne Boleyn, promised well. She was probably the most attractive of those whom at one time or other he had selected to be his Queen. She was a Catholic, which would have tended to mitigate the excesses of religious persecution in the country. She was also a young woman of brains. Had she survived she might have been a great help to the King. They were probably much devoted to each other and it seemed an ideal marriage. In addition to her other qualities, she bore him a son on 12th October 1537 at Hampton Court.

In view of his previous disappointments, the King was exceptionally delighted at the birth. In the rest of the country there was also much rejoicing, since an heir born to the King held out some hope of a peaceful transmission of power on the death of the sovereign. The people had seen, and suffered too often from, the wild scramble for power while a monarch's corpse lay cooling in the palace. Henry already had two daughters to succeed him: Mary, by Catherine of Aragon, and Elizabeth, by Anne Boleyn, but the people would naturally be apprehensive about a young girl's chances of being able to seize and hold the keys of government on her father's death.

The birth of the baby Prince was not effected without the aid of the surgeon's knife.[11] One shudders to think of a sixteenth-century Caesarean operation, but it looked at the time as if mother and child might both survive. According to rumour, based on flimsy evidence, Henry replied to the doctors who asked him which it was to be if they had to make a choice: '[Save] the child by all means, for other wives can easily be found.'

However, after three days both were still surviving. The baby was christened Edward after his great-grandfather Edward IV, and succeeded his father ten years later as Edward VI.

It was curious that Ralph was apparently not invited to attend. His fellow Grooms of the Chamber were all present. Ralph may have wondered uneasily whether he may have incurred the royal displeasure at being absent from Court rather more often than the King thought necessary. At one time it seemed as if he might even be dismissed from Court, which would have been a disastrous blow. But the explanation may be that some of his servants were known still to be slightly affected by the plague epidemic which had swept London and it was thought wiser for the baby's sake that he should stay away.

Hampton Court was in an uproar of celebrations after the

christening.[12] Bands, singing, primitive fireworks, all manner of jollification, enveloped the Palace. Noisy processions assembled in the Queen's bedroom, and went careering along the passages. Doors banged, windows were flung open – and left open. Icy midnight winds streamed through the lofty rooms, and penetrated to the Queen's own chamber, bearing on their frosty breath all the tumult of rejoicing. Sitting up bravely and pretending to enjoy it all, the young Queen caught a chill. During the next few days she became seriously ill. The King cancelled a visit to Esher and stayed in the Palace to be near her.[13] But within a fortnight she had died.

It was two years before Henry could bring himself to think of marrying again. Writing his will nine years after Jane Seymour's death, and a year before his own, he left instructions for her bones to be placed beside his. In 1813, when the Prince Regent, later George IV, was digging about in the Windsor vaults during his search for the body of Charles I, the slim coffin was found lying close to Henry's gigantic skeleton.

3
'Letters for a Spy'

By the beginning of 1540, Henry had begun to receive disquieting reports of French intrigue in Scotland, ultimately directed against himself. He was friendly enough with King James, but the bar to even closer friendship was James's Prime Minister, the wily, resourceful and influential David Beaton, one of the Pope's most valued Cardinals. It was not possible to imagine a person more wholeheartedly opposed to Henry in every way. James set much store by his advice and opinions. It is not surprising that Henry therefore never lost an opportunity of trying to create a rift between James and the Cardinal. He even toyed with the idea of having him assassinated, as is proved by several letters still preserved. Beaton's eventual murder was not Henry's doing. This was only because he could not think of any suitable method.

Cardinal Beaton's power over James and Scotland was steadily growing, to Henry's consequent alarm. He determined to make another great effort to persuade James to seize all the monastery lands and revenue in Scotland as he himself had done in England, to make away with Beaton and all the Papal element in Scotland, and to assume leadership of the Catholic Church in Scotland. In short, to bring about a similar Reformation to Henry's in England. If no meeting between uncle and nephew could be arranged, then an envoy must go up again and try to get the idea accepted in principle. Ralph Sadleir was the natural choice once more – a personal friend of the Scottish

King, and well known in Scotland. At a time when the average Scotsman's distrust of the English, always present but aggravated by Flodden, exacerbated relations between the two countries, it was especially valuable to Henry to be able to use Ralph as an envoy, with his high personal standing at the Scottish Court.

His standing at Henry's Court seemed fully to have recovered the setback it received at the time of Edward's christening. For in the list of King Henry's gifts for 1539 we find Sir Ralph being presented with a silver cup. The King expected something in return for his presents: Ralph is recorded as having given him a gold signet 'with a draft therein'.

Ralph now set off yet again on the tedious journey to Edinburgh. And yet again he had to go at the worst time of the year, leaving London on 28th January 1540.[1]

His task was much the same as on previous occasions, only this time the instructions were more specific. He was to persuade James definitely to agree to some sort of Reformation in Scotland and above all to get Cardinal Beaton thoroughly discredited.

Ralph had up his sleeve what he hoped would be two high trump cards, one a positive ace. This first was his authority to hint to James that Henry was fully empowered to appoint his own successor to the English throne. The little lad Edward, born to Jane Seymour in 1537, would naturally succeed in due course. But supposing he were to die before Henry himself – and Edward did not, even then, look too sturdy – let it be whispered in James's ear that Henry was thinking about appointing his 'dear nephew' to succeed him. This would surely give James something to ponder over when Cardinal Beaton next came sidling up to 'evilly report, backbite and slander' his loving uncle.[2]

The second trump was something more tangible. The previous November, Cardinal Beaton had written a letter from Kelso to the Reverend Mr Oliphant, Vicar of Foulis, the Cardinal's 'man in Rome'. Oliphant was an agent or spy, and regular letters passed to and fro between them. Through Oliphant the

Cardinal kept closely in touch with the Vatican. The courier between them was a man called Brunstoun. On this particular occasion, Brunstoun's ship was overwhelmed by a wintry North Sea storm and wrecked on the Northumberland coast quite near to Bamborough Castle. Whereupon Captain John Horsely, Keeper of the castle, had rushed out with a body of men and snatched the survivors from the boiling surf. Taking them back to the lonely castle for examination, Captain Horsely had found a packet of letters on Brunstoun, among which was the one from Cardinal Beaton. The Captain astutely recognised it as of possible value and sent it at once to London. Here its diplomatic value was fully confirmed and it had been given to Ralph to take up with him.

The letter itself was not as scurrilous or treasonable as Henry had hoped.[3] In fact, it only urged Oliphant to make no more use of two men whom James had caught and imprisoned as rebels and told Oliphant 'to solicit nothing . . . that may in any way irritate the King's Majesty, considering the time is perilous' – i.e. there was a definite hint of a possible Reformation in the Scottish air – 'and . . . we are labouring to have them' – the two rebels – 'freed and put to liberty for the conservation of the liberty of the holy Kirk'. By 'the holy Kirk' was meant Catholicism as administered by the Pope.

It was not the sort of letter which, when disclosed to King James, would necessarily brand the Cardinal as an underhand traitor, but Ralph hoped to work it into something more sinister when he actually saw James. The surprise element, Ralph calculated, would surely shake the King into taking action against the Cardinal.

In addition to these diplomatic shafts, Ralph was also to take up another of Henry's famous presents to James.

But unfortunately, as we have seen, Henry was no expert at winning friends and influencing people by the bestowal of gifts. This time he had collected half a dozen horses to send up North. This could have been an acceptable present – some well-bred mares and stallions would have been much appreciated in Scotland, where neither land nor conditions were conducive to the breeding of fine-quality horses. But what did Henry choose? Six geldings, one of which was not even a whole horse, being a jennet, a cross between a horse and a donkey.[4] By contemporary accounts they were an undersized and ill-sorted lot. Ralph set little store by their appearance himself. He was a fine judge of a horse and evidently did not rely greatly on these geldings to create a useful atmosphere for his negotiations.

He did not take them with him, but sent young Christopher Erington, a sort of trainee, off ahead in charge of them. Sore-shinned and spavined, the motley group eventually came clumping into Edinburgh. Three days afterwards, on Tuesday, 24th February 1540, Ralph himself arrived.

Ralph was by this time quite a grand figure, carrying the full status of Ambassador. He was therefore able to collect Henry Ray, the Berwick Pursuivant, and send him on in advance to Edinburgh with one of his own staff to book rooms. But Edinburgh was rather full, the King's Council being in session and many noblemen and their attendants thronging the timber-terraced city. The place suggested for Ralph by the Provost, who was the official Billeting Officer, was therefore not up to the normal standard. Ralph described it later as 'a mean lodging in a poor merchant's house', and fully approved his servants' protest to the Provost. The Provost had done the best he could, and said as much, but suggested that they should go round the city and see if they could not find something more suitable themselves. 'If it be possible to have it,' he added, 'ye shall.'

The Pursuivant therefore set off on a tour of inspection. Before long he came across one of the Queen Dowager's retainers whom he knew, and explained the trouble to him. The Queen Dowager was James's mother, widow of James IV.

'Marry,' said the Queen's servant, 'the King hath appointed the Provost to see [the Ambassador] lodged.'[5]

On being told that the Provost would 'appoint none that is meet', the retainer went off at once to tell the Queen Dowager, who was also staying in the city. She in turn told the King, and the King straightaway sent a special instruction to the Provost to billet Ralph in a certain house in one of the best districts. That all this could be carried out in a few hours showed in what esteem Ralph was held by the Court circles in Edinburgh, and how anxious James evidently was not to give any offence to his uncle Henry.

The Provost sent word back to the King that unfortunately this particular billet was already occupied by the Bishop of Ross, down from his Highland diocese of Ross and Cromarty. An interesting comment on the King's opinion of the Catholic hierarchy is revealed by James's outburst at this information. 'I say,' he said, and can be presumed to have stamped his foot in a fury on the uncarpeted boards of his Palace of Holyrood, 'I say, in the foul evil, dislodge the Bishop and see that the house be fairly furnished against the Ambassador's coming.'[6]

Whereupon the reverend Bishop and his staff were unceremoniously bundled out, and the place prepared for Ralph's arrival. Ralph commented that the lodging was then 'honestly appointed for me, both with beds and hangings of coarse tapestry, and all other things necessary'. The now roofless Bishop had evidently not set up in any great style there. From such peremptory treatment, it appears that Henry's incessant anti-Vatican propaganda over the last few years was beginning to take effect upon James, despite the vigorous counter-measures of Cardinal Beaton and the French.

Ralph certainly enjoyed King James's confidence, which the Cardinal's men did their utmost to shake on every occasion. They made little headway, despite all manner of cunning approaches. They were indeed the only group of educated people surrounding the King. He was therefore forced to rely upon them as ministers and councillors since he had nobody else. They tried spreading malicious gossip about Ralph, taking care that it reached the King's ears in a roundabout way. They started a rumour that Ralph and his men were eating meat and other foods forbidden in Lent, and were therefore 'no better than heretics and Jews'. Cardinal Beaton lost no time in issuing a proclamation that anyone in his diocese buying or eating an egg in Lent would be burnt as a heretic and all his property confiscated.[7]

This incensed Ralph, who was still a Catholic, as was, of

course, King Henry and most of the rest of England, despite the Reformation. Only the Pope's authority had been dispensed with, not the Catholic religion. Ralph would have been just as guilty of heresy in England as in Scotland had he eaten forbidden foods in Lent, and he at once complained to some of James's courtiers about this scurrilous rumour. As soon as James heard of it – and the Cardinal's men saw to it that there was little delay – he sent his Rothesay Herald to tell Ralph that, 'whatsoever publications were made, the King's pleasure was that [Ralph] should eat what [he] would and that victuals should be appointed for [him] of what [he wished to] eat'.

Another reverse for the Papal party. Ralph duly thanked the King, admitting that he did eat eggs and white meat in Lent because he was what he described as 'an evil fish-man', meaning that fish disagreed with him. He saw no offence in this. 'For if it were [an offence],' Ralph told the King, 'I would be as loath to eat it as the holiest of your priests that have thus belied me.'

'Oh,' replied the King, 'know ye not our priests? A mischief on them all.'

Such words must have struck a chill note into the heart of the Cardinal when reported to him.

Another cunning slander spread about was that all Ralph's servants were in fact dispossessed monks, press-ganged into menial service. To give credence to this sinister report, the Cardinal's men pointed out the Greek motto which the classically-minded Ralph had embroidered on the sleeves of all his men: ' 'μονῳ 'ανακτι δουλευω' ('I serve the King alone').[8] Either as a joke, or through ignorance, the priests had translated this into 'monaculus' meaning a 'little monk', making the motto read something like: 'I am served by little monks', or words equally ridiculous. Ralph permitted himself and his associates a good laugh at the expense of the Cardinal's less subtle intriguers. He might not have detected if his leg were being pulled.

Despite these minor happenings, Ralph had lost no time after his arrival on that last cold Tuesday of February to get settled in. First thing next morning, Rothesay Herald arrived from King James to bring Ralph greetings and to say that the King looked upon him as 'one of his familiars', as he would anyone who came from his uncle's Court. He 'was not minded to use him as a stranger'.

This was a promising start. Ralph told Rothesay that he would come round to the Palace that very afternoon. The Herald was not ready for such an immediate response and said he would have to go back to see if that would suit the King. He returned within an hour to say that the King would like Ralph to have a good rest after such a long journey, and that he would send for him the day after.

Rothesay added: 'I assure you ye are right dear unto him, and so be all that come from his uncle. . . . Call for everything that ye want, as boldly as if ye were in England, for so is the King's pleasure.'

After such an amicable start, Ralph was justifiably in a most optimistic state of mind about the outcome of his mission.

Accordingly, sharp at nine o'clock next morning, a distinguished little party knocked on Ralph's door. This was composed of Sir William Ogilvy, the King's private secretary, Captain Borthwick, officer in charge of the French Royal Guard in Scotland, and Sir David Lindsay of the Mount, who, in addition to being a celebrated poet and anti-clerical playwright, was Lyon King of Arms. There was also the Rothesay Herald whom Ralph had already met. After friendly greetings, they all went back to Holyrood, taking Ralph with them for his promised audience of the King.

On entering the Palace they went to the Chapel where they found the King in the middle of hearing mass, surrounded by courtiers, noblemen, monks, priests, bishops and others. Ralph was conducted up through the throng and placed close behind the King. When the mass was over, the King rose and turned to greet Ralph, who gave him briefly the more general salutations from Henry, assuring him of his uncle's concern for his health, welfare and prosperity and generally exchanging platitudinous good wishes. Ralph handed him

Henry's letter of greeting which James opened and read at once. Ralph at that moment had no opportunity to start conveying the more delicate part of his mission, since it was most secret: James was packed about by priests and Cardinal's men as he stood there in the Chapel. He therefore arranged to meet the King again the next day and James went off to his dinner leaving Ralph in the care of Sir William Ogilvy's party as before.

Captain Borthwick then suggested that if Ralph would stay there in the Chapel he would see the Queen coming to hear mass, which she used to do privately, not in company with the King. Ralph did have messages from Henry, both for the Queen and for the Queen Dowager, and did want to see them. But it would not have been in accordance with protocol if he had done so without first obtaining the King's assent. This, he told Captain Borthwick, he had quite forgotten to do, so would wait another time. The Captain, however, offered to go quickly after the King and seek his approval. He came back in a few moments with the news that the Queen was 'something crazed, and came not abroad'.[9] The King had accordingly thought it better for Ralph to see both Queens the next day. The Queen's condition was probably not so alarming as the report would suggest. Any slight indisposition might have been so described, and when Ralph did see the two Queens the next day they seemed well enough.

After Captain Borthwick had brought the royal reply, Ralph took his escort party back to his lodgings and entertained them to lunch there. He was thus on the best of terms with these influential members of the King's household.

The next morning, Friday, 27th February 1540, Sir William Ogilvy and his friends came round again, between nine and ten o'clock, and conducted Ralph back to the King's Chapel.

This time he found the Queen, Mary of Lorraine, in company with her ladies, listening attentively to a sermon being preached in French. Ralph was pushed forward to the same seat he had occupied the day before. As soon as the sermon was over, Sir David Lindsay introduced him to the Queen.

They chatted for a few moments, exchanging the usual

formal greetings, Ralph professing Henry's 'most hearty commendations' and congratulating her on the 'good, virtuous and honourable Life between her and her husband, of the continuation whereof [his] Grace would be most joyful and glad, etc. etc.' The Queen replied with suitable thanks and messages of goodwill.

Rothesay Herald then came up to say that the King was ready to receive him.

This was Ralph's great moment, probably the most testing of his career so far. His confidence apparently did not fail him as he was taken before the King in his Privy Chamber. James greeted him most kindly, and with a conspiratorial air drew him aside into a bow window where there was less likelihood of being overheard.

When he was not rambling about his country properties by himself, disguised in rustic dress as some form of farm bailiff or 'gudeman' as he called it, James took quite a pride in his clothes.[10] On this occasion he would probably have been wearing his low doublet, not heavily quilted against an assassin's knife as affected by James VI, but with embroidered collar and plunging neckline, offering a glimpse of a well-laundered fancy white shirt beneath. On his feet were probably the sort of ankle-length boots called 'brodikins', from which will have arisen scarlet or russet tights, kept creaseless over his fairly shapely legs by garters knotted in the form of a rose. A little bonnet, or perhaps a flattish hat or cap, completed his formal attire, together with scented gloves or mittens and a handkerchief with a gold tassel at each corner.[11]

Ralph might have taken up the very smart outfit which he is known to have possessed at one time when sitting for a portrait.[12] This consisted of a close-fitting long-sleeved green jacket with broad gold bands running lengthways and merging imperceptibly into knickerbockers of the same material, like a pair of very elaborate combinations. These in their turn gave on to white stockings caught at the knee by a thin gold buckle. Fluffy red felt shoes with thin laces kept his feet warm. Round his waist could have been his narrow gold belt worn stylishly loose, a concession to fashion and not, as with his royal employer, fighting a losing battle to support a pendulous gurgling abdomen. Confining his straight blond hair might have been his favourite green skull cap with a handsome brooch at front.

But, whatever his dress, he will have worn it with an air. He started off by reaffirming the messages of goodwill which he had given the day before in the Chapel. He then told the King that his uncle's present of horses had got as far as Leith, where they were staying the night, and that he would bring them to the King after they had had a day or two to recover from the journey.[13] Getting then well into his stride, Ralph said that his next points required, by Henry's express instructions, a strict promise of secrecy from James, which James duly gave. The King must have been wondering by this time whatever it could be that needed all this secret palaver between them.

Ralph, however, continued such a long-winded preamble, perhaps unable to bring himself to the actual point, or perhaps deliberately building tension that the King could no longer contain his curiosity.

'I pray you, what is it?' he burst out, and Ralph plunged into an account of the affair of the secret letters of Cardinal Beaton, seized by Captain Horsely of Bamborough Castle.

Since this was expected to produce a shattering effect on the King, Ralph had probably rehearsed well how he would put it, in order to make the best impact. He started off well enough.

'It fortuned late,' he reported, 'that a subject of yours, being servant, as it is reported, to your Cardinal here, was by the rage and tempest of the sea driven a-land in the north parts of England, very like to have been drowned.'

What could have been Ralph's astonishment and chagrin when the King interrupted him with: 'Yea, that was Brunstoun: he is now newly come home'?

This was the first blow to Ralph's carefully prepared case. The King already knew all about Brunstoun.

But more awkwardness was to come. Ralph plunged on with his set speech: 'This Brunstoun, when he was thus on land, by chance left certain private letters and copies behind him.'

Once more the King interrupted him. 'No,' he said, 'the letters were taken from him by the King mine Uncle's officers!'

This was worse than ever. Ralph tried to brazen it out. 'Indeed, sir, the letters were found by the King my master's officers, and sent up to his Majesty.'

James must have been secretly amused at the way things were going. 'Well,' he said, 'it is no force.' He knew well enough what had happened, and left poor Ralph to struggle on with the whole prepared story which both knew to be nonsense.

Ralph developed the case as best he could against Cardinal Beaton and what he described as the 'crafty dealings of those Prelates'. He told the King how worried his uncle Henry was at the possible effect on his nephew and on the realm of Scotland of all these foreign intrigues. Ralph closely watched James as he retailed this, and noted that James 'looked very steadily . . . with grave countenance . . . [and] bit the lip and bowed his head'.[14] Some of his shafts were evidently getting home.

James then reaffirmed his faith in leaving spiritual matters to the care of the Pope, declaring himself in favour of confining his own authority to purely temporal matters.

Ralph pressed home his attack, urging action against such a dangerous influence as the Cardinal and again quoting the Brunstoun letters. But the Cardinal, one of the astutest men in Scotland, had anticipated this whole manœuvre, and had shown the King copies of the letters long before Ralph had arrived in Edinburgh. The King had been convinced there was nothing exceptionable or unreasonable in them.

In a last effort to make something of the whole Brunstoun episode, which appeared to be falling so flat, Ralph, groping about in his jacket, offered to produce the actual letter taken from Brunstoun which he had brought with him and to read it then and there to the King.

At this moment, Cardinal Beaton himself sidled into the Chamber with miraculous timing. James, at once dropping his voice very low, hurriedly whispered to Ralph: 'No, keep the letter still, we will take another time for it. Let this matter pass at this time, we shall talk of it more at our next meeting.'[15]

The raising of their voices to normal pitch again must have caused a smile to crease the crafty Cardinal's face as he leant nonchalantly against the loose-tapestried wall.

Ralph was a determined man, however, and was not to be thrown out of countenance by the unfortunate turn of events. He thought it prudent to drop that particular phase, which was evidently not being a success, and try the next. This was to persuade James that it would be far more profitable for him to take into his hands the revenue of some of the religious establishments in Scotland, which, he alleged, amounted to a great part of James's realm and were merely being squandered on the voluptuousness and idle life of the bishops and clergy. This would be a far more becoming way for a king to maintain his dignity and estate than by 'meddling with sheep and such mean things', as his uncle Henry had 'heard it bruited'.

This must have been a sore point with James, for the joke struck home. He indignantly denied such activities. 'In good faith,' he protested, 'I have no sheep, nor occupy with such things.'

This time it was Ralph's turn for a secret smile, since he knew that James had in fact a fine flock of some ten thousand sheep grazing in Ettrick Forest in Peeblesshire, in charge of Andrew Bell, the royal shepherd.[16]

Having thus seized the initiative, Ralph returned to the attack on the priesthood, castigating them as 'a kind of unprofitable people that live idly upon the sweat and labours of the poor', maintaining that nowhere 'reigned there more Carnality, Incontinency, Buggery, Sodomy, with Leachery and other abominations than is used in Cloisters among Monks, Canons, Nuns and Friars etc. etc!'[17] These were strong words to use to the King, or indeed to anyone, and Ralph must have been wondering whether he had not overstepped the mark.

But the King's defences remained unbreached by this wordy assault. With simple dignity, he dismissed Ralph's argument. 'God forbid that if a few be not good, for them all the rest should be destroyed,' he remarked, adding, 'though some be not, there be a great many good, and the good may be suffered and the evil must be reformed.'

But Ralph was undaunted. 'By my truth,' he struggled on, 'ye must weed them up by the root, as the King your uncle hath done, or else ye shall never redress them.'

The King stood firm. 'No,' he replied. 'I am sure my Uncle will not desire me to do otherwise nor my conscience serveth me.'

And so Ralph argued on with the King, trying to shake his faith in the Cardinal and his bishops, and to loosen his links with the King of France.

'There is a good old man in France,' replied James, 'my good father [father-in-law] the King of France: I must needs call him so, for I am sure he is like a father to me, that will not see me want anything.'

Ralph charged James that he was at the beck and call of the Emperor and of the King of France and of the Pope, and that he was even conniving at their plans for an invasion of England.

'No, no,' said James. 'I am no bairn. Neither Emperor nor French King can draw me to do what they list.' He insisted his good faith towards Henry on all of Ralph's charges.

Ralph finally summed up the advantages accruing to James if he would only keep closely in with Henry. At the end he produced as bait the possibility of being nominated as Henry's successor to the throne, Henry being 'well stricken in years'. Henry was then forty-eight.

For all these blandishments, James preserved an unruffled resistance. Ralph's last effort was to get him to agree to a meeting with Henry, which he had nearly brought off before. James denied that he had defaulted over this the previous time, affirming that he would be glad to meet Henry, but suggesting that the French King ought also to be invited to attend.

On a note of smiling friendship, achieved and maintained by Ralph with his unexampled tact throughout the whole of a most difficult and danger-fraught interview, the King and the Ambassador parted company.

Ralph, by no means exhausted by this lengthy performance,

then sought the King's permission to visit James's mother, the Queen Dowager.

'Marry,' said James, 'I pray you at your leisure [visit her]. Ye needed not my licence for that, but ye may boldly see and visit her at all times.'

Whereupon Ralph obtained admittance to her apartment in the Palace, her normal abode being at Linlithgow. His tact and charm were again in demand, for the Dowager 'took it the most unkindly that might be' that he had brought no letter for her from Henry.

Was it with genuine pathos that, she complained, she perceived Henry 'set not much by me', adding, 'but though I be forgot in England, never shall I forget England. It had been but a small matter' — and here a tear coursed down her raddled cheek — 'to have spent a little paper and ink on me, and much had it been to my comfort'?[18]

The touching effect was surely spoilt when she added, 'and were it perceived that the King's Grace, my brother, did regard me, I should be the better regarded of all parties here'.

Ralph smoothed all this over somehow, leaving the Dowager in a happier frame of mind than he had found her. She had told him that James was genuinely working for a closer understanding with Henry, and also that she was getting on well with the new Queen, Mary of Lorraine. Altogether she was quite cheerful by the end of his short session with her.

Thus ended an anxious and exhausting day for Ralph: he must have been glad to get back to his lodgings to rest in preparation for the next day's effort.

The following morning, being Saturday the 28th of February, Rothesay Herald came round early to say that the King would like to receive Henry's present of horses formally at the Palace on Sunday morning between nine and ten o'clock. This was at a time when all the lords and noblemen and people of importance would be up and about: by having a rather ceremonial presentation, James would be able to demonstrate to everyone how much his uncle held him in esteem. This would be a politically useful display for James, calculated to preserve the loyalty of any of his followers whose support might be waning. Proof of what great friends James was with his powerful uncle might also help to keep the Cardinal's ambitions in check.

But Ralph declared that the horses had only had two days' rest: he had probably seen what a state they were in, and was anxious to gain some time in which to make them as presentable as possible. 'It required a time to train them,' he told Rothesay; could he not bring them round next week?

'By God,' replied Rothesay, 'the King would fain have them tomorrow.'[19] The assembly of nobles was obviously dispersing that day and by Monday would all have left Edinburgh. The full effect of the present-giving would be much diminished if they waited until next week. And what is more, said Rothesay, 'His Grace would have you be with him by nine o'clock of the morning, and the horses to come within half an hour after.' So James had already got the plan worked out. Rothesay knew well how much store he was setting by the whole performance.

Ralph was equally anxious for it all to go without a hitch, and asked young Christopher Erington, who had brought the horses up, whether they were fit to be handed over. Erington told him that, if he really had to, he could deliver the horses at once. Ralph probably took this as meaning that they were looking as good as they could ever be made to look: he decided to make the presentation in accordance with James's plans. Rothesay took this message back with relief.

There is no record of how Ralph passed the rest of that Saturday. He may have been taken out for a day's hawking by one of his Scottish friends, who knew of his great interest in the sport. Or he may have stayed at home writing up his notes and thinking what he would say to James on Sunday.

However, later that evening came a knock on the door and there was Rothesay again. This time he brought a present of a useful parcel of wine for Ralph from the King. There was both white wine and claret, a most considerate present and doubtless very welcome, since Ralph was a connoisseur and might otherwise have had to rely on rough claret or some local brew. He invited Rothesay to spend the evening gossiping with him while they sampled the various bottles. From the variety of detailed information which Ralph was always able to send back to Henry and to Cromwell when he was away on these missions, he must have been very adept at extracting snippets of interesting news from all whom he met. A glass of the King's wine on a Saturday evening would provide just that sort of occasion.

But, however late they sat that night, it did not prevent Ralph being up and dressed in good time on Sunday morning. This was just as well, for the King's party arrived at his lodgings before nine o'clock. They were the same people as had come on the previous occasions, with the addition of seventy-year-old Sir John Campbell of Lundy, one of James's personal envoys.

Leaving word with Christopher Erington to bring the horses on half an hour later, Ralph accompanied the party back to the Palace, where he was again taken in to the Chapel. Here he observed the now familiar sight of the Queen listening to a sermon in French. Coinciding with the end of the sermon came the clattering of hooves outside: the gift horses had arrived. Ralph was at once whisked out of the Chapel and hurried in to the King, to whom he was able to declare that the horses sent by Henry were awaiting his acceptance in the courtyard below.

James thanked Ralph and took him into another room over-looking the courtyard. The window was flung open. With every-one possible collected together at other windows and in the courtyard itself, Christopher Erington paraded the horses round. There were loud praises and complimentary remarks, doubtless prompted by Ralph and echoed by the King, who will have kept one eye on the assembled nobles to see how impressed they were with his uncle's generous solicitude.

Christopher Erington showed them all off in turn, riding each one round and putting them through their paces in the limited square of the courtyard. Ralph gave a running commentary on their breeding, ages and names, and could have been relied upon to make this sound as impressive as possible. James's favourites were the jennet, an oddity even in those days, and a little Barbary horse. He confessed that he 'liked them the better because they be of mine Uncle's own breed'. He was perhaps trying not to look them too closely in the mouth when he confided rather wistfully to Ralph, 'If the Barbary Horse were bigger he were worth much good.' 'But by my troth,' he concluded bravely, 'he is a bonny beast, and so be they all.'[20]

Whereupon there was a general acclaiming and approving of all the horses, James enthusing again over the splendour of the gift and on the qualities of each individual horse, not forgetting the jennet. Everybody naturally joined in with a chorus of praise, and both James and Ralph must have been relieved it had all gone off so well.

Immediately afterwards the Master of the King's Household came up and told James that his 'dinner was on the board'. The King thereupon went into his private dining room where, before sitting down, he washed his hands. In this practice he was not followed sixty years later by his grandson King James VI (and I of England), who was reputed never to have washed his hands in his life, merely on occasion to have 'moistened the tips of his fingers with a damp napkin'.[21]

Ralph was left in the charge of the various lords who were to dine in the Palace that day. It was none other than Cardinal Beaton himself who tenderly took Ralph's arm and guided him into the main dining room used on such occasions. If it took the edge off Ralph's appetite, to be treated like an old friend by the one person against whom his whole mission was directed, he did not betray it. The Cardinal would have delighted in placing him in such an embarrassing position. He at least will have enjoyed the spectacle of Ralph having to make bright conversation with some of the very subjects of his intrigue. He was made to sit at the top of the table, and, as he recorded, they entertained him 'very gently'. There is no mention of the menu.

In addition to the Cardinal, there were others present, distinguished either then or later in the various factions which kept Scotland in turmoil for several decades. There were the Bishops of Glasgow and Aberdeen, the Earls of Huntly, Erroll, Cassels and Athole, Lord Erskine, Sir Walter Ogilvy, Sir John Campbell and two or three more.

The meal passed off quite happily, and afterwards Ralph was

taken once more into the King's private chamber. This was the last time Ralph was to speak with the King. At James's death two years later Ralph was genuinely sorry. They had got on well together; there existed between them a firm understanding and personal friendship which was doubly remarkable considering the nature of Ralph's several missions to the King. Ralph could not have said half the things he did to James, and in the manner in which he put them, without risking serious offence had not their relationship been much closer than that of monarch and mere envoy.

For the last time, Ralph was drawn into the window recess by the King, who started at once to say how much he wished that all those who passed between Henry and himself would retail only the truth, 'as I know ye have done'.[22]

Ralph was naturally gratified at this, and also saw an opening to start up his favourite theme of Cardinal-baiting again. King Henry, said Ralph, was often having stories told him about James, which he knew to be untrue. As long as such friendship existed between the two Kings, he was sure neither would feel disposed to believe any malicious gossip of the other. 'But,' he hinted darkly, 'I think there be some who would not have you over great friends.'

At this, James saw that the Cardinal was about to come under fire again. It is evident that Beaton had been having regular discussions with James all the time Ralph had been in Edinburgh. The Cardinal had been astute enough to foresee that an awkward situation might arise over the Brunstoun affair. As soon as the King had got news of the shipwreck and of the loss of the packet of letters (not before, however) and had asked about it, Beaton had come forward at once with copies of the Brunstoun letters to show to the King. This the King now told to Ralph, to his discomfiture. There was one last chance of retrieving something from the Brunstoun fiasco. Perhaps the Cardinal had shown the King a conveniently altered copy of his letters to Oliphant in Rome, missing out the phrases which might have needed awkward explanations.

Ralph quickly weighed up the chances and decided it was

worth a last throw of the dice. 'Did your Grace see the double of a letter that he [the Cardinal] wrote to his Clerk and Agent in Rome?' he asked.

'Yea, marry,' replied the King. 'To one that is all his doer over there.'

'Well, sir,' said Ralph, doubtless keeping his fingers crossed for the success of this last shot, 'if your Grace do see the very original, then shall ye perceive if the double and it agree.'

Perhaps incredulously, James then asked him: 'Have ye the original here upon you?'

'Yea, that I have,' replied Ralph, his spirits rising at the renewed interest he had aroused in the King over this now well-worn theme.

Then the King lowered his voice. 'Take it out privily,' he hissed, 'as though it were some other paper, and let me see it.'[23]

For, incredible to record, the Cardinal had again appeared out of nowhere, like Mephistopheles, and was sauntering about the King's Chamber with, probably, a most innocent expression on his face.

With much rustling of paper and secret looks round the curtain, like two schoolboys in fear of being found making their first cigarette out of brown paper and tea leaves, James, King of Scotland, and Ralph Sadleir, His Majesty of England's ambassador, furtively carried on their business. Ralph pulled the letter out of his inner breast pocket and handed it to the King, who took it and 'read it softly, every word, from beginning to end'. How he made it appear 'as though it were some other paper' is difficult to guess. It is a pity there was no one present to record the expression on the Cardinal's face as he casually watched the two whispering figures in the alcove.

To Ralph's supreme disappointment, the King then told him that he had in fact seen an exact copy of the letter. But nevertheless he was very grateful to his uncle, he added, for he saw by the action he had taken over the letter that Henry would not hesitate to let him know of anything which might adversely affect him. 'And, by God,' he added, 'I shall do suchlike to him.'

Some little good had perhaps come out of it all by this

protestation of good intentions towards Henry by James. But the Cardinal, the chief target, remained unscathed and apparently impregnable.

James would not hear a word against him, even when Ralph lamely kept up the attack, asking James if he did not 'perceive by this letter the crafty pretences of the Cardinal'.

'No, no. Why? Wherein?' replied James, and would not accept any censure on the Cardinal and his men. 'I may tell you, they dread me,' he added, with more hope than truth.[24]

At that, Ralph saw he could make no further headway on those lines. It was just as James pleased, and he could take it whatever way he liked. But King Henry, he concluded, had felt bound to let his nephew know about what had seemed such a sinister business affecting James's security and safety. If James wanted to do anything about it, then it was up to him. But if not, Ralph reminded him, he had promised at the outset to treat the whole matter as a secret.

James, by no means out of humour, reaffirmed his promise of secrecy.

Even the collapse of this lengthy argument did not deter Ralph from a supreme final effort.

Searching once more in his 'bosom', he produced this time a document laying down the principles and method whereby Henry had given a semblance of legality to his reorganisation of the Church at Canterbury.

That was just the sort of arrangement James should make in his own Church, urged Ralph. Before the King could protest he had started to read out the whole document to him. James's patience was running out by this time, and although he allowed himself to comment that Henry's arrangement sounded 'both godly and charitable', he was plainly becoming exasperated by the persistent Ralph. And when Ralph once more 'began to reprehend [the] idle life, vices and . . . abuses' of the Cardinal's men, urging James to suppress the religious houses, the King could stand it no longer and made to bring the interview to an end.

But Ralph was not to be dismissed so readily. After a short

pause, he raised again with the King the question of arranging a meeting between him and Henry.

King James, however, his friendship and patience strained to breaking point, could not be drawn into further discussion. Promising that he would send a reply to Henry which he hoped the King would find acceptable, he gave Ralph 'a gentle countenance, with his cap in his hand', and beckoned Sir Walter Ogilvy and Sir John Campbell to take Ralph back to his lodgings.

Even Ralph could not keep the conversation going after this. He went back with the others to pack his bags for the return to London.

He had been told that James was anxious to set off on one of his elaborate hawking expeditions into the interior, but that he did not want to go until Ralph had left, for fear he should follow him into parts of the country where he would be able to act as an effective spy.

Ralph accordingly wasted no more time. About 2nd March he left Edinburgh and arrived uneventfully in London, where he found the Court installed at Greenwich.

4
The Men of Solway

IT WAS NO placid scene of country life to which Ralph returned in mid March 1540. There was a frenzy of activity on all fronts, headed by the King's latest matrimonial fiasco. Whom a king married was of greater consequence than in later times. If his marriage proved unsatisfactory the repercussions were widespread.

Henry had been obliged to go through with his wedding to the tow-wigged Anne of Cleves, a lady of limited attractions and barely recognisable in the portrait which the King had commissioned Holbein to paint of her. At the grand parade to welcome Anne of Cleves, Henry had invited Ralph to ride out in front on a jet-black stallion, both horse and rider superbly decked in specially designed finery. Ralph wore a huge gold chain newly presented to him by the King.

Holbein survived Henry's disappointment and aggravation at the sight of her. But Cromwell did not: it was he who had contrived the wedding, and he did little to expedite the immediate divorce which Henry demanded.

Matters were not improved by the Hapsburg Emperor Charles V and Francis I, King of France, preparing an alliance of their own against the Protestant Smalcaldic League, to which Henry was now indirectly linked through his unwilling entanglement with Protestant Anne of Cleves. He became increasingly incensed at Cromwell having embroiled him in such a ragamadoglio and not extricating him at once. Little encouragement was therefore needed for the ardently Catholic Duke of Norfolk, Lord High Treasurer, to arrest Cromwell unexpectedly on the afternoon of 10th June 1540, when all the Privy Council were in committee in the Council Chamber.

The mighty Cromwell was then hustled to the Tower and held without trial on an unproven charge of treason. With what must have been an uneasy conscience, Henry signed an order for his execution. On 23rd July an amateur executioner – deliberately, so it was said, provided by the Duke of Norfolk and his cronies – hacked off the great man's head in company with that of Lord Hungerford, a notorious homosexual.

Only the previous May Cromwell had been created Earl of Essex. Ralph himself, on his return from Edinburgh, had been promoted to be one of the two Principal Secretaries of State, together with his friend Thomas Wriothesley. Cromwell had become Lord Privy Seal.

Soon after his important appointment Ralph was made a Privy Councillor, and knighted. This was a considerable honour in those days, and Ralph must have been very gratified. He would therefore have been doubly dismayed at the catastrophe which overwhelmed Cromwell so shortly after they had both received great honours. He could not have felt very secure. But being a most loyal and high-principled man, he made no effort to dissociate himself from his fallen friend. When Cromwell, as Earl of Essex, lay deserted in a dungeon on Tower Hill, no one could be found who would dare take a letter to the King which the great man had written in his cell.[1] But as soon as Ralph—Sir Ralph—heard of it, he went fearlessly to the King to ask if he could bring it. On the King agreeing, Sir Ralph fetched the letter which he read three times over to Henry. Although much moved by the noble appeal for mercy, Henry made no effort to save him, ignoring a strong intercession by Archbishop Cranmer.

After this disaster Sir Ralph applied himself most studiously to the many affairs of state with which he was now much involved. He had become a Member of Parliament for Hertfordshire,[2] probably by some form of appointment involving no campaign or bribery, which latter was not unusual. No reliable records of Sir Ralph's parliamentary speeches survive, but it is clear he was a vigorous and polished speaker, at his best in dealing with crises of a highly controversial nature. Sir William Petyt, the seventeenth-century parliamentarian, recorded in the margin of a copy of Sir Ralph's speeches on other occasions that he 'excelled in dangerous speeche'.[3]

The office of Principal Secretary brought in a useful income in the form of all manner of fees and duties, which Sir Ralph shared with Wriothesley. They also shared their parliamentary work, which was considerable. They took it in turns to attend the House of Lords or Commons, one being in the Upper House while the other was in the Lower, turn and turn about each week. As part of the perquisites of office, they had free furnished apartments, including meals, in whichever Palace the King was occupying.

While Cromwell lay in the Tower, a fortnight before his execution, the House of Convocation – the ruling body of the clergy – declared that Henry's marriage with Anne of Cleves had anyway been illegal, since it was 'discovered' that she had already been betrothed to the Marquis of Lorraine before she came over to England. The union was therefore conveniently nullified. Anne was offered Richmond Palace in which to reside, and an allowance of £3000 a year. She showed no emotion at any of the goings-on and lived happily, in some style, at Richmond until her peaceful death in 1544.

During all these troubles several of Cromwell's former associates and close friends were arraigned on various charges. On 17th January 1541 Eustace Chapuys, the Imperial Ambassador, reported to his sovereign Mary of Hungary that various of Cromwell's men had been arrested. Among them, several had been identified as servants of Sir Ralph. De Murillac, the French Resident in London, also reported this news to Francis I on 18th January, but neither of these two correspondents declared that Sir Ralph himself had been put under any restraint. Significantly, Sir Ralph's name does not appear during these few days in the usual Court attendance lists. De Murillac did mention, however, that an eye-witness had told him the following story.

He had, he said, seen a gentleman of the King's household who had recently been on a mission to Scotland, one of the men whom Cromwell had made Principal Secretary, being escorted to the Tower of London in company with Sir Thomas Wyatt, both with their wrists firmly bound.

This description, if true, could hardly have applied to anyone but Sir Ralph. But a few days later, on the 25th of the month, de Murillac wrote again to report the collapse of the Cromwell persecutions and the release of some of the detainees. On this date, Sir Ralph's name abruptly reappears on the attendance list of the Council.

Unless there was a case of mistaken identity by the unknown witness, possible but unlikely owing to the detail of his description, Sir Ralph is shown not to have escaped entirely unscathed from the consquences of his loyalty to Cromwell. The King himself may have intervened to protect Sir Ralph and reinstate him. Whatever the facts, which may never be known, Sir Ralph's career does seem to have received a check from this point.

It is a miracle how he survived, having been so close to Cromwell for so long. It is possible that he enjoyed such a close confidence of the King that no one dared start anything serious against him for fear of repercussions from Henry. The King had personally invited Sir Ralph to enter his service some years before, had known him for a time before that, and had a real liking for him. Sir Ralph was evidently a man without lust for power and never appeared to strive for high public position. It is difficult to judge whether this was his own choice, or whether some black mark lay against him. But almost certainly he preferred to be behind the scenes where the real power tended to lie. He had no inclination to be ennobled, which would have been his for the asking at some stage in his long career. He was close to the monarch at all times and amassed enormous wealth. The fact that he never bore a high-sounding title probably contributed to his longevity, since it would have been more difficult to avoid the limelight had he been obliged to parade as the Earl or the Duke of this or that.

He was a most efficient administrator. Soon after his

appointment as Principal Secretary, he set up the foundation of the present State Papers Department, whereby all the important state documents are carefully recorded and preserved. He appointed his friend William Paget, a Clerk of the Council, to be the first Registrar.

Meanwhile, Henry had married a wayward niece of the Duke of Norfolk, bright-eyed, coquettish, Katherine Howard. With a giggle and a toss of her tumbling curls, she had often romped about the Palace in the days of Anne of Cleves. The Duke, her uncle, made sure she caught – and held – King Henry's eye on many recorded occasions.

Latterly, this had not gone unnoticed by keen-eyed purveyors of society chit-chat.[4] Richard Hilles, voluminous correspondent of the time, wrote off excitedly to his friend Bullinger, that he had 'observed the King to be very much taken with another young lady of very diminutive stature, whom he now has. It is a certain fact,' he scribbled on, regretfully admitting he had not seen this next episode himself, 'that about the same time many citizens of London saw the King very frequently in the day time and sometimes at midnight, pass over to her on the river Thames in a little boat.' Nor was that all. 'The Bishop of Winchester,' he went on, 'also very often provided feasting and entertainments for them at his palace. But the citizens,' he concluded severely, 'regarded all this not as a sign of divorcing the Queen, but of adultery.'

Henry, exasperated by marriages arranged for political purpose, probably took little Katherine as his wife by way of relaxation. But little Katherine already had her own ways of relaxation. These she continued despite her royal marriage, but not for long.

The next year, 1541, Henry's sister Margaret Tudor, the turbulent Queen Dowager, died in Scotland in Methven Castle, the comfortless home of her wastrel husband. She had lived to the full her hectic life of fifty-two years. She was buried with the greatest pomp and ceremony in the Carthusian church at nearby Perth, in the same tomb as James I.

His matrimonial and political affairs being quiescent, Henry set out on a grand Progress through the Midlands to Yorkshire on 1st July 1541. There had been several risings in this part of the country, chief of which had been that led by Sir John Neville. The strong body of Papists had expected a reversal of the Reformation after Cromwell's downfall and a return to their previous forms of worship under the direct guidance of the Pope. They were encouraged in these hopes by the accession of Katherine Howard as Queen, since she was a professed Catholic. Anne of Cleves had of course been a sturdy Protestant.

But their hopes had all been dashed, and Henry had shown no signs of looking again to the Vatican. The northerners had taken matters into their own hands, restoring images and Latin texts in local churches and generally trying to turn the religious clock back. On finding that they had no official support, they banded together in a rebellious army in an effort to enforce their wishes. A small but highly trained body of royal troops had therefore gone north to suppress them. The rebels were soon dispersed and the leaders imprisoned or hanged.

It was through restless Lincolnshire and the Midlands that Henry now went on Progress, to hearten his supporters and discourage potential rebels. His new Queen accompanied him, together with some of his Council. Sir Ralph remained in London with the rest of the Council and helped carry on the nation's affairs.

Henry's tour had a good effect upon the latent loyalty of the northcountrymen. He was well received, and even presented with a gift of £900 in gold raised by public subscription.[5] This could have been either a genuine token of loyalty or an attempt by the local gentry to smooth over their past indiscretions.

While he was at Pontefract, an envoy from James of Scotland named Bellenden arrived to make arrangements for the long-proposed meeting of the two sovereigns, and to assure Henry of James's peaceful intentions. He was evidently in earnest this time, since a safe conduct pass was made out for James and his party. They were expected on 20th September. But, although Henry waited from the 20th to the 26th, nobody appeared from Scotland again, much to his annoyance.

It is evident that James did intend to come south to meet his uncle, but before his arrangements were complete Cardinal Beaton arrived back in Scotland from his latest jaunt to Rome. He could think of nothing more unsatisfactory than the impending visit by James to Henry. He therefore set about dissuading James from going. He had little difficulty in this, since James trusted and believed in him implicitly. It is curious that no word was sent to Henry advising him of this change of heart. Some excuse could have been trumped up; anything would have been preferable to defaulting and saying nothing. Apart from bad manners, it was obviously impolitic to insult Henry openly by totally ignoring the arrangements. That James was so ready to risk a break with Henry over a matter so easily altered was a good indication of the Cardinal's power over James. However close James and the Cardinal now thought their ties with France, their strategy was seriously at fault in offending Henry in such a cavalier fashion.

Henry returned to London in October incensed by James's behaviour. His temper was not improved by the exposure of his new Queen's scandalous antics. Two of her clandestine lovers were caught and done to death with astonishing cruelty at Tyburn on 1st December. Two months later, on 13th February, she was herself beheaded in the Tower of London, together with Lady Rochford, who was widely believed to have acted as procureuse for the Queen's pleasure.

Sir Ralph had been busily preoccupied with his duties at Court and the seat of government during the first half of 1542, during which year he first sat in Parliament as Member for Hertfordshire. On 14th May, family tradition avers, he was granted armorial bearings. Although no factual evidence of this has come to light, there is no reason to reject this possibility. It is most likely that he was then in a position to bear arms, and the lack of any grant in the College of Arms is not conclusive proof that no grant was made. In 1575 he applied for a variation of his arms, which is fully documented at the College.[6] In December 1569 he certainly sealed a letter to Cecil with a lion rampant, which makes it appear that he was in possession of arms legally granted to him before then.

However, at this early stage in his career, he was more concerned with the rapid deterioration of relations between England and Scotland, relations which he had worked so hard to establish on a basis of lasting friendship. He will have heard with dismay of the outbreaks of skirmishing and raiding on both sides of the Border, culminating in the capture by the Scots in August 1542 of Sir George Bowes and a band of his officers and men at Halydon Rigg, not far from Carlisle.

A contemporary gossip writer maintained that Sir Ralph was one of this band, and was duly captured with all the others.[7] The sources from which gossip writers obtain their information are notoriously difficult to check, and this snippet of news is no exception.

It is possible that Sir Ralph had gone north at this time to advise on the handling of the Scottish situation. But it is not very likely that a man of such importance in state administration would have spent his time galloping about the Borders brandishing weapons. He may have come up later when more serious operations were under way, but there is no record of this. We can only note that someone at the time thought Sir Ralph had been at Halydon Rigg, and presumably had some grounds for thinking so.

Henry's patience with James was rapidly becoming exhausted. The news of the constant Border raiding, together with that of Sir George's capture, consumed the last drop. Henry sent the Duke of Norfolk up at once with twenty thousand men. Storming over the Border that next October, 1542, the Duke, victor of Flodden in 1513, laid about with a will and devastated the valley of the Tweed.

King James was intent on giving battle at once, but could get no support for the project from most of his nobles. But Cardinal Beaton, in the offing as usual, encouraged him to ignore the nobles. Ten thousand men were mustered together and sent off under Oliver Sinclair, a roving bandit turned courtier and become a favourite of the King. His appointment as leader was greeted with no enthusiasm, obedience or loyalty. As a result, the army broke up into commando bands, James himself having been prudently directing operations from his lodging at Caerlaverock Castle, ten leagues away.[8] In the early hours of a November dawn, the 24th of the month, this loosely cohesive force descended upon the outskirts of Carlisle. Their operations then developed into individual pillaging.

The English Warden of the West Marches was well accustomed to dealing with raiding parties, of which he believed this latest attack to consist. Gathering a sturdy force of five hundred Border horsemen within an hour or two, and turning out with the promptness and dash of a municipal fire brigade, Sir Thomas Wharton, supported by Thomas Dacre and John Musgrave, galloped his men full tilt out of Carlisle.

Tearing along the dusty lanes in compact little groups, they made for each party of undisciplined Scots. The vigour and hustle of their assault soon routed the roving bands of clansmen, who thought they had been caught by the whole of Norfolk's army. Flinging away their dirks and broadswords, King James's men went scampering back to the Border in a wild, dishevelled rout. To add to their discomfiture, the tide had run high up the Solway Firth that afternoon, filling the River Esk to its banks, which they had crossed at low water earlier in the day. The bellowing and shouting of the lusty Borderers added to their panic and alarm.

The casualties were desperately heavy among the ill-led Scotsmen as they struggled about in the great marsh which lies between Gretna and the river. This march, or moss, trapped the remainder of Oliver Sinclair's army. The rout at Solway Moss was over before night had fully closed in. Among the estimated thousand prisoners, many of the principal officers were made captive and sent to London. Among these were the Earl of Glencairn, with the Earls of Cassels and Maxwell, and Lords Somerville, Gray, Oliphant and Fleming, with others of similar rank. They were to play an important part in later developments between the two countries.

It redounded little to the credit of James, who received the news at Lochmaben Castle. Although only thirty years old, he looked half as much again. His body and mind had not stood the pace of his dissolute life. He had burnt the candle at both ends – and in the middle.

Leaving Lochmaben he made his way to Edinburgh, where he stayed for eight days, 'with great dolour and lamentation for the tinsel and shame of his lieges'.[9] From Holyrood House he went to Falkland Palace, 'and there became heavy and dolorous and never ate nor drank that had digestion: and so he became vehement sick that no man had hope for his life'. Remorse, frustration, shame and jaundice overwhelmed him; he may also have been poisoned. Uncertain what to do next, he sent for some of his lords and heads of the Church to ask their advice, 'but ere they came he was nearhand strangled to death by extreme melancholy'.

Bowed down by depression, he died soon after, on 14th December 1542. But before he expired two events are recorded as having occurred. One definitely did happen; evidence for the other is not so strong. First, the news was brought to him of the birth to his wife, Mary of Lorraine, of a baby daughter, later known as Mary Queen of Scots. John Knox averred that Cardinal Beaton was the father of the child.

Second, the Cardinal, who was standing by the bed of the dying King, pulled out from his robes a blank piece of paper and some form of pen. Before James lapsed into his final coma, the Cardinal got him to sign his name at the bottom of the sheet.[10] As the King turned on his back with a smile and a gentle wave of farewell to the few assembled lords and personal servants, the Cardinal stuffed the valuable blank signed will back into the folds of his costly garments.

In the drama of James's death and the birth of a baby daughter, King Henry saw a chance of success for one of his dearest dreams – the peaceful and prosperous union of England and Scotland.

Deciding against wholesale invasion of Scotland over the body of the dead King, Henry intensified plans for the future marriage of his five-year-old son Prince Edward of England with the weeks-old Mary Queen of Scots.

5
'As goodly a child as I have seen . . . and as like to live . . .'

HENRY DIRECTED THE whole attention of his volatile mind
to the fulfilment of his plan. He was determined to do this
by peaceful means if he possibly could. He most handsomely
rewarded the special herald who came down from Scotland to
return the insignia of the Garter and Order of St George which
he had given to James, and sent him back with every show of
peaceful intentions towards Scotland.

He then conceived the idea of turning the influential prisoners
of Solway Moss to his service.[1] Calling Glencairn, Cassels,
Maxwell and the others before him from the Tower, he explained
his high-minded longing for lasting friendship between their
two nations. He was sure they longed equally for such a happy
state of affairs. Fortunately, they were in a position to do much to
bring this about, he explained. Convinced of the desirability of
the eventual marriage between Edward and the infant Mary, they
were to go back to Scotland and work by all means in their
several powers to bring it about. They were to persuade their
fellow nobles of the great benefits which would thereby come to
Scotland: they were to break down the prejudice felt in some
quarters against England: they were to win over the members of
the Regency Council to whole-hearted approval of the scheme.
Furthermore, said Henry, he would like them all to keep
him regularly posted of all events in this connexion, and to in-
form him of the various opinions held on it by all the influential

people with whom they would be coming in contact. If they undertook to do all this, he would be most happy for them all to depart as friends. They were to think this over and let him know.

Meanwhile they were regally entertained and shown the sights of London, after which the most comfortable billets in the city were found for them. Sir Ralph put up Lord Monkeith, an important leader of Scottish opinion at the time. From the fact that such people as the Earl of Hertford and the Bishop of Winchester had only commoners billeted upon them, it is apparent that Sir Ralph was living in considerable style by then.

This flattering treatment had the desired effect. Whatever the Scotsmen thought in their own minds about the marriage question, a safe conduct home laden with all manner of gifts which had suddenly been showered upon them precluded too close an examination of their consciences.

'They were so entertained,' writes a contemporary, 'that they confessed themselves never to be better used, nor to have greater cheer in all their life-time.'[2]

Headed by that turbulent exile the Earl of Angus, not a prisoner of Solway but an exile and pensioner of Henry's, and his brother Sir George Douglas, who now considered their exile at an end as a result of James's death, the prisoners readily agreed to do their utmost to help Henry. They all told him the proposed marriage was an excellent idea. Henry was delighted. On 25th January 1543 they were accordingly provided with new clothing, fresh horses and a safe conduct and trotted gaily out of London. They did, however, leave behind them various sons and other close relations as hostages who must have joined them after their capture. For generations after, their families bore the stigma of being descended from the Men of Solway.

They arrived in Edinburgh just in time to start lobbying before the Great Convention, arranged for 10th February. This was a meeting of all the principal figures interested in the government of the country, including the Queen's party, the nobles and the clergy. It was an important meeting, the first since James's death.

Future policy was to be discussed and the conduct of internal affairs settled.

There were two main contestants for the office of Governor or Regent of Scotland. There was Cardinal Beaton, who supported his claim to be Governor of the Realm and tutor to the infant Queen Mary by flourishing the 'last will and testament' of King James. This will had duly appointed the Cardinal to all the chief offices. It will be recalled that when the dying King had signed this 'will', it had been a blank sheet of paper. Beaton lost no time in filling it up with advantageous directives as to his own future status. He had then set up at once as Regent before the Convention, hoping to consolidate his position before the return of the Solway prisoners.

The other contestant was the Earl of Arran, the closest male relative of the late King, and next heir after little Mary. He was in fact a second cousin, his grandfather having married Mary Stuart, sister of James III. He was also the son of the Cardinal's aunt, and a Protestant. He was not otherwise a great character, which was particularly unfortunate when Scottish affairs were in such a state of flux. There is some doubt as to how sound he was in his mind. People at the time certainly considered him 'facile and simple – unmeet for Government', and 'not turbulent, but inclined to quiet and rest'.[3] The Earl of Glencairn, the Solway prisoner, described him as 'a bastard, undoubtedly'. This was meant literally, rather than as a general insult, for Arran's father had taken as his third wife Janet Beaton, Arran's mother, while his second wife was still alive. The divorce which his second wife had obtained against him was largely unacceptable to the stricter Catholics of the time.

However, Arran succeeded in winning a majority of votes at the convention and was duly appointed Regent, Protector and Governor of Scotland. The Cardinal was consumed with anger and determined on a course of unrelieved mischief. He won over to his side the Queen Mother who, being a Frenchwoman, would naturally favour the most ardent Catholics. He also made easy allies of all those with leanings towards France, among whom were such influential men as the Earl of Argyll and Lord

Seaton. A liberal distribution of gold and silver from his bulging treasury won him other adherents to whom the integrity of Scotland was a matter of indifference.

At the Convention, an outline of Henry's general proposals for peace was set out. The chief condition was that the little Queen Mary should be sent at once to England to be brought up and educated as the future wife of Prince Edward. Other conditions were that English garrisons should be put into the castles of Edinburgh, Stirling and Dumbarton, and that Cardinal Beaton should be delivered to London as a prisoner. Humiliating as these demands were, the Scots had no option but to agree. They also prepared a safe conduct for an ambassador, Sir Ralph, to come and discuss details. The Cardinal's fraud over James's will was exposed by one of the friars whom he had made a party to his scheme. This resulted in some loss of face and popularity to Beaton, and gave Arran an opportunity to arrest him without appearing to be acting on the direct instructions of the King of England. It took some time for particulars of the King's demands to filter through to the mass of the people. As Arran and his Council must have known, these were received with astonished indignation. The French King's reaction, when he heard what terms had been accepted, was unprintable.

It was additionally unfortunate for the Cardinal that news of one of the schemes he had been hatching with the Queen Mother should have broken at this stage. Although confined to Dalkeith, and then Blackness Castle, near Linlithgow, he was under no more than house arrest. His gaoler was his ally, Lord Seaton. Between them, the Cardinal and the Queen Mother had sponsored a plan whereby her father, the Duc de Guise, should come over from France in some force and carry her back to France, together with her baby, Queen Mary.

The Cardinal would be released and reinstated at the same time, the Regent Arran overthrown, and Scotland secured for France. Henry's arrangements would thereby be completely thwarted.

This idea thoroughly recommended itself to the Frenchman. The Duke hurriedly started fitting out a fleet at Rouen, and collecting an army together. News of this enterprise soon leaked out and was made known in London. Henry's reaction was swift. He sent reinforcements to the troops lying along the Scottish Border under Lord Lisle, Warden of the East Marches, to prevent any sudden invasion.

He then set up a council in the north country, consisting of the Duke of Suffolk, Lord Parr, and Sir Ralph, with the co-operation of Cuthbert Tunstall, the Bishop of Durham. They were to get ready a small heavily-armed but speedy force of ships, at Newcastle and Hull, and keep them poised for an attack on the French as soon as their sails appeared over the sky-line.

That winter the frosts were exceptionally hard. Sadleir's ships were frozen tight into their harbours.

'Notwithstanding all the policy and good means possible used, as well in breaking of this ice by men's labour and other-wise, the said ships be not yet gotten out,' he reported in reply to anxious enquiries from London.[4] He could, however, have spared his worried scanning of the horizon; the weather at Rouen was just as sharp, and the Duc de Guise equally firmly frozen in. By this time, the Duke realised that everyone knew all about his secret expedition and that he had been forestalled. He then wisely abandoned the whole plan.

Henry then turned his attentions back to Scotland and the progress of his marriage project. The promising start made by the Scottish Convention had petered out. Henry had heard no more from the Regent, and had received none of the promised letters and reports from his released Solway prisoners. He accordingly wrote on 13th March to the Council in the North with instructions for Sir Ralph to go up at once to Edinburgh. The Convention was assembled again, and Henry was sure that Sir Ralph could find out exactly what was going on, and why the Earl of Angus and the rest of them had stayed so strangely quiet since their return. He was to go at once, with only two or three servants, 'for,' added the King, 'in your speedy repair and sud-den arrival there shall consist the great benefit of your journey'.

Lord Parr was instructed to hold a large number of the best Border troops at Alnwick at one hour's notice to leave on call by Sir Ralph should he get into difficulties in Scotland. For his personal requirements he was given a most handsome allowance, enabling him to maintain a state appropriate to the importance of his mission. It is not easy to calculate what his forty shillings a day would be worth in modern currency, but certainly not less than £150 a week.

Sir Ralph was always a quick mover. Six days after the King had written his letter of instructions in London, he had carried out all the necessary preliminaries and had arrived in Edinburgh by the next Sunday afternoon, 19th March 1543.

He discovered that the Parliament had broken up the day before, and would not be called again until April or May, according to necessity. He went at once to seek out the Governor, the simple-minded Earl of Arran, whom he found pacing up and down in the garden of Holyrood Palace accompanied by a great throng of his friends and supporters, all trying to influence him to do different things.

Sir Ralph was warmly greeted by Arran, who must have had some difficulty in disguising the concern he felt at the sudden arrival of this powerful envoy in the midst of all the plotting and scheming.

Sir Ralph handed him letters from Henry. While the Governor was reading them, the Earl of Angus and the rest of the more important Solway prisoners came hurrying up to embrace Sir Ralph, telling him how pleased they were to see him and asking after his health.[5] Their delight was doubtless tinged with unease as they thought of the unwritten letters and reports which they had promised to send to Henry. The family of Douglas, headed by the Earl of Angus, had again become a force to be reckoned with: the Earl's brother, Sir George Douglas, was as much involved in the political intrigues as the Earl. He was also by far the more forceful character. There was considerable fear and ill-feeling among several factions, principally that led by Mary of Guise, James's widow, and the Cardinal. They were incensed that a man banished into England for over fifteen years should, a matter of weeks after the death of the King, suddenly reappear as bold as brass, taking an important part in the affairs of State, and breathing down the Governor's neck on all occasions. He had also taken back most of his confiscated properties. The Douglases were irrepressible. The Cardinal longed to find some safe way of eliminating him.

Sir Ralph cut short the Governor's fulsome welcome and came quickly to the point: what was Scotland doing about the promises of treaty arrangements? Arran assured him that he wanted nothing better than to do all he reasonably could for Henry. As a matter of fact, he said, two ambassadors were just about to set off to the King, which would surely please him.

At this point, all the nobles and the rest of the company who were thronging the garden saw that Arran was about to get involved with Sir Ralph. They pressed round at once to hear what he was saying, and doubtless to interrupt should Arran start making promises or other arrangements unbeknown to the rest of them.

This reduced Arran to silence. 'As indeed,' observed Sir Ralph, 'he is a man of no long communication or great discourse.'[6]

The Governor then brought the short interview to an abrupt end, saying that he thought his visitor should go and get some rest after such a long journey. He would see him the next day.

Sir George Douglas and one or two friends escorted Sir Ralph back to his lodging. Chatting in a friendly way as they went along, Sir Ralph as usual did not miss the opportunity of sounding his companions for some unofficial information about the recent Parliament. Sir George told him all he could, being evidently on the best of terms. There had been general agreement among everyone present, he reported, 'although in the beginning,' he said, 'one began to grin at another, yet there was none that would bite'.[7] They had realised it was a question of United We Stand, Divided We Fall.

When they reached the lodging, Sir Ralph invited him in for a more private talk. Sir George readily agreed: he even appeared anxious to talk to Sir Ralph. He maintained at once that he had been working as hard as he could to carry out the King's instructions, and in his own opinion had not done too badly, considering the enormous difficulties.

'I slept not three hours in one night these six weeks,' he added, as if to prove the measure of his zeal.

The chief difficulty, he explained, was that many influential men were thoroughly opposed to any of the King's proposals even to the extent of nearly joining up with the Cardinal's party and setting up a separate Parliament at Perth.

He himself had prevented this, he said, and had got the Governor to send all the nobles an express command to attend the Edinburgh Parliament under threat of treason. As a result of his splendid efforts, he went on, the whole Parliament had agreed honourably together that the marriage should eventually take place, and that Scotland and England should be friends for ever.

This glowing report made little impression on Sir Ralph, the seasoned diplomat and negotiator. That was all very well, he replied in effect, but what happened to the rest of the Solway men, with all the regular letters that they were supposed to be sending?

His brother and he, said Sir George, had written from time to time, and given all the news, but many of these others were a poor lot at the best of times, and would never anyhow have been able to keep their promises, even though some of them meant well.

'The rest,' he declared, 'are mean men, and the others that be of any power are slipped and gone, so that there is no hold of them – specially the Earl Bothwell: [he] is the worst that may be.'[9]

But as long as they could keep a good hold on the Governor, he went on, they could make themselves stronger than all the others. Many friends were joining them all the time, he concluded optimistically.

Sir Ralph was still unimpressed. It did not look to him as if things had been going at all satisfactorily. He hoped the envoys who were shortly going down to the King were fully authorised to negotiate.

'Well, Mr Douglas,' he said at last, '. . . if your ambassadors should now come with mean things, not agreeable to His Highness, ye know what may ensue thereof!'[10]

And with this sinister observation Sir Ralph fixed his blue eyes steadily on Sir George.

This put Sir George on the defensive. He protested that everything would be all right, and had been thoroughly agreed. The Governor was virtually under his influence, he claimed.

'I have so insinuated myself with the Governor, that I am in chief credit with him.' What is more, he went on, 'I have caused him pull down the Cardinal who was . . . chief enemy to the King's purposes.' But things must be done bit by bit, he said, adding that he had 'brought the said Governor also wholly to the King's Majesty's devotion . . . and clean altered him from France'.

It had also been suggested, he said, that, to begin with, Henry should appoint a small group of men and women of good standing to be with the baby Queen for her general education and upbringing, until she was nearer time for marriage. It would be no good at all trying to take her into England at present, he said. No one would agree to such a suggestion.

'There is not so little a boy,' he added vehemently, 'but he will hurl stones against it, and the women will handle their distaffs.'[11] If the plan were insisted upon even after this weighty threat, the whole country would be opened wide to France, whose army would be invited over without delay. This would precipitate the use of force on both sides, whereas by patience and caution, he claimed, the whole thing might be concluded peacefully.

Sir Ralph was not convinced, and made arrangements to see the Earl of Angus the next morning. After supper that same evening, when Sir George Douglas had gone home, Lord Somerville – another of the Solway men – arrived at Sir Ralph's lodging to give his version of what had transpired. He was more cautious than Sir George.

'Things [have] not succeeded in all points,' he said. Otherwise the story was much the same. Not only had the Earl

Bothwell slipped away from their party but he now called them the 'English Pensioners',[12] a joke which obviously riled them all considerably. Lord Fleming was 'not all the best', he said, 'but the Earl of Angus, though he be too much led and directed by his brother George, was perfect good and assured'.

About the rest of his colleagues he was less flattering.

The next morning Sir Ralph duly met the Earl of Angus, together with the Earl of Glencairn, with whom he talked both separately and together. They both made various excuses why they had not been able to do all that they had promised the King, the Earl of Angus claiming that '[my] friends came not in to [me] at the first'. They both assured Sir Ralph of their fervent goodwill, declaring they would fight to the end for Henry against any French invasion and reaffirming their belief that everything would work out all right in the end. The Earl of Angus added that he thought 'to be every day more and more able to serve His Majesty, as I shall ever be a true Englishman and faithfully serve the King's Majesty, while I live, to the uttermost of my power'.[13]

After further talk, and giving information to Sir Ralph about the state of the various strategic castles, the two 'English Pensioners' went away.

But in the afternoon the Earl of Glencairn came back to escort Sir Ralph to his promised second meeting with the Governor. The Earl launched into another personal apologia, and said that he wished he were with the King so that he could explain everything personally. Sir Ralph astutely suggested that he put it all down on paper, which the Earl did there and then. But, not being much of a scribe, the Earl's effort was quite illegible and 'he prayed me to write it out again', reported Sir Ralph, which he did and sent it off at once to the King.[14]

When Sir Ralph was eventually brought to the Governor, Arran was most solicitous. Sir Ralph explained again the gist of Henry's plan, adding that he hoped the ambassadors to London were fully briefed and authorised to conclude the arrangements.

The Governor changed the subject abruptly, saying that he had heard the King wanted the Cardinal delivered up to him. Ralph reaffirmed that the Cardinal was, in his opinion, a menace to the peace of the realm.

'By God,' Arran burst out, 'he shall never come out of prison whilst I have mine own will, except it be to his further mischief.'

Within a week, however, the Cardinal had been allowed to saunter back to his stronghold at St Andrews, a handful of gold coins having encouraged Lord Seaton, his gaoler, to turn a blind eye.

After these few words the Governor went in to the Council which was assembled in a nearby room, leaving the Earl of Cassels to keep Sir Ralph company. This was another man of Solway, and Sir Ralph had a few questions for him, too.

In a short time, Sir George Douglas emerged inviting Sir Ralph to come into the Council. He accordingly went into the Chamber where he 'found a great number of noblemen and others at a long board, and divers standing, but not one Bishop nor priest among them'.[15] Arran gave him a seat beside him, and the Earl of Huntly then invited Sir Ralph to address the Council.

Sir Ralph went briefly over the now well-worn ground of Henry's proposals, saying the King had sent him up to stay in Scotland in order to be ready at all times to assist them in any of their deliberations concerning England. If the Lords of the Council felt like telling him what instructions they had given their two ambassadors due to leave so shortly for Henry's Court, he would be glad to 'assist them with [his] poor advice'. He felt this would be beneficial to both sides, and hoped that the ambassadors had been given ample authority.

This evidently took the Council by surprise. Being unable to decide what to do, they asked Sir Ralph to leave the room whilst they had a discussion. On his return, they assured him the ambassadors were amply briefed. They were not prepared to tell what instructions had been given the envoys, from which Sir Ralph rightly deduced that their instructions were inadequate and that their mission was bound to be a failure.

When the meeting broke up, Sir Ralph went back to his lodgings to write up his dispatches for the day. After nightfall, who should arrive but that home-spun hero the third Earl of

Bothwell, coiner of the happy phrase 'English Pensioners' and branded by them as having 'slipped away' on his return to Scotland. This was Patrick, known as The Fair Earl, and father of the better-known James who married Mary Queen of Scots. His carefully worded excuses as to why he had defaulted on his promises to Henry must have sounded a little naïve to Sir Ralph – how everything had been so different when he got back, and how he could not get on with the Governor, but that he would not fail to keep all his promises, unlike those other 'mean personages'.

He confided that several people at the Parliament that afternoon had in fact been in favour of disclosing the ambassador's instructions to Sir Ralph. Sir Ralph pricked up his ears at once, and asked if he 'might be so bold to know who they were who would not have [him] made privy to [the instructions]'. Bothwell neatly side-stepped this and took his leave, assuring Sir Ralph that everything would come out all right in the end.

No sooner had the door banged shut than it opened again to admit the Earl of Glencairn bringing further written assurances of his loyal devotion to Henry. Following closely upon this, however, came a plea from the Earl that his son, who had been left in London as a hostage, should be sent home. His father's affairs were in difficulties without the son, in addition to which the hostile Earl of Argyll, a neighbouring landowner, was taking full advantage of the absence of father and son. Sir Ralph evidently knew the son and held a high opinion of him, there being 'few such Scottish in Scotland, both for wisdom and learning and well dedicate to the truth of Christ's word and doctrine'. This rider by Sir Ralph undoubtedly procured the young man's release from the household of the Earl of Westmorland by whom he was being loosely detained.

Sir Ralph received no more visits that night from any of the English Pensioners. Indeed, they appear to have made themselves scarce, possibly not being anxious to submit to Sir Ralph's penetrating enquiries.

The next day, 23rd March 1543, the Scottish ambassadors,

with all the inadequacies of their instructions, were supposed to be setting off for London. But, discovering that a religious festival intervened, they delayed another two days before getting on the road.

Ten days after his inconclusive meeting with the Scottish Parliament, Sir Ralph took horse to the Palace of Linlithgow, twelve miles from Edinburgh, in company with Sir George Douglas and some others. Here he had an appointment with Mary of Guise, the Queen Dowager as she was known at the time, widow of James V and mother of the infant Mary Queen of Scots.

Only twenty-eight years old, but already an accomplished intriguer and plotter, the young Queen added good looks and a polished cosmopolitan charm to her skill as a negotiator. Yes, she considered the proposed marriage of her little daughter to Prince Edward an excellent plan. How lucky she herself was, to have a daughter whose safety and well-being were so splendidly assured. How fortunate for the prosperity of the realm, how beneficial the arrangement for everyone; the Parisian diplomat smiled her wholehearted approval of everything.

A lesser man than Sir Ralph might have been excused for taking his departure convinced that the Queen Dowager was entirely on Henry's side, and that any whispers to the contrary were malicious gossip. But Sir Ralph had also been to France, and was well versed in the ways of diplomacy, apart from being a very perceptive judge of character. Mary's unqualified approval of all these difficult problems merely set him on his guard. She continued by trying to throw doubt on the Governor's integrity and reliability in Sir Ralph's eyes. She told him that the Governor and his parliament were quite determined not to allow the little girl to be taken to England. In this she was proved right.

But her motives were probably more dislike of Arran's faction fostered by the Cardinal's hatred of it than a desire to keep Sir Ralph helpfully informed. She had, of course, no sympathy for Arran. She even said that he would certainly not let the marriage take place because he fancied his own son as a husband for the infant Queen. She then went on to deny two things, at least one of which Sir Ralph would have known to be true. The first was that Mary had been toying with the idea of marrying the Earl of Lennox, a leading member of the French faction and as anti-English as possible at that time. The second was that her father had ever thought of preparing ships in which to sail against England via Scotland. Since Sir Ralph had so recently been busy preparing counter-measures against this very expedition, he will doubtless have made a private note to treat all her statements with considerable reserve.

Thinking she was making good headway with Sir Ralph, she then said in an off-hand way: 'The Cardinal, if he were at liberty, might do much good. . . .'[16] It would have been a triumph for her had she been able to get Sir Ralph to sponsor his release.

Sir Ralph merely replied that he thought exactly the opposite. His professional charm prevented any unpleasantness clouding the conversation.

She next returned to the subject of the Governor, implying that her daughter was not safe from Arran, who was the next heir, and that the little girl would indeed be safer with Henry. She felt Arran was paving the way for the baby's sudden death which could be put down to ill-health.

'He said,' she declared, 'that the child was not like to live', being too delicate. 'But you shall see whether he saith true or not.'

And she took Sir Ralph up to the nursery to show him the three-month-old baby.[17] The nanny was told to take all the child's clothes off, whereupon she was displayed naked and shivering. Some imagination was probably needed to picture her as the beautiful young woman into which she grew. Sir Ralph's powers of imagination were equal to it, and he declared to Henry that 'it is as goodly a child as I have seen of her age, and as like to live, with the Grace of God'.

He then left the Queen Dowager and prepared to return to Edinburgh. But before he left she called Sir George Douglas into her privately: he had not been present when she was talking

74

to Sir Ralph. After a short time Sir George came out and they set off home. On the way Sir George divulged that the Queen Dowager had asked him whether he thought the baby ought to be sent to England or not. She was very against it herself, she told him, because it was too far for such a little girl. She had added that she was in fact quite opposed to all Henry's ideas.

Sir Ralph was not over-surprised to hear this interesting information. The young Queen Dowager had not deceived him in spite of the expert act which she had put on.

His suspicions were also roused about Sir George Douglas himself. For on the previous morning Sir Ralph had been told that Cardinal Beaton was at liberty again at St Andrews. He now asked Sir George whether this was true.

Douglas replied that, by his faith, he could not tell, but if he was in fact at St Andrews he was in 'as sure a prison there as any place in Scotland'. Compromising his assertion of ignorance of Beaton's whereabouts, Sir George went on to reveal his previous knowledge of a plan to let the Cardinal back to St. Andrews. 'And yet,' he went on, 'he shall not tarry thither long, but as soon as they [the Governor and Lord Seaton] have [the Cardinal's] house and goods in their hands . . . he shall be conveyed to Tantallon.' This was an almost impregnable stronghold of the Earls of Angus and the rest of the Douglases, on the coast three miles from North Berwick.

Bearing in mind the Governor's strong promises about never letting the Cardinal out 'unless it were to his further mischief' Sir Ralph was naturally a little confused about the whole matter. He was now thoroughly suspicious of all his informants, and realised that he could rely on nothing he had been told by anybody during the last few days.

'Thus your Majesty may perceive,' he wrote to Henry that night after trying to make sense of the whole situation, 'that some juggling there is, which with the grace of God a little time shall reveal to your Majesty.' His letters took an average of only four days to reach the King from Edinburgh.

In order to assist in the interpretation of all these events, and on the chance of discovering occasional confidential information,

Sir Ralph had suggested that Henry should ask Arran to give the office of Governor's secretary to a man called Drummond who had been acting as his courier between Edinburgh and London. It was hardly to be expected that the Governor would take such a nominee into his close personal service. When he read Henry's letter asking him to take Drummond on, the Governor replied that he was 'right sorry' to have to disappoint the King, since he had already appointed a Mr Henry Balnaves to that office. A curious illustration of how well informed Sir Ralph was in all the Governor's affairs is shown by his report to Henry in which he said that he 'commended much [to the Governor] the wisdom and qualities of the said Mr Drummond', although he 'knew well enough . . . that the office was gone . . . before the arrival here of the said Drummond'.[18]

The Governor, with whom Sir Ralph was chatting of this and that, then changed the subject, asking him 'how he had liked the old Queen and the young Queen'.

Sir Ralph answered non-committally that he 'liked them both well'. Arran would readily have passed on any unguarded comment. Sir Ralph then slyly said that he thought the young Queen 'a very goodly child *and like to live*'.[19] He added the '*like to live*,' he said, 'to hear what he [the Governor] would say, because I had heard before, both by the Queen Dowager, and otherwise, that he was of a contrary opinion!'

Arran was heir presumptive to the little Queen; if any mischance befell her, he would himself be King. However, he did not fall into the trap and show his inner feelings. He merely agreed, his face probably as near a mask as the ever-twitching muscles would allow. Dappled with beads of sweat, a tiny drool of saliva constantly seeking a landfall on his doublet, the Regent may not have presented a very attractive appearance in moments of conversational stress.

He reiterated his sincerity and strength of purpose over the question of the marriage, although, he said, he could do nothing alone: such decisions were made by Parliament. Anyway, he added, 'if I had not earnestly minded that the King's Majesty should have the marriage of our young Queen I could have had a contract between her and my son passed or established by this Parliament, wherein I am sure no man would have been against me'.

Sir Ralph's constant suggestion that the Governor was perhaps not heart and soul on the side of the King at last goaded him to a point of exasperation. The King should certainly be friendly to me, he added in effect, 'for I have had mickle cumber among the Kirk-men for his sake'.[20] By this, he intended to convey that he had been put to a great deal of trouble and unpleasantness by the Cardinal's faction on account of his show of adherence to Henry.

He was evidently restraining his temper as best as he could: Sir Ralph could be very provocative, although in the politest of ways, as was seen during his conversations with James V three years earlier.

As for the marriage and other questions, Arran went on, everything could perfectly well be left to the ambassadors who were at that moment with Henry. Within twenty days he expected to hear from them, and they would then know how matters stood. And he returned to the attack, asking Sir Ralph how Henry was getting on in his relations with France.

Sir Ralph said diplomatically that as far as he knew all was well. An ambassador from France had just arrived at Henry's Court, so everything must be all right.

They soon got on to the subject of the Cardinal, who was never very far from Sir Ralph's thoughts, nor indeed from the Governor's. Arran again maintained that he had allowed Beaton to be taken to St Andrews 'for a policy', so that the Cardinal's castle of St Andrews should fall into the Governor's hands. 'He is in as sure prison in his own house, and as strongly looked unto as he was before.' This was not, as Sir Ralph knew, saying very much. Arran 'could not put him in a stronger place in all Scotland', added the Governor, more to comfort himself by a fantasy than by way of stating a fact. 'Were he at liberty,' he went on, 'I should surely go to the fire as, when the King lived, he [the Cardinal] told him I was the greatest heretic in the world.'[21]

After this bout with the Governor, Sir Ralph sought out the Earl of Angus and put some awkward questions to him. Chief among these was: how did he reconcile the appointment of a Governor with all the promises he and the Solway men had made about the future direction of Scotland's affairs? 'He was much perplexed,' noted Sir Ralph with some satisfaction, 'and could almost say nothing to it.'

Give them a little time, prevaricated the Earl, and everything would work out right.

Sir Ralph had heard this suggestion before: he was no more impressed by it than on previous occasions. He said he was surprised that one having such a close interest in the succession to the throne as the Governor himself should be appointed custodian of the little Queen. Angus revealed that Parliament had appointed eight people to be her tutors and bodyguard, of whom two were always to be with her.

Sir George Douglas, the Earl's youngest brother, then appeared. Sir Ralph tackled him on the question of the appointment of a Governor being inconsistent with promises given to Henry. Sir George lightly brushed that aside, saying that he himself had made no promise about it, and that those who had were quite unable to keep them.

When Sir Ralph told him that he felt sure Henry would want the young Queen in safe keeping in England, Sir George said that if the ambassadors reported Henry adamant about this, he would go down himself to the King if there were any chance of making a satisfactory agreement. 'But,' he added, 'I will not go to my master with an unpleasant message.'[22] He would only go if there were solid grounds for agreement.

Sir Ralph then went back to his lodgings with the Earl of Cassels and Lord Somerville. To these also he put the same complaints. They maintained that they had only promised to do what they could: they had in fact done all within their power. They were equally sure the Governor was in earnest about the marriage proposal, and added that they thoroughly agreed that the young Queen should be put into Henry's keeping. They had told everybody that Henry would certainly not conclude a peace if she were not delivered up. But what were their two voices among so many? They had resolved to await the ambassadors' report; they would then see what they could do to meet any objections that Henry might have declared.

Sir Ralph had formed a good opinion of these two men. 'I take them both to be very plain and true Gentlemen to your Majesty,' he decided, 'but I fear their power, as far as I can perceive, accordeth not with their good wills.'

On his way out, Lord Somerville whispered to Sir Ralph that if Henry held out, he would be bound to get all he wanted. Scotland was in no fit state to maintain a war.

Sir Ralph then enquired for more of the defaulting men of Solway, and others of the 'English' party, but discovered they were all out of Edinburgh. There was nothing to do but wait until they came in to the capital.

Meanwhile, word had reached him from the Sheriff of Ayr that the Earl of Lennox was about to return from France to take a hand in home affairs. This twenty-seven-year-old 'plain-hearted and credulous' Adonis eventually became son-in-law of the Earl of Angus and Margaret Tudor through his marriage in 1544 with Margaret Douglas. He had hoped to marry the Queen Dowager and to lead the French faction in Scotland. On these two suppositions he was now preparing to return home from France, where he had become a naturalised Frenchman.

When Sir Ralph gave the Earl of Angus and his brother George this information, they declared they would do all they could to resist him. Since he would be a dangerous rival to the Governor himself, they asked Sir Ralph to arrange for English ships to intercept him at all costs. They would be very grateful, they said, as would the Governor. Sir Ralph did not commit himself on this, but went off to interview the Earls of Huntly and Murray. He found them ostensibly in agreement with the proposed marriage, although doubtful how it could be brought about. They suggested that a marriage contract, made now, might give the best chance of success. They would do what they could to help, but were not optimistic about their own contribution.

Sir Ralph found the twenty-nine-year-old Earl of Huntly 'a

jolly young man, and of a right good wit'.[23] His opinion was not shared by Sir George Douglas, who described him as 'the falsest and wiliest young man in the world'. He had been brought up by the Earl of Angus with James V, who was only two years older. Victor of Halydon Rigg the year before, he subsequently led a turbulent life, which culminated in lying unburied, for three years after his death, at the Bar of Parliament, while an Act of Attainder was passed against him.[24]

He was already a young man of character, as Sir Ralph was quick to note, and 'far more frank than the Earl of Murray'. The latter, Sir Ralph gloomily observed, 'was a great Beadsman, and noted here to be a good Papist, wholly given to the old ceremonies and traditions of Rome'. Forty-three years old, a former tutor of James V and a close associate of the Cardinal's, Murray, mumbling over his rosaries, was a poor companion to the lively Huntly.

Next on Sir Ralph's visiting list was Earl Marischal, a Privy Councillor at the time. On his death in 1581, he was accounted the richest Scotsman of his time. He seemed 'a goodly young gentleman, well given to your Majesty, as I take him', Sir Ralph reported guardedly to Henry. But he was against the Queen leaving the country until she was of the lawful age to marry.

From this, Sir Ralph realised that they all had the same deep-rooted objection to their young Queen leaving the country while still a child. They would have no objections to the two countries being joined together by her marriage to the English Prince when she became old enough. But taking her away before then would, they feared, mean the loss of their national sovereignty and freedom which they held dear above all else. This was to be the stumbling block which thwarted Henry's plans. Over a hundred and sixty years were to pass before the peaceful union of England and Scotland became a fact.

6

The Queen and the Cardinal

KING HENRY VIII had many virtues, but patience was not one of them. He was exasperated by the uncertainty of affairs in Scotland and what he considered the double-dealing of his 'Men of Solway'. The tone of his instructions to Sir Ralph became increasingly irritable: a firmer hand altogether was to be taken in all his dealings. He was to visit the Queen Dowager again and see what she had to say this time. He was to tell whatever nobles could be tracked down of the King's general dissatisfaction and, if necessary, 'allure them with promises and rewards' to speed up arrangements for the marriage alliance and a general peace. But he was also to let it be known that Henry was making considerable preparations on the Borders for the powerful enforcement of his plans 'in case these promises, gentle handling and reasonable communication take not effect!' Since this last threat was no idle one, Sir Ralph was to show the actual instructions to anyone who doubted Henry's serious intentions.

Henry was fully aware of the difficult nature of the negotiations. His dissatisfaction was by no means extended to his ambassador, whom he commended for his 'discreet comportment and ingenious pregnancy',[1] a compliment which at first sight reads curiously today. The King's 'hearty thanks' were accorded Sir Ralph throughout his mission. Sir Ralph's next step, on receipt of these more vigorously worded instructions, was to send as usual for Sir George Douglas, with whom to discuss them.

Sir Ralph had been dourly amused to receive a message from

Cardinal Beaton by one of his chaplains, which had been delivered to Sir Ralph's landlord, himself also a priest. The message read that the Cardinal, being again at liberty, 'would be glad
to welcome [me] into the country, offering his lawful service
unto the King's Majesty'. This was understandably 'not a little
to my marvel',[2] as Sir Ralph observed. Only a day or two before,
the Governor had vowed to keep the Cardinal under lock and
key, only removing him 'to his greater mischief'. And now the
Cardinal was residing comfortably at home in St Andrews, issuing belated messages of welcome to Scotland to Sir Ralph. In
addition to this, he was even offering his services to Henry, to
whom everyone knew he was implacably opposed in every way.

Sir Ralph blandly observed to Sir George that he 'perceived
the Cardinal was now at liberty'. What had he to say about that?

Sir George was caught off his usual diplomatic balance.
Flying into a rage, he inveighed against the Governor, calling
him among other things 'the most wavering and unstable person
in the world . . . altered and changed with every man's flattery
and fair speech'. He had conveniently ignored the fact that it
was usually the fair speech and flattery of Sir George Douglas
which made the Governor so unstable. The Earl of Huntly next
fell under Sir George's lash: he was accused of persuading
Arran to remove the Queen Dowager and the little Queen Mary
to Stirling from Linlithgow. The Earl, declared Sir George, was
working for the Governor's 'overthrow and utter confusion.
But,' he went on, and was observed to give a triumphant grimace,
'I have changed the whole purpose and have said my mind at
large to the said Earl.' By this it was implied that Huntly's
plans had been set at naught.

That sounded all very well, said Sir Ralph, noting that Douglas 'seemed to be in great heat'. But what had actually happened
to the Cardinal?

Again Sir George, according to his own estimation, had risen
splendidly to the occasion. A document, he said, had been prepared authorising the Cardinal's complete release and was lying
on a desk awaiting the Governor's signature. 'I did tear [it] in
pieces,' he answered, 'and went to the Governor with one of the

pieces in my hand [and] declared my mind plainly [to him] .... And with such like words I changed him again clearly from that purpose.'³ Under Sir Ralph's sceptical scrutiny, Sir George did not wait for any admiring approval but at once suggested that he should rush off and tell the Governor of the King's menacing new instructions to Sir Ralph.

There would be no point, he added, in saying anything to Arran about getting the Cardinal sent down to England since the Governor would be bound not to agree. Also, it would only engender suspicion in him.

That was nonsense, replied Sir Ralph. There was nothing in such a suggestion which could possibly engender any suspicion. But Douglas was adamant. Sir Ralph accordingly sent him off but made a mental note to raise the matter with the Governor on the first possible occasion. He had realised some time before that his Scottish friends were perhaps not entirely frank with him on all occasions, and that their vehemently expressed intentions were liable to remain no more than vehement expressions.

Meanwhile, the Queen Dowager herself had written asking Sir Ralph to pay her another visit. She particularly requested him not to bring with him the same companions as he had brought the last time. These had been the disreputable Lord Methven, Lord Ochiltree with James Stewart, possibly his son, and the ubiquitous Sir George Douglas. She wanted a private discussion with Sir Ralph: she knew well enough that such a thing would be impossible with Sir George anywhere in the vicinity.

Sir Ralph accordingly replied that he would go up to Linlithgow as soon as he could. He asked Sir George to obtain the Governor's approval of his intended visit, prudently not divulging the Queen Dowager's stipulation about his travelling companions who had in fact been appointed by the Governor himself on the previous occasion.

Obligingly enough, Douglas went to see Arran and returned that evening. He repeated that, had the Governor known Henry disapproved of the Cardinal's removal, it would not have taken place. But Beaton was perfectly safe, he said, and there was little point in doing anything about it now that he was actually at St

Andrews. He was thinking about sending his Treasurer, the Laird of Grange, over to St Andrews to see how things were going: this man would 'take order for [the Cardinal's] sure guard and custody'. The message ended with the Governor's assurance that Beaton was 'in as sure and strong a prison and as straitly kept in his own house as if he were within any other stronghold in Scotland'. If this included the previous stronghold in which he had been detained, Sir Ralph must have reflected, it was not likely to prove much restraint. Sir Ralph knew as well as the Governor that Beaton had ridden freely out of Blackness Castle, tossing a golden coin to his guardian, Lord Seaton, who had accompanied him to St Andrews. There was no reason to suppose that the Cardinal was not at that moment free to go wherever he chose. His previous message to Sir Ralph strongly suggested this. It is additional proof of the Governor's simple mind that he thought such nonsensical information would be accepted by Sir Ralph. He either genuinely had no notion of what he had done the day before or was likely to do the next, or had hopelessly underrated the efficiency of the Englishman's intelligence service. He had even added to Sir George's message that the Cardinal 'may hereafter be removed to Dunbar or Tantallon, as the case shall require'. The torn-up fragments of his authority for Beaton's complete release probably still lay on his desk. He can only have imagined that Sir Ralph was ignorant of most that went on round him.

However, he did not want Sir Ralph to go to Linlithgow at the moment, since he had just arranged for the Earl of Huntly to go up there with Douglas. He wanted Huntly himself to tell the Queen of the change of plan about her transfer to Stirling. It had been Huntly's plan originally. The Governor doubtless feared that, if he told her himself, she would imagine it was some plot of his own. He would therefore prefer Sir Ralph not to visit her until they had returned. 'The Governor,' added Sir George, 'was very sorry [Sir Ralph] had no better cheer nor entertainment here, trusting [he] would ascribe the same to their business . . . but the said Governor desired [him] heartily to take the pain to dine with him tomorrow'.[4] The fact that 'tomorrow' was 1st

April was doubtless a coincidence. Sir Ralph readily accepted, making a note that he would 'feel him thoroughly touching the Cardinal'. He would also see if he could get some agreement on sending Beaton to England.

The dinner party was an acceptable diversion for Sir Ralph. Being a convivial soul and the best of company, his leisure time – of which there had been little – hung heavily on his hands. His friends were all 'business friends', whom he was obliged to regard with deep suspicion while yet putting on an adequate show of good humour. He had little opportunity of relaxing in cultured company. He must frequently have sighed for some of the good conversation to which he was so accustomed, and of which he was such a master. The food was abominable, although there was no excuse for that. The raw materials were not in short supply, and he appears to have had his own cook with him. Drink was almost non-existent. The rough red wine which occasionally came in to the port at Leith was hardly the drink for a discerning palate at that chilly time of year, or indeed at any time. White wines were scarce, and it is doubtful whether he had close enough liaison with the Frenchmen in the capital to be offered anything from their private and superior cellars. He was regarded with increasing suspicion by the ordinary people and knew that no one enjoyed his presence in Edinburgh. He could not even have the satisfaction of being able to claim any real progress with his mission. It was altogether a dismal state of affairs, with no prospect of any improvement.

He therefore made the best of his dinner party with the Governor. It took place in the early afternoon, not at the time normally associated with dinner today. His host made him 'great cheer and countenance', but marred what might otherwise have been an enjoyable occasion by 'all the dinner-while hold[ing] purpose with me against the abuses of the Church, the reformation of which he most earnestly pretend[ed]'.[5]

He even asked Sir Ralph to order him some Bibles in English, and copies of all the statutes made by Henry during his suppression of the monasteries.

After dinner Sir Ralph plunged again into the topic of the

Cardinal's detention at St Andrews. Henry had asked him to try to prevent the transfer from Blackness Castle, but the instructions had come too late.

The Governor reaffirmed that he would have done something about this had he known in time. But having the Cardinal in St Andrews, said the Governor, was by far the best way of getting hold of the castle itself, which he – the Governor – was most anxious to do.

Sir Ralph could hardly believe this, unless, as he said later, the Governor 'be the greatest dissembler that ever was'. Arran would not yield at all to the suggestion that Beaton would be safer in England. He just laughed and said: 'The Cardinal had lever go into Hell.'[6]

Sir Ralph suggested that he was a potential menace to the peace of the realm with all his many adherents, virtually holding court once more in St Andrews.

Arran replied that he was safe enough in Lord Seaton's hands.

Sadleir suggested he would be safer still in England, out of reach of his many friends from land and sea.

Arran countered by pointing out how strange everyone would think it if the authorities in Scotland were not able to punish any transgressors on their own, even if it were the Cardinal himself. Arran was so adamant that Sir Ralph almost believed his sincerity.

An additional point came out after dinner. During the Cardinal's detention, all the priests in Scotland had refused to say mass or to administer the sacraments. This was distressing to everyone, the majority of the population being devoutly Catholic. It was also getting very near Easter. If the Cardinal were thought to be still a prisoner, there would be no Easter celebrations either. Such a major disruption in the pattern of religious life might well have threatened the stability of the Governor's own position. He would not willingly have risked such an upheaval. He therefore thought that if the Cardinal were back home in St Andrews it would be easy to put it about that he was in fact at liberty, whether this were actually the case or not. The priests would accordingly resume their religious duties.

Sir Ralph appreciated this argument, and reported it for what it was worth. He probably thought it a little curious that the Governor, in some difficulty over what appeared to be the actual release of Beaton, had not seen fit to mention this useful argument earlier.

However, Sir Ralph at last managed to change the subject, although to an equally well-worn theme: what did the Queen Dowager think about it all now? There had never been any love lost between her and the Governor.

'[You] will find her in end, whatsoever she protesteth, a right Frenchwoman,' he declared.[7] She was French herself, and of course thoroughly committed to the French party. She was always plotting to bring him into disrepute with King Henry, he said, and now he had heard that she had sent one of her servants to Henry to say that he, the Governor, was planning to marry his son to the infant Queen Mary, thereby confounding Henry's great plan. This was malicious nonsense, he said, and 'sware a great oath, no less than by the wounds of God, that she belied him'. If it were in fact true, he said, he could easily have arranged it before then, and 'not a nobleman in Scotland could or would be against [me] in it'. But he admitted that he had discussed the possibility with the Queen Dowager. After the return of the Solway prisoners, he went on, when Henry's plan became known, he had of course abandoned all such idea, seeing how much more beneficial to the whole country would be a marriage to Henry's son.

He warned Sir Ralph against the Queen Dowager. 'She studies nothing more,' he asserted, 'than to set the King's Majesty and [me] at pick, and so keep both realms from unity and agreement. . . . She hath a vengeable engine and wit to work her purpose,' he declared, 'and still she laboureth by all means she can to have the Cardinal at liberty.'[8]

All this argument only increased the complexity of the situation. Sir Ralph was undecided in his own mind, but faithfully reported back to Henry everything that might enable the King and his counsellors to form a sound opinion.

7

Governor Arran 'at his wits' end'

SIR RALPH CONTINUED his interminable round of visiting,
questioning, guessing and probing. He went again to Linlithgow
to see the Queen Dowager at her request. The Governor had told
her 'he would rather die than deliver the child into the King's
hands'. He had tried to set her against Sir Ralph, urging her to say
anything that might keep him happy for the time being, and
calling him 'an haughty fellow'.[1] This jibe riled Sir Ralph, and
will have increased his growing animosity towards the vacuous
Arran. The Queen Dowager reiterated most of what she had told
Sir Ralph on his previous visit, adding that the Governor was
still intent on marrying his own son to the young Queen, despite
his denials. She said she was wholly in favour of going to
England herself with her daughter, since she feared for both
their lives in the present turmoil. She made yet another plea for
the release of the Cardinal, and warned against the Earl of
Angus, who was 'of no policy or engine', as she called it. He was
'altogether ruled by his brother Sir George, who was as wily and
crafty a man as any was in all Scotland'.

Her protestations accorded with the normal pattern presented
to Sir Ralph wherever he went. This general procedure he must
by now have accepted as standard. It began by assuring him that
Henry's plans were ideal, continued by urging either the release or
continued detention of the Cardinal according to which side was
favoured, and ended by denouncing in scurrilous terms various
people on the other side. They were all 'mean personages', or

'crafty' or 'wily' or 'dissemblers'. Sir Ralph was warned against everyone in turn by one person or another. He must have been heartily tired of them all by the end of two or three months.

Lord Maxwell came round the next day to Sir Ralph's lodging with the opinion that the object would only be achieved by force. 'There is no other way to his Majesty to come by his purpose,' he declared.[2] It was he who had been virtually in charge at the rout at Solway Moss and been duly captured. He had written several times to Henry, he said, as promised, but all the letters must have got lost in the post, since he never received any acknowledgment. His chief purpose in coming round was to ask for the release of his eldest son, then a hostage with Henry. His second son would do just as well, he suggested cheerfully, and he himself would go down to Carlisle and place himself in the hands of Sir Thomas Wharton until the changeover had been effected. His eldest son was needed at home to look after all the family affairs, he added.

Later in the week Sir Ralph was entertaining the Earls of Glencairn and Cassels to mid-day dinner when fresh dispatches arrived from the King. He understood that the Earl of Lennox, newly come from France, was consorting with the Cardinal and was beginning to 'assemble and gather a power', proposing to abduct the Queen Dowager and her daughter. What did the Earls think about that?

They agreed Lennox might easily try to get hold of the Queen, but they thought she was too well guarded. The rumour about Lennox was laughed away. It was uneasy laughter, however. On reflexion, they decided to go to the Governor and 'see what they could work in the matter'.

As usual, on the receipt of any new instructions, Sir Ralph sent for Sir George Douglas. Douglas told him he had tried to persuade the Governor to take the Queen to Edinburgh for additional safety, but that he would not hear of it. The Governor was preoccupied with reports that Henry had refused to see the Scottish ambassadors sent down in March, and that English troops were massing on the Borders. Was Henry contemplating a sudden coup? wondered Arran.

Sir Ralph hurried round at once to the Governor's house. Without waiting for Arran to start any questions, he attacked straightaway. The King had already been completely deceived over the matter of the Cardinal, he complained, and now there was some story about the Earl of Lennox being in league with the Cardinal to kidnap the Queen Dowager and her daughter. The Governor would be well advised to remove them to safety in Edinburgh, said Sir Ralph sternly, allowing himself a little 'haughtiness' in view of the Governor's recently disclosed description of him.

But Arran was again doubled up with extraordinary oaths, protesting that he knew nothing about anything and that all was for the best whatever happened. The Earl of Lennox had no 'force and assembly'. He was even coming to Edinburgh next Sunday for a talk with Arran. The Cardinal himself proposed to look in one day soon, although he was at present remaining in St Andrews, 'feigning himself sick'. The young Queen was as safe as could be at Linlithgow with trusty men round her. Probably then catching Sir Ralph's eye, he added hurriedly that the business about Lord Seaton and the Cardinal had indeed been most unfortunate: it was surprising what could be done with a handful of coins.

He eventually agreed that the Queen would be safer in Edinburgh, but that it was in the hands of Parliament to order her transfer. He could do nothing himself.

After some further talk Sir Ralph got the first hint that the Governor was considering going over to the Cardinal's party. Although Arran had said nothing definitely to this effect, Sir Ralph's keen mind had perceived a chink in the Governor's rusty mental armour through which the skilful Cardinal was working a wedge. 'I did as much as I could,' wrote Sir Ralph afterwards, 'to cause him smell the danger which must needs ensure to him if he should fall from the devotion of the King's Majesty to the other party.' Arran reasserted his utter and permanent loyalty to Henry.

This had evidently not been taken for granted by Henry. He redoubled his efforts to keep a grip upon the Governor, sending by return masses of the Bibles, tracts and copies of statutes for which Arran had asked Sir Ralph at dinner a few days before. He also offered to give his ten-year-old daughter Elizabeth in marriage to the Governor's eldest son James, then an unpromising lad of thirteen. This was a weighty bribe indeed. Had the Governor not still been cherishing the idea of having the little Queen Mary herself as a daughter-in-law, he would surely have taken the offer up at once. He was very tempted. An English princess at the altar, he possibly thought, would be worth two Queens in the cradle. But before anything could come of it, the turmoil of state affairs had swept the chance away. Later on, in 1560, the son himself initiated advances to the then Queen Elizabeth, but she was not interested. He ultimately married nobody at all, dying a little out of his mind at Linlithgow in 1609.[3]

After Sir Ralph's formidable interview and constant questioning the Governor said that 'he was at his wits' end'. That would not have been a long journey.

Later that day Lord Fleming came to see Sir Ralph. Another Man of Solway, he was a brother-in-law of James V. His target was the Douglas family, whom he started to denounce as being 'most to blame . . . if [the King] had not all [his] desire and purpose'. Sir George was specially singled out. 'If he had not taken upon him to work all things, as he did, after his own fantasy and appetite,' alleged Lord Fleming, then all the King's plans would by now have been successfully concluded.[4]

Sir Ralph was mildly surprised at this outburst, but soon discovered the reason for it. The Douglases and the Flemings were rivals for some Sheriff's office, and Lord Fleming thought that by hurrying round to Sadleir he might be able to discredit Sir George somehow. But Sir Ralph was not so naïve as most of the people whom Lord Fleming was accustomed to lobbying.

Seeing that this tirade had not had the desired effect, Lord Fleming unburdened himself of more gossip. The Governor had just told him, he said, that 'he would rather take the said young Queen and carry her with him into the Isles and go dwell there, than he would consent to marry her with England'.[5] Look what a liar he must be. burbled Lord Fleming.

He saw that he was on better ground now. If the Governor did do this, he went on, the King 'for the value of £10 Scots could have one of the Irish lettericks bring you his head'. £10 Scots was worth less than a sovereign in England, so this must have been a bargain, except that it would have given the Cardinal free rein. A letterick was a kind of country ruffian.

He had also just been talking with the Queen Dowager, said Fleming. She had asked him to tell Sir Ralph that the Governor had asked her whether Henry had made any proposals of marriage to her. She had replied that he had not, but that she would feel bound to accept if he did make such an offer. It is surprising that Henry never made a serious move in this direction. Such a marriage would have been very advantageous to both sides, provided the religious difficulties could have been overcome.

At this same interview, the Governor had also told her that Henry anyway passed on to him everything she wrote to the King, so that Henry was 'dissemble[ing] altogether with her'. This was a particularly crude attempt to divide the Queen Dowager and Henry, between whom there existed a certain feeling of mutual trust and understanding. But Arran was a stranger to subtlety: it was the best he could do.

On the same day, 9th April 1543, the Earl of Angus married Lord Maxwell's daughter, Margaret, overcoming the Governor's opposition. Arran had performed one more of those noted reversals of decision which he applied to domestic affairs as well as to those of state. This item of society news Sir Ralph passed on to Henry as light relief from his more weighty dispatches.[6]

8

Mary, Queen of Scots

AT HOME HENRY had been busy readjusting his domestic affairs after the unsatisfactory outcome of his two-year marriage with Katherine Howard.

His Council had despaired of seeing him happily and permanently married. They gave up suggesting that he should remarry: he had suffered their promptings regularly during his celibate or widower days. They despaired of his producing another male heir to the throne. Their hopes were now fastened on pale Prince Edward, whom they were dismayed to find growing up distinctly anaemic.

Henry's zest for life had at last reached the stage where he wanted a woman's company, but did not want to pursue her, nor have other people pursuing her. He was determined to marry once more. But this time he wanted her to be a reasonably presentable and above all companionable and sensible woman. No throwing of garters into tournament lists, no mad galloping through Windsor Forest, no uproarious parties in barges on the river.

Henry himself resembled an over-ripe pear, lying split at the seams at the foot of a creaking tree. Flatulent, cystular, yet mentally as sharp as a rapier, he picked upon Catherine, Lady Latimer, as his final partner. Intelligent, well educated, with handsome features and gentle nature, thirty-one-year-old Catherine had already enjoyed some matrimonial adventures of her own. The daughter of Sir Thomas Parr, an undistinguished

North Country squire, Catherine had been married against her will to the feeble-minded Lord Borough of Gainsborough. On his death in 1529, which was much to everyone's relief, she married John Neville, Lord Latimer, as his third wife. After a few years she felt this had been a mistake. She accordingly made arrangements to marry Sir Thomas Seymour, brother of Jane Seymour, Henry's third Queen, as soon as the tiresome Lord Latimer should be out of the way. He died at last in 1542, but before she could have the banns called with Sir Thomas, she received a royal command to come to the palace and marry the King. Tactful hints that she did not wish to consider herself available for such an honour were brushed aside, and on 12th July she was married to Henry.

She had the brain to realise that the best she could do was to make herself as good a wife and consort as possible. A moderate Catholic, she was a considerable success to begin with, and a worthy comfort and companion to the King. As time went on she came to know too much about the affairs of state and became critical of Henry's handling of affairs.[1] He plotted to ensnare her as a heretic and send her to the dungeons, but death thwarted him of this plan. Then, after three months of royal widowhood, the emancipated Catherine married the faithful Sir Thomas Seymour, later Lord Seymour of Sudeley.

Meanwhile, towards the end of April 1543, Sir Ralph had been obliged to relinquish his joint post of Principal Secretary through his continual absence in Scotland, being succeeded by Sir William Paget. The loss of this post would have been a considerable financial blow in itself. It is typical of Henry's concern for the well-being of those servants able to retain his favour that he at once made Sir Ralph Master of the Great Gardrobe, or Wardrobe, an office which had just been relinquished by Lord Windsor.[2] There were many useful fees and perquisites attached to this post. Sir Ralph asked the King to appoint his great friend, Sir Thomas Wriothesley, later Earl of Southampton, to be joint holder of the office. Wriothesley was the other Principal Secretary, and Sir Ralph could, as he confided to the King, fully trust him, 'he [being] so much my friend, not [to] take any part of the fee from me, nor yet meddle with the office'.[3]

It was not only Henry who was appreciative of Sir Ralph's constant efforts. The Duke of Suffolk, Chairman of the Council in the North, sent a special recommendation to the King that he should be substantially rewarded. On this advice, Henry granted him some more property formerly belonging to the dispossessed Priory of St John of Jerusalem at Temple Dinesley, Hertfordshire, together with Temple Chelsyne. When bestowing such handsome gifts from his store of Church property, Henry never allowed his generosity to interfere with his sense of business. The lucky recipients of these title deeds were given a bill for their present. In this case, Sir Ralph's came to £843 2s 6d.[4] It was a 'once-for-all' payment unlike the normal custom, and fat revenue accrued thereafter to the holder of the land. Sir Ralph left this property in his will to his second son Edward who married a daughter of Sir Richard Lee, the fortifications expert.

Therefore in spite of being away in Edinburgh, Sir Ralph suffered no material loss. But during that chaotic April and May he must often have wished himself back in London. There was, he thought, no escaping the mesh of crazy intrigue in which Scottish men of affairs were constantly entangled.

The bewildered Governor, the Earl of Arran, had no sooner decided on one course of action than he was instantly threatened so severely by objectors that he would swing back at once. With the Cardinal cajoling and scattering gold on the one hand, and the Earl of Angus rattling his sabre on the other, the indeterminate Regent was half out of his mind. A crisis was reached on the receipt in Edinburgh of the dispatches sent back from London by the Scottish ambassadors. Henry, they reported, was insisting on the transfer of the young Queen Mary to England at once. The Scottish Parliament would not accept this at their meeting in spite of the Earl of Angus summoning as many supporters as possible, including all the 'English' party. The Governor was resigned to war with Henry over it. But heavy and skilful pressure by Sir Ralph resolved the awkward moment into a decision to send more influential ambassadors down to London, namely Lord Maxwell and the formidable Sir George Douglas. At this stage the Governor came back fully in support of Henry, and hopefully awaited an easy outcome to the negotiations by the second lot of envoys. Sir George Douglas managed to have Lord Maxwell replaced by his bosom friend the Earl of Glencairn, whom he accounted to be 'a man of deep judgment'.

They reached agreement with Henry that the little Queen should stay in Scotland until she was ten, at which age she should marry Prince Edward. During that time, an English couple should be with her to bring her up in the way of the English Court. In July, Henry appointed Sir Ralph and his wife to this position. Sir Ralph demurred, begging to be relieved of this appointment on the grounds that his wife was 'most unmeet to serve such a purpose . . . having never been brought up at Court . . . [and] for lack of wit and convenient experience in all behalfs she is undoubtedly not able to supply the place'.[5] In addition to this, Sir Ralph respectfully protested that she was about to have a baby, so would not be able to travel the long distance to Edinburgh that summer nor the following winter. He suggested the widowed Lady Edgcumbe as a substitute, 'a grave and discreet woman, of good years and experience'.

This throws a little further light on the curious history of Lady Sadleir. Even after several years of marriage, she was still not to be trusted in courtly circles to behave in a manner reflecting credit on her husband. It could be supposed that any uncouth ways or gaucheness would have been smoothed out by now, and that Sir Ralph would have raised no objection had he really wanted to settle in Edinburgh. But it is more likely that the idea of having to spend ten years there, with only occasional visits to London, so appalled him that he vigorously pleaded the inadequacy of his wife, determined at all costs to avoid the assignment. As matters turned out, neither his wife nor Lady Edgcumbe was ever called upon to fulfil the exacting office of guardian-companion to the little Queen of Scots.

While the Scotsmen were parleying at Hampton Court, an envoy from the King of France arrived in Edinburgh. His visit was happily timed. He brought promises of ships, soldiers and money for the Scots provided they resisted all Henry's blandishments.[6] Bearer of this important message – and a handsome sum of money with which to ensure the Governor's ready ear – was Monsieur Montgomery, Seigneur de l'Orgue, who later achieved notoriety through inadvertently killing King Henry II of France when jousting with him at a tournament. A splinter from his shattered lance ran into the King's eye and mortally wounded him. To back up the promise of support, eleven French men-of-war arrived in the Firth of Forth. They stood off at a discreet distance and after a day or two anchored out of sight behind the Isle of May.

The French sailors were not too pleased with their Scottish friends at that moment. On the way across from France they had been attacked by English vessels off Lowestoft and their force of seventeen or eighteen ships battered into dispersal. The little navy behind the Isle of May thus lacked some six or seven of their original party. The blame for this naval ambush was laid at the Cardinal's door, because rumour had it at the time that he and the young Queen were on board one of the ships, being hustled away to France.

Sir Ralph and his party were becoming increasingly unpopular in Edinburgh. The ill-feeling was reciprocated. 'Such malicious and despiteful people, I think, live not in the world as the common people of this realm towards England, as I have well found and proved since coming here,' he protested.

His life even became in danger. For as he was strolling in the garden one day, on what he later described as 'the backside of my lodging', in company with some of his people, someone stole up behind the hedge and fired a small matchlock gun at him. It missed one of his men by '. . . I dare say four inches', he noted dramatically.[7]

With this general deterioration in relations, the Governor was again swinging away from Henry over to France and the Cardinal. To swing him back again, Sir Ralph was sent £1,000 to give him. Arran recovered his staunchness at once, accepted the money readily and swore – with his customary shrill vehemence – all manner of oaths of loyalty and support to Henry. He had been urging Sir Ralph to withdraw from the scene altogether to the greater safety of the Earl of Angus's stronghold of Tantallon Castle on the coast north of Berwick. Sir Ralph had stoutly declined to leave, much to Arran's annoyance. But the £1,000 so much influenced him that on 25th August 1543 he actually signed and ratified the Treaty on the terms agreed, in Sir Ralph's very presence. This was solemnly accomplished at High Mass specially celebrated in the Abbey Church of Holyrood House, 'by the authority of the Queen and Three Estates of the Realm, in the presence of the greater part of the nobility of the same, and notaries also present'.[8]

Significantly, the Cardinal was not there, nor any of his cronies.

It must have been with a feeling of profound relief, tinged with apprehension, that Sir Ralph dined that day with the Governor. This was the day for which he had worked so hard: now it looked as if everything had been accomplished. He would doubtless have felt happier had the Cardinal been one of the signatories. Nor would he have been any easier in his mind when he learnt that the next day the Governor had gone to St Andrews to see the Cardinal, and had been refused admittance to the castle. Arran then proclaimed the Cardinal a virtual outlaw together with all those associating with him, and hurried back to the quieter atmosphere of Edinburgh. There, he planned to denounce the Cardinal's party as rebels and traitors.

But within a very few days news came to Sir Ralph that the Governor had ridden out of Edinburgh again and met the Cardinal in privy conclave at Callendar House, near Falkirk, the home of Lord Livingston. They had fallen on each other's necks and 'every friendly embracings were betwixt them, and also a good long communication'. After this tender tryst they had all clattered off to Stirling, to which the Queen Dowager had previously removed herself and her baby daughter. There the baby was crowned Mary Queen of Scots, 'with such solemnity as they do use in this country', reported Sir Ralph, 'which', he added sourly, 'is not very costly'.[9]

Sir Ralph was now being subjected to increasing 'public lewdness' and general abuse. 'I assure you,' he wrote to Lord Parr, one of his fellow members of the Council of the North, 'there never was so noble a prince's servant as I am, so evilly entreated as I am among these unreasonable people, nor do I think never man had to do with so rude and inconstant and beastly a nation as this.'[10]

The Governor was growing anxious about him, and again sent messages urging him to withdraw to greater safety. But, if the Governor were anxious, Henry was beside himself with wrath at the turn of events, especially after the many concessions he had made in the whole affair.

Finally, less than a fortnight after the solemn ratification and signature of the Treaty in the name of the 'Three Estates', the Governor publicly renounced it and all its implications. The sanctity of Treaty and bond had endured little longer than the echoing chant of the priests at High Mass and the twanging chords of shawm and sackbut, dwindling up through the raftered beams of Holyrood Abbey, on that solemn day of the signing.

At the news of the renunciation, Henry issued a declaration of war. Sir Ralph showed no sign of the depression which must have surged over him. He had feared the worst throughout the long and difficult negotiations, and now the worst had happened.

It was to be war, and his mission had been transformed overnight from success into failure through no fault of his own. He was now in serious danger of his life. Henry was well aware of this, and was determined to protect him as best as he could.

He issued a fearsome proclamation to the people of Edinburgh, threatening extermination of the whole city 'to the third and fourth generations' if his ambassador should suffer the slightest injury. Knowing that Henry was not accustomed to speaking idle words, the city fathers made a desperate effort to avert disaster, sending round a 'small present of wine' to Sir Ralph as a rather pathetic little gift. They also took strenuous steps to prevent the customary jeering in the streets at members of his party. Fewer stones were thrown, and life became a little less hazardous for the undaunted envoy.

The Solway prisoners, led by the Earl of Angus, had joined the Governor in his new alliance, but professed to Sir Ralph that they were now working in a body for Henry. They maintained that by joining the Governor they had the best chance of rescuing something from the wreckage of the Treaty. They declared they had every intention of fulfilling as many of their original promises as they could. They were not powerful enough anyway, they said, to stand out alone as a separate party, despite the money which Henry paid them. Their position was certainly awkward, and they were in some personal danger all the time.

But confusion was still the main theme. On 23rd September, the Earl of Lennox, chief accomplice of the Cardinal and leader of the French party, suddenly defected, sending word to Sir Ralph that he was now entirely in support of Henry and the English party against all others. He was also a suitor for the hand of twenty-eight-year-old Margaret Douglas, daughter of Margaret Tudor and her second husband, the Earl of Angus. This project doubtless governed his actions. Through such a marriage he saw his way to power and influence. He succeeded in marrying her within a few months. One of their children became the ill-fated Lord Darnley.

9

Sir Ralph at Tantallon

HENRY'S DECLARATION OF war had no immediate effect. It was too late in the year to start an invasion of Scotland: the climate and nature of the ground along the Borders made the passage and maintenance of an army a difficult matter at the best of seasons. In winter, with a hostile population, large-scale manœuvres were not an attractive proposition to any commander. Henry contented himself with planning a punitive expedition in the spring. In the meantime he laid hands on several Scottish merchant ships lying in English harbours, which had either discounted news of the outbreak of war or remained in ignorance of it. Their cargoes were mostly salted salmon and other fish for France and the Netherlands. Henry justified himself through Sir Ralph to the Governor and his national party – of whom the Cardinal was now spokesman – by saying that supplying anything to France was in direct contravention of the Treaty between England and Scotland. The fact that the Treaty had been recently renounced by the Governor was ignored.

For Sir Ralph, life became even more difficult. He was treated as an influential spy and *agent provocateur,* a charge amply borne out by a study of his activities. He continued to send secret messengers scurrying round Scotland collecting information and opinions from members of all factions. At the same time he was still at liberty to have interviews with the Governor, the Cardinal and anyone whom he chose, or could persuade to see him. His presence was most irksome to the Governor, since his intelligence service and the efficiency of his postal arrangements were far superior to those available to Arran. His letters were on one occasion waylaid and subjected to the closest scrutiny, being detained two or three days while the Governor's staff attempted to crack the cypher in which the more important communications were written. Sir Ralph was 'credibly informed' that they were successful in this particular branch of counter-espionage.

At last he began to have serious doubts as to whether he could perform any more useful purpose by staying in Scotland. He had hitherto resisted the entreaties of both the Governor and King Henry to remove himself to Tantallon Castle, a place of reasonable safety, 'wherein I might be sure from [the] malice' of the King's enemies. A strict sense of duty and disregard for personal convenience had kept him at the capital despite the constant hazards. The people of Edinburgh would not by now have hesitated to lay hands upon him if a suitable occasion arose, despite Henry's threats of annihilation. They were determined to keep him in Edinburgh as a hostage against the return of the merchant ships of Leith which had been detained by Henry with their foreign-bound fish cargoes. At night his lodging was ringed about with murmuring bands of self-appointed vigilantes, determined to keep the valuable Ambassador within the city confines.[1] He was, they were sure, worth money to them. Sir Ralph himself, peering out upon the unlit street and hearing the stealthy tread and muttered brogue as the ruffians changed over watch, wondered how he was ever to get out of Edinburgh unscathed. On commenting to a city authority about the unofficial guard on his lodging, he was told that it was for his own safety, to protect him against any untoward incident. Reporting to the Lords of the Privy Council about his difficulties, Sir Ralph wrote: 'Surely . . . I have been as ill treated here as was any man, and in no little danger of my life.'

Meanwhile the comings and goings continued among all the various factions of which articulate Scotland was then composed. Sir George Douglas continued to purvey the latest gossip to Sir Ralph, and to avoid involving himself in any situation requiring action. The general request by the loosely bound English party was for more money with which to keep their followers loyal and to influence others. 'The Captain of the Castle of Edinburgh,' said Sir George, for instance, 'is one of the Hamiltons which be all false and inconstant of nature and [I doubt not] what might be wrought and practised with *him* for money.'[2]

Henry's terms for a conclusion of the whole squabble were formidable. The Governor and the Cardinal were both to be delivered into his hands, or deprived of office; a council of twelve nobles to be appointed to govern the country, and eight others to replace those now in charge of the young Queen.

There was little enthusiasm from any quarter for these proposals and no one came forward to suggest how they could be carried out.

On 6th October a diversion occurred near Dumbarton.[3] Sir Ralph got to hear of it the same day. This was the arrival in the Clyde of five or six well-appointed French ships. On board was James Stewart of Cardonald, whom the Earl of Lennox, in his days of loyalty to the French cause, had sent to France to raise money and munitions for the support of the Cardinal and the French party in Scotland.

Also on board was the Legate of Pope Paul III, one Marco Grimani, Patriarch of Aquileia. He was described by a contemporary commentator as 'a bishop of notable piety, Peter Francis Contarini, Patriarch of Venice', but Vatican records show this description, at least as far as the name is concerned, to be inaccurate.

There were also two emissaries from the French King, Monsieur de la Broche and Monsieur Menager. The 60,000 crowns of gold ('for all their brags, not past 30,000,' said Sir Ralph) and £10,000 worth of munitions presumed to be in the holds of these vessels were presents from the King of France to help Lennox keep Henry at bay and to strengthen the anti-English party in Scotland. It was not until this little treasure fleet had set sail for the Clyde that the French learnt of the Earl of Lennox's change of allegiance, that he had turned from 'being noted a good French-man [and] is now become a good English-man'.

By that time it was too late to recall the ships. They dropped anchor under the lee of Dumbarton Castle. In charge of this stronghold was George Stirling of Glorat, Hereditary Keeper of Dumbarton Castle, a close friend of the Earl of Lennox. He at once sent word of this windfall to the turncoat Earl, who dashed up to Dumbarton with all speed to take delivery.

Sir Ralph could hardly believe that Lennox was prepared to take the money and munitions from the French and divert them to the opposite purpose for which they were sent to him.

But the Earl had promised that, if he could in fact get hold of the money, he would spend it all on the joint enterprise in the English cause on which he had embarked with his new-found friend, the Earl of Angus. 'This he saith,' observed Sir Ralph caustically on hearing of the promise, 'but what he will *do*, knoweth God.'[4]

The French at first were reluctant to land their valuables until they saw how they could best be 'employed for the purpose and benefit of France'. Where they derived their information is not revealed. The fact that the Earl of Lennox got most of the money and munitions in the end supplies an adequate answer. Lennox at once went off and fortified Glasgow Castle against the Governor, from which he had been taunting the Cardinal's party.

He had still been hoping to marry the Queen Dowager, and had virtually won the protracted wooing match which he had been conducting with the consequently impoverished third Earl of Bothwell, father of the more famous James, Earl of Bothwell. Lennox was a dashing, sprightly character. He was also rich. Bothwell was a gallant but shambling figure, pale-faced, mousy-haired, droopy-shouldered, rather over at the knee. His slender funds were soon exhausted by the daily efforts to surpass his rival at the Court for the hand of the Queen Dowager. While Lennox, decked with jewels, sported new and costly clothes, different every day, the fully fashioned silk stockings from France showing off his shapely calves to advantage, Bothwell had to rely on the same old cosy homespun, with woolly stockings knitted from his own raggedy sheep, and an occasional ill-fitting velvet doublet for best. The Queen Dowager, who was not minded to marry anyone at the time, found the cosmopolitan Lennox, veteran of France's battlefields, with his winning ways and fluent French, more appealing than the gentle but ageing and self-conscious local laird.[5]

The next year, Glasgow having been overwhelmed by the Governor with twelve thousand men, Lennox took refuge with Henry, who had received him kindly. Margaret Douglas, whom he had also fancied, was living at her uncle's Court at the time. Henry readily arranged a marriage since he observed that they seemed genuinely in love. He had always determined, he said, that his favourite niece should only marry under those conditions.

In Edinburgh, Sir Ralph at last received definite instructions to get away to Tantallon Castle. He was down with some sort of fever at the time. Henry asked him for news of some French ships which had been chased by English men-of-war into the shelter of Montrose and Dundee harbours. One of these was the renowned *Sacre* of Dieppe, and another the *Faucon*. The *Sacre* had covered herself with glory by defeating the English *Primrose* and *Minion,* although her own losses and damage were heavy.[6]

There was now no sign of the great *Sacre*. The *Faucon* had stayed in Montrose for some time before departing precipitately one day with her full complement of soldiers and sailors but leaving the captain behind. It is not recorded why the ship sailed without him. Had he slipped ashore for some last-minute commission, and the company cast off at a prearranged time thinking him on board, or had he been deliberately abandoned? However, he turned up later in Edinburgh saying that it was perfectly true she had sailed away and that he had no idea where she had gone. There was also no sign of the two smaller vessels which had accompanied the dreadnoughts. The party was not thought to have had any connexion with those carrying the Earl of Lennox's treasure, although word had been sent at once to the Navy to come and capture the Frenchmen.

Meanwhile, skirmishing and raiding was in full swing on the Borders. So much damage was being done by the English that

Sir Ralph was now openly threatened and dared not ride abroad at all. When it was made known that Sir Ralph dared not venture out, the Provost of Edinburgh came round with a large body of citizens to see him. They much regretted the reports that he was afraid to stay behind in Edinburgh when the lords left for the West Country, and thought it reflected most unfavourably on the good name of the city. For this they were most apologetic, and maintained that they would rather it cost the life of a thousand men than that Sir Ralph or any of his men should come to harm. Sir Ralph thanked them, replying that he wished to leave not through fear of his life but 'for mine own recreation'.[7]

The Earl of Angus was reluctant to let him go to Tantallon, since during the Earl's fifteen years of exile the place had been virtually abandoned. Sir Ralph had sent a servant to reconnoitre it; he brought back a depressing report on it being 'clearly unfurnished both of bedding and all manner of household stuff, and none to be bought nor hired, nor no manner of provisions to be made thereof, nor any kind of victual nearer than this town [Edinburgh] which is twenty miles off'. A daunting prospect for a man not yet recovered from fever. Sir George Douglas was lying at Pinkie, four miles from Edinburgh, also stricken down: he recovered, although for a time was more seriously ill.

Sir Ralph had suggested travelling westwards with the Earl of Angus. But even the Douglases could take no responsibility for having such an eminent representative of the English King among them at that time. They would not guarantee his safety. It would also have been inconvenient for them to have shown publicly that their allegiance lay with England. Their supporters would, they thought, melt away if Sir Ralph rode about with them so openly. Tantallon was therefore preferable from their point of view.

Meanwhile, the French Ambassador was doing the rounds with a roving commission to bestow yearly pensions on anyone who could be of service to the French cause, and to tighten the much relaxed understanding between England and France.[8] The Pope's Legate was also stumping the country, armed with all manner of Bulls, Faculties and Pardons for sale in an effort to raise money. He met with little success, and Sir Ralph noted 'some say that finding the people and country here so wild, he wisheth himself at home again'.

The Patriarch was evidently the more popular of these two peripatetic envoys. He remained in Edinburgh as long as he could, and was given a banquet or some sort of entertainment almost every day of the week.[9] Whether it was pride of hospitality or uneasy conscience which prompted them, all the resident nobility vied with each other to divert the envoy of the Pope. Both the Queen and the Governor received him regularly. Among the Edinburgh hosts doing a short season in the capital and anxious to get such an eminent visitor into their guest list was the Earl of Moray, an illegitimate son of James IV. He devised a plan with which to impress the sophisticated visitor from the Continent. He decided to load up a sideboard before dinner with all manner of glass and crystal objects, calculated to dazzle his guest with such a costly display. Then, at a secret signal during dinner, one of his servants was to trip forward as if by mistake and lurch against the sideboard. This would crash to the ground, and if the servant carried out his instructions correctly every piece would be dashed to fragments on the floor. Then, as if this were no more than an unfortunate lapse, the sideboard would be set up again and laden with a fresh collection of rare objects previously stacked next door. By this demonstration of plenteousness and wealth, the Earl hoped to convey to the Patriarch the idea that Schotland was as well provided with aids to gracious living as any of the countries of Europe.

One can imagine the preparation for this dinner party, the scouring of the meagre shops of Edinburgh for matching glasses, decanters, plates and goblets, all to look well in display, but all to be thoroughly breakable: the discussions on the position of the sideboard; the trial lurchings: 'No, no, much too obvious; do it with your elbow'; the practising of the secret signal.

And then the dinner itself. All eyes, except those of the guest, are on the sideboard as course succeeds course. There is venison, done up in several different ways, some brawn, maybe some salmon although it was not much thought of in those days. Jams and jellies are much in evidence, all washed down with aqua-vitae or brandy and local ales. On the tablecloth of 'dornick' are several 'bosses' or half-gallon bottles of Gascon wines imported at Leith. Plenty of highly spiced bread helps to take the edge off any keen appetite. Soon, the great moment draws near. Conversation gradually ceases round the table, except from one guest deputed to keep talking loudly and naturally. The Earl grows more and more nervous for the success of the plan. At the moment the signal is given – the Earl's fist pumping up and down behind his back ('*Now,* you fool, *now* . . .') – a bejerkined servant runs at the sideboard – down it goes, a fearful crash. Cries of dismay as everyone rises to his feet, and the Patriarch is loud in outspoken commiseration with his host.

And then, as the glittering fragments are swept away with brushes standing ready against the wall, the gasps of admiration and astonishment as an even more brilliant collection of objects is instantly crammed upon the righted sideboard.

The ruse came off without a hitch, a triumphant success. The Patriarch, doubtless most astonished at the unaccustomed display, expressed with tactful effusion his admiration of such a demonstration of the richness, both of his host and of Scotland, who could between them produce such sumptuous ornaments. He added that he 'never did see better in Venice where [he himself] was born'.

Shortly after this proud stroke for the honour of Scotland, the Earl retired to his castle of Darnaway with severe gout and gravel stones of which he died the next year.[10] After this famous dinner, the Patriarch went off with the Cardinal to St Andrews.

By the end of October, Sir George Douglas, without whose aid Sadleir's inside information had been seriously curtailed, was recovered from his illness. He asked Sir Ralph to 'take horse and ride out of this town into the fields to speak with him', since there was nowhere secret enough to meet. At some risk, Sir Ralph went out to keep the rendezvous, and was well briefed on the latest gossip.[11] Douglas concluded by saying that Tantallon was being got ready, and that he would escort Sadleir there as soon as it was convenient.

Accordingly, about 6th November, Sir Ralph arrived safely at Tantallon, which, although habitable, was still most meagrely appointed. However, it had the merit of strength, and he reported that he needed not 'fear the malice of mine enemies, and therefore do think myself now to be out of danger'.[12]

On his departure the pace of internal intrigue accelerated. Two Men of Solway, Lord Somerville and Lord Maxwell, were caught by the Governor and the Cardinal and imprisoned in Edinburgh Castle. Sir Ralph was sceptical about the degree of this disaster.

'Lord Maxwell', he reported, 'some men think was taken by his own consent . . . though it be not true, both he and Somerville used much folly to put themselves in such danger as to come so slenderly furnished within the bounds and strength of their enemies.'

The Earl of Lennox was reported to have gone back over to the Cardinal's side and about to be made Lieutenant-General of the Realm, a sort of deputy to the Governor.

The Governor now felt more secure. In his new-found courage, and with Sir Ralph safely out of the way, he assaulted and captured the castle of Dalkeith which belonged to the Earl of Angus's brother, the Earl of Morton. Sir George Douglas's second son, James, heir to Morton and later Regent of Scotland, happened to be in the castle at the time.[13] With typical Douglas enterprise, he barricaded himself into one of the towers and defied the Governor and all his army, although he had no weapons and very little food. He held out so long that the Governor had to raise the siege and allow him to march out unmolested, accompanied by his handful of colleagues, and such baggage as he had.

Arran next attempted to lay discreet siege to Tantallon itself, but confined his operations to the arrest and search of all messengers going in and out of the castle. Sir Ralph was naturally aware of this and wrote his letters in a cypher which had been altered since the disclosure of his previous one. In addition to this, Oliver Sinclair, scapegoat of Solway Moss, was lurking in ambush in a little house within two miles of Tantallon.[14] He had sixty horsemen with him and hoped to waylay Sir Ralph or any of his party should they stray beyond the radius of the castle's defences. During the fifteen years' exile of the Earl of Angus, Sinclair had got himself appointed Keeper of Tantallon. Latterly, he had allowed it to lie empty and abandoned, but he was well acquainted with the castle and its immediate neighbourhood. Sir Ralph was aware of all this, and kept within bounds.

Meanwhile, in grim Tantallon, where there were no dinner parties, no crystal goblets and no sideboards on which to put them even had there been any, Sir Ralph prepared to fight a diplomatic rearguard action.

The country was, he reported, 'in great garboil'. Members of the English party, doubtless wondering whether it had been a mistake after all to have formed such a party, rode about the country with as many supporters as they could muster, in constant fear of being attacked by the Governor's men or his agents. Reports came in daily of one or more of their friends being captured or imprisoned. The Governor, the Cardinal and the Queen Dowager formed a temporary but powerful alliance. The English party sent urgent pleas to Henry through Sir Ralph for more money with which to bolster the morale of their dwindling bands of supporters. The Earl of Angus, who had incurred considerable odium by lending his castle to the English ambassador, conferred with Cassels, Glencairn, Lennox and the others on what they should do. They planned to weld their forces together, attack the Governor and burn his home town of Hamilton. But they had not enough money to maintain an army of any size, so they were fortunately relieved of the necessity of putting any such bold projects into action.

The Governor finally wrote to Sir Ralph insisting that he come up before the Governor and give some adequate explanation of why he should be allowed to remain any longer on Scottish soil. Failing this he was to depart at once. 'You daily receive and direct writings privately to and fro from sundry and small men within this realm and send thereupon advertisement to the King's Majesty,' protested Arran, 'being both very suspicious and hurtful to the commonwealth of the same . . . and is of such weight and importance as may not be permitted.'[15] The Governor, fired with boldness at the new support he was receiving, summoned quite a threatening attitude to Sir Ralph, concluding that he was 'constrained by [his] strange behaviour and practices to pray and also charge [him] to depart forth of this realm with diligence'.

Sir Ralph addressed a lofty reply, denying in true diplomatic fashion that he had ever written a single thing to anyone which he would not readily have 'your lordship and the whole realm privy unto'.[16] The fact that many were written in code was conveniently ignored. He added that there was 'such division in this realm, and such change and alterations as I daily see chancing amongst you', that he did not even know to whom official communications should be addressed.

This final shaft deeply wounded the Governor's pride and resolved him to get rid of Sadleir at all costs.

He was newly encouraged by promises from Monsieur de la Broche, the French Ambassador, that six thousand troops from Denmark, to be maintained by France, would be available at the Governor's command to land in either Scotland or England, in addition to ships of war. The French King also promised to pay for the wages of ten thousand Scottish soldiers during any campaign against Henry.[17] The Governor was therefore full of confidence and determined to carry the war right into England without waiting for Henry's anticipated springtime operations.

The Laird of Brunstoun, one-time employee of the Cardinal, had taken the place of Sir George Douglas as courier to the English party. He kept Sir Ralph informed of the increasing difficulties in which the Earl of Angus and his associates now found themselves. Had Henry poured money into Scotland at this time, he might possibly have enabled the English party to form such a useful army of their own that, had they been so minded, they could have routed the Governor's and the Cardinal's parties and substantiated the broken treaty of peace and marriage. But, with several previous examples of the cavalier way in which loyalties were apt to be treated in Scotland, Henry doubtless had adequate reasons for sending only the most meagre sums for distribution among his allies north of the Border.

The reliability of all the information still filtering through was suspect. Sir Ralph had formed a good opinion of the Laird of Brunstoun, his new go-between, 'except' – and his cynical reserve was never broken down – 'there is no truth in Scottishmen'.[18]

The Governor commanded the Earl of Angus to send Sir Ralph away from Tantallon. True to tradition, the Earl disdainfully took no notice, although it must have been most inconvenient to have been host to such a troublesome nest of spies.

Henry suggested that Sir Ralph should leave the castle and go wherever Angus and his allies were to be found. This would be quite impossible, replied Sir Ralph at once. In the first place they were always twenty or thirty miles apart from each other, and secondly the Earl's house had only two habitable rooms, one for himself and one for his wife. The others were equally badly off for accommodation. He had no intention of camping out in midwinter or trailing round hostile Scotland in imminent danger of his life. He also knew what an embarrassment his presence would be to his friends.

Finally, on Saturday night, the 8th December, Sir Ralph received a letter from the King recalling him to London. His sigh of relief must have echoed round the comfortless walls of Tantallon as loud as the breakers in the surf below. He got in touch at once with Sir George Douglas, who had nobly offered to escort him the forty-three miles to Berwick whenever he wished. Accordingly on Tuesday, the 11th December, 'an honest company of gentlemen and their trains, to the number of 400 horses or thereabouts', arrived at the bleak stronghold.[19] Sir Ralph, with his few retainers and bulging briefcases, rode out in their midst and came safely to Berwick-on-Tweed.

From there he wrote his last dispatch to the Duke of Suffolk, Chairman of the Council in the North. The Governor was already having trouble with his supporters, he reported optimistically, and it seemed that the Cardinal's high-handed treatment of those nobles whom he was regularly catching up in the name of the Queen and committing without trial to prison and worse was straining new friendships beyond breaking point.

With a little more money to distribute, he suggested, it might be possible to set all the factions at each others' throats so that by the time the King was ready to invade, there would be no effective resistance from any quarter.

On this hopeful note he left Berwick, and reached the Duke's headquarters the next Saturday night. The first phase was over.

IO

The Rough Wooing of the Queen of Scots

SIR RALPH'S DEPARTURE from Scotland was the signal for all manner of tortuous intrigue. The Governor little knew how temporary his absence was to be. The vision of his return enthroned on clouds of vengeance was one which would have deprived the inconstant Regent of many nights of rest. As it was, the Earl put Henry out of his mind for the time being and set about destroying the remnants of the English party. He saw the Earl of Lennox as the biggest obstacle and plotted with the Cardinal how best to eliminate him.

But Lennox was well able to look after himself. His friends, of whom he had no lack, brought him a rumour that some hidden mischief was brewing against him, and that, unless he were careful, he would find the Governor and the Earl of Angus joining forces again. In order to give such an alliance a basis for tentative negotiation, the Governor managed to arrange for Sir George Douglas and the son of the Earl of Glencairn to be detained as hostages, the former as pledge for his brother the Earl of Angus, the latter for his father. This was done reasonably amicably, on the understanding that they would very soon be released. But the Governor held them indefinitely until the pre- cipitate arrival of the English army some six months later. Had the army not come, they might never have regained their liberty. That left the Earl of Angus himself still warily at large, as well as Lennox, Maxwell, Cassels, Glencairn and the other Men of Solway.

Angus was not so much of a warrior as his brother. He preferred to see the country at internal peace – provided, of course, the terms were not disadvantageous to the house of Douglas. He could himself have made a satisfactory pact with the Governor and smoothed everything out. But Lennox was a difficulty. He was a serious contender for the Governorship and was well known to be intent on wiping out Arran and all his establishment. Not for nothing had he spent the French gold on bolstering his own defensive stronghold against the Governor's forces. The Earl of Angus decided therefore to attempt a mediation between Arran and Lennox. Taking Lord Maxwell with him he rode off one day to Glasgow, where Arran and his Council were maintaining a centre of government.

Governor Arran himself probably bore few grudges against anyone wishing to make up a quarrel. He would have been happy enough to forgive and forget. But his Council had been heavily infiltrated by the Cardinal's persuaders, men dedicated to the establishment of Beaton's unchallengeable authority. Here was their arch enemy, the Earl of Angus, riding into their camp unaccompanied for once by a heavily armed striking force of Douglases. It was, they urged the indecisive Governor, a heaven-sent chance to seize him for treason. Without further reference to Arran, the Council pounced on Angus and his colleague.[1] To avoid the outcry among the people which they knew would follow the disclosure of their dishonourable action, the Council hurried their prisoners out by the back entrance to Glasgow town and off to Hamilton Castle. The actual castle of Glasgow was still held against all comers by Lennox's men. Hamilton was the headquarters of the Governor; never did a gaoler hold prisoners in his dungeon more reluctantly. Against this master stroke by his Council he was incapable of making an effective protest.

The underhand trick lost the Governor the few traces of popularity remaining to him in all but the most Cardinal quarters. Even his associates despised him for his feebleness of character and lack of resolve.

However, it effectually disposed of Lennox's right-hand man. It only remained to capture Lennox himself and his Glasgow fortress. Safe from all possibility of counter-attack the Governor assembled an army of twelve thousand men, all summoned by proclamation, since he could not count on getting any volunteers. Lugging along a selection of brass cannon and other pieces of heavy artillery from Edinburgh, he ranged this sledgehammer force before the nut of Glasgow Castle, and attempted to crack it by siege on 8th March 1544. Ten days afterwards the little castle was still intact, and the Governor's huge army disgruntled and mutinous, with all its powder, ammunition and arrows spent.

Unable to make headway by military skill, the Governor sent word in to the keepers of the castle that he wished to treat with them. Agreeing to the Governor's terms, whereby all the defenders should be granted safe conduct in return for the surrender of the castle, the keepers handed the place over. Whereupon the Governor, the noble Earl of Arran, imprisoned the keepers and hanged every single survivor upon the castle walls.[2]

Lennox himself was invited to appear. Not unnaturally he declined the invitation, whereupon he was, in accordance with a practice of the day, 'put to the horn', or declared a rebel and outlaw with accompanying blasts of a trumpet, and his property confiscated. Shortly afterwards, leaving his surviving stronghold of Dumbarton Castle in safe hands, he departed for London against the advice of many of his friends, who thought he could have eventually won the country over to himself if he had stayed and fought it out.[3] Soon after his arrival in London, he married Margaret Douglas, daughter of the Earl of Angus, who was then living at her uncle King Henry's Court.

The Governor's tawdry successes in battle spurred him to new levels of cruelty and confiscation on many people linked by land or blood to his opponents. The spring of 1544 found him still balanced precariously but now jubilant at the head of the State. But the month of May, usually accounted a merry one, brought the Governor a shock, as severe as it was unexpected. On the morning of the third of that month, the citizens of Edinburgh and district awoke to find a fleet of two hundred English men-of-war lying at anchor off the harbour of Leith.

Such a spectacle seemed at first like a mirage. Everyone who saw this doom-laden armada must have rubbed his eyes hopefully. But it was no mirage. It was the first manifestation of England's new-born navy, the forerunner of a mighty tradition which was to endure, usually triumphant, for four hundred years. It was also King Henry's reply to the spurning of his treaties and the mocking of his ambassador, Sir Ralph Sadleir.

*   *   *

After his return to London at Christmas the previous year, 1543, Sir Ralph had barely had time to enjoy a quiet family holiday before being plunged into further activity. His friend Wriothesley, who had been running Sir Ralph's office of Clerk of the Grand Wardrobe for him in his absence, was promoted to Lord Chancellor. Moving up the ladder of fame together, as on previous occasions, Sir Ralph in his turn now received the lucrative office of Clerk of the Hanaper. This post had to do with the keeping of various registers and records, hanapers being wicker baskets in which such papers were kept. But he had to relinquish, or was deprived of, the very important office of Principal Secretary. It is not clear whether enemies were working behind his back to get him out of his high positions, or whether his continued absence in Scotland made it physically impossible to keep up with the work.

In February he was again selected for important work. Henry had decided to strike a vengeful blow north of the Border, well calculated to put new heart into the survivors of the English party.

A large fleet was already being commissioned to transport an army to France, principally for the siege of Boulogne. This could be used for a trial run to Scotland, carrying a striking force capable of dealing a lethal blow at the heart of Scotland and returning in time for the French campaign. The Earl of

117

Hertford, who later became the temporarily omnipotent Duke of Somerset, was put in command and Sir Ralph was appointed to the important post of Treasurer of the whole army.[4]

As in 1542, a Council of the North was established, consisting of Hertford, Sir Ralph and Cuthbert Tunstall, still Bishop of Durham. Headquarters were set up at Newcastle as before. Lord Lisle, the Lord Admiral of England, duly set sail from London and arrived at Tynemouth on 18th April. He had brought up a large force of soldiers who joined up with those recruited by Hertford and Sir Ralph in the North Country. The total had now reached ten thousand men. All that was needed was a favourable wind: everything was ready. The plan was for this navy to sail direct to Leith, where they would disembark and be joined by four thousand cavalry under Lord Evers, at that time mustering his squadrons at Berwick-on-Tweed.[5]

Day after day went by, and the wind persisted in blowing from both the north-east and occasionally east-north-east, hopeless directions for the square-sailed vessels. It was no easy task to keep such a large body of men disciplined and harmlessly amused in sixteenth-century Newcastle. As day succeeded day with no change in the wind, the ingenuity of the junior officers and NCOs was highly taxed. At last – but not until the first of May – the laggard wind veered to the south. So eager for action was the whole encampment that within the short space of two tides every man had embarked and the great fleet was clearing the mouth of the Tyne.

It must have been a noble spectacle as the unheard-of number of ships dipped to the North Sea swell. Security ashore had been very good. No hint of destination had been whispered in the country taverns, and no word of the fleet's objective filtered through to the Governor as he sat at his Holyrood desk, cackling over the results of his latest tyranny. It was generally thought that the army had been prepared for France.

On the 3rd of May after an uneventful passage the armada entered the Firth of Forth. As a preliminary, several ships went across to the little port of St Monance on the north side. After landing and setting fire to that fishing township, they returned to the fleet towing a number of fishing boats to be used for the next day's landing.

That night they dropped anchor some three miles off the port of Leith, in the lee of the island of Inchkeith. By curious chance this particular spot had always been known as the English Roads. It was now considered an aptly prophetic name.

The next day, within the space of only four hours, the whole army of ten thousand men was put ashore at Grantown, two miles west of Leith. They formed up at once into the vanguard under the command of the amphibian Admiral, Lord Lisle, the centre under the Earl of Hertford, and the rearguard under the Earl of Shrewsbury. There were also some pieces of artillery drawn along by manpower. Sir Ralph took a command under Hertford. The first objective was the town of Leith, and the army accordingly set off in good order.

At the first stunning news of the fleet's arrival, the Governor had collected whatever he could in the way of an army. Accompanied by the Cardinal himself, the Earls of Huntly, Moray, Bothwell and many others, they had hurried along the coast to oppose the invaders.[7] The Governor had taken this opportunity of releasing at once the Earl of Angus, Sir George his brother, and the others of the English party whom he had locked up. If the English overwhelmed the country, he knew he would have even less chance of survival if Henry's friends were found in prison. Sir Ralph in these circumstances could certainly not be counted upon to intercede on his behalf.

However, by urgent proclamation, five or six thousand horsemen had been gathered together, and a considerable number of infantry. These were arrayed with some supporting artillery in a defile on the approaches to Leith.

The English soldiers, cooped up so long in camp and then in the cramped quarters of a ship, fifty to a vessel, could hardly be held back from getting to grips with the enemy. The Scots had been totally unprepared for such a major assault and put up no serious opposition.

An English captain observed at the time that 'the first man that fled was the holy Cardinal, like a valiant champion, and with him the Governor. . . .'[8] This heavy sarcasm is scarcely warranted on the part of Beaton, since he could hardly have been expected to do battle in the field as a Cardinal of the Church. The Governor may have realised at once that resistance in the field was hopeless and that he would be better employed organising the defences of Edinburgh.

Hertford then took Leith without difficulty and camped in it for the night. The next day the heavy ordnance was unloaded in the harbour, in which several good ships were discovered.[9] Chief of these were the *Salamander,* which had been given to James V by the King of France on his marriage to the French King's daughter, Madeleine de Valois, in 1537, and the *Unicorn,* home-built pride of James's navy.

The next day, 5th May, the army issued out towards Edinburgh, leaving fifteen hundred to hold Leith.

The capital was soon captured and set on fire, including Holyrood Palace and Abbey. Fearful destruction was done the whole length of the country from Stirling to the mouth of the river and untold damage was wrought.

Leith was eventually destroyed. *Salamander* and *Unicorn* were put in ballast with thirty thousand iron cannon balls found in the town and sailed off as prize ships.[10]

By 15th May the work of destruction was complete and part of the army moved along the coast to Berwick, laying waste everything in its path. A savage delight was taken in the destroying of Lord Seton's 'chief castle, called Seaton, which was right fair: [we] destroyed his orchards and gardens, which were the fairest and best in order that we saw in all that country. We did him more [damage],' reported one of the English, 'because he was the chief labourer to help the Cardinal out of prison, the only author of their [the Scots'] calamity.'[11]

The wanton ruin continued without opposition. The lords had in fact kept a large force hovering about, reported by a captured lancer to be ten thousand men. But, on the only day when the lie of the land offered a suitable advantage of position, a thick sea mist lay over the district and did not disperse until two o'clock in the afternoon. The invaders were so spoiling for battle that they rushed forward as soon as visibility allowed.[12] The Scotsmen withdrew hurriedly to the hills behind. An observer noted that those slopes were 'covered with flocks of their people' at the time, civilians fleeing from their ruined homes.

On 18th May, the army re-embarked at Berwick and sailed away, leaving a pitiful trail of death and smoke as a memorial to the misdirection of the nation's affairs.

The expedition had cost the lives of only forty of Henry's men. The main body, after tidying up at Newcastle, then sailed direct to Calais to be ready for Henry's joint campaign with the Emperor Charles against France.

Sir Ralph, after making up his accounts for the expedition, returned to London. He was rewarded by Henry with the grant of the manor of Standon in Hertfordshire, where he later built the noble house he made his home.[13] But he had little time to examine his new property, for on 14th July he embarked at Dover with Henry and crossed the Channel to France, where the King assumed full command of his army.

I I

Death Comes to Cardinal and King

SIR RALPH HAD proved his ability in handling the financial administration of armies. It was a highly skilled and responsible job. He was probably appointed Treasurer-in-Chief to the forces in France, although there is no definite proof.

When they arrived across the Channel, the King and Sir Ralph interested themselves in that section of the army which had just started to lay siege to Boulogne. The Duke of Suffolk was the corps commander. The other army corps, under the Duke of Norfolk, had set off for Montreuil, an important stronghold lying across the main route to the heart of France.

This was part of a major plan conceived by Henry and the Emperor Charles, whereby they should jointly crush Francis, King of France. The enterprise was only a partial success. After a vigorous siege of two months, the Duke of Suffolk's blockade obliged the garrison of Boulogne to surrender. Sir Ralph's younger brother John had commanded a company throughout the operations.[1] The Duke of Norfolk had no success to report, and Montreuil remained in French hands.

But Henry was delighted with the capture of Boulogne, in which he had himself taken command.[2] One cannot imagine that any great tactical skill was required in sealing off the town from outside help. Provided no ships were allowed into the harbour, and a deep ring of troops remained established round the town walls, it was merely a question of waiting until the defenders were starved out. Henry cut a noble figure in his daily inspection of the troops. No other manœuvres were necessary. Direct assaults were soon abandoned in favour of a policy of masterly inactivity. The King was well satisfied with his generalship and, when the town eventually capitulated in mid September, he felt he could afford to treat the vanquished with princely generosity.

He accordingly returned to England in triumph together with Sir Ralph. But it was not a completely satisfactory scene which he left behind him in France. The Duke of Norfolk had achieved nothing, nor had the Emperor Charles himself done much better. Since Henry had declined to join with Charles in a dramatic thrust to Paris, he had felt unable to make headway on his own. He had accordingly made a separate peace with Francis of France. Encouraged by this, the French made strenuous efforts to recapture Boulogne and erase the effects of Henry's invasion.

Towards the end of January 1545, they launched a force of fourteen thousand men against the stubbornly held little town. Their initial impact spent itself in the suburbs. To their surprise, before dawn the next morning the gates flew open and the Earl of Hertford rushed out at the head of his garrison.[3] Laying about them with skill and vigour they routed the whole French force which prudently abandoned the siege.

Henry thus remained on bad terms with Francis, who was stimulated by these reverses into encouraging the Scots to stir up fresh trouble. Francis thought that, if he could get enough diversion created by Scotland, the way would be free for a massive French invasion of England.

Throughout that winter and during the early spring of 1545, Lord Evers had taken upon himself to conduct large-scale offensive operations along the Borders against the quiescent Scots.[4] This seemed merely to rub salt in the wounds of the previous Hertford invasion, and to serve little purpose from a national point of view. He did much damage, and the Scots became increasingly indignant against their Governor, who took no action.

Eventually the Earl of Angus, his promises to Henry and the

English party set aside at last, had a stormy interview with the reluctant Arran. Brushing off the Governor's pleas that he had been deserted by the nobility and could do nothing on his own, Angus stormed away at him.

'As for us two,' he raged, 'I know that I am accused by my enemies of treason, and you of cowardice. But if you would do that speedily which you are not able to avoid, 'tis not a fine-spun oration but the field and dint of sword shall wipe off both these criminations.'[5]

Wilting before this blast, the Governor agreed to get a force together. Since most of the property suffering from the English depredations belonged to Angus himself or to the Douglas family in general, Angus's concern at the Governor's inaction was understandable. Without waiting for reasonable forces to assemble, Angus and the Governor set off the next day with all they could collect in the time, which amounted to less than three hundred horsemen.

They were joined on the way down to the Border by a handful of others, and came eventually to Melrose, on the Tweed. Here discretion tempered their valour: they decided to wait for more forces to accumulate. But the English commander, Lord Evers, was occupying Jedburgh only thirteen miles away. Spies brought him word of the tired and diminutive army ranged against him. With five thousand men he therefore prepared to make all speed to Melrose, hoping to extinguish the Scottish force and catch up the Governor himself in the lodgings pinpointed by informers. As night fell Lord Evers got on the move. But so did the Governor. Lord Angus's counter-espionage had revealed the Englishman's purpose. The Governor slipped out of the town with his loyal followers and put up for the rest of the night at The Shiels, a roomy house beyond Melrose Bridge.[6]

The English duly arrived at Melrose, but too late to catch the Governor. Spitefully sacking the town they returned to Jedburgh.

In the early morning, Angus and the Governor were delighted to receive reinforcements from Fife, who had ridden all night. More high-spirited than numerous, they added only two hundred to those assembled, bringing the army to a total of five hundred.

Without further ado they set out the morning of their arrival to avenge themselves upon the invaders. By cunning use of their ground, of the strong sun, and high wind – which latter blew all the fumes of gunpowder straight into the enemy's faces – they lured the invaders into an ambush on Ancrum Moor.[7] Their victory was as complete as it was unexpected. For the loss of only two men, killed inadvertently by their own artillery, the Scots slew a hundred of the enemy and took about a thousand prisoners. Lord Evers was killed as well as his second-in-command.

This was indeed a notable victory. The Governor, a good soul at heart, at once called for the Earl of Angus and sincerely praised his courage, determination and wisdom in the whole affair. He also thanked Sir George Douglas for his valiant service, declaring that after such a battle the family of Douglas was thoroughly purged of any aspersion cast upon its loyalty to Scotland in favouring the English. He personally commended all the people who had brought troops and helped him. Had there been medals to issue, there would doubtless have been a generous share-out.

That evening the Governor and his friends rode in triumph to Jedburgh and had a grand supper on all the stores which had been collected into the town by the English.[8]

The next morning heralds went through the country proclaiming that all the lands annexed during the winter by Lord Evers had, by this battle, been released from the English yoke and were duly Scottish again.

Flushed with their brilliant success, several of the junior commanders were in favour of pressing on into England to attack the various forts held or abandoned by the English troops. Wisely enough, the Governor insisted the Scottish force was too small to do any good; also, they had hardly any artillery. He therefore persuaded them to go back to their homes and himself returned to Edinburgh.

Meanwhile, Henry had not been inactive. He was well aware

of the impending pincer movement on England which the King of France was trying to organise. As in previous emergencies, he lost no time in setting up another Council of the North composed of the Earl of Shrewsbury, Sir Ralph and, as usual, Cuthbert Tunstall. With its customary accuracy his intelligence service reported that the Governor of Scotland had sent an ambassador to France to acquaint the King of the glorious battle of Ancrum Moor, to imply that Henry was heavily harassed on the northern borders and that it would be just the time for a large French army to arrive in Scotland. Coupled with the impending invasion of the coast of Hampshire, it seemed an opportune moment for Papist Europe to combine in dealing a mortal blow to the villain of the Reformation.

The French King was kindly disposed towards the idea, but, because Henry was rumoured to be preparing a further assault on France, he said he could spare no more than three thousand footmen and four hundred horsemen under the command of Monsieur Montgomery de l'Orgue, the same man whose splintered lance later accidentally killed his King, Henry II, at a tournament. These troops duly arrived at Leith. They were considered by the French more as a diversionary irritation for Henry than as the spearhead of a future Franco-Scottish attack.

Henry had already heard that France was sending forces to Scotland. The threat was taken seriously, especially after the reverse of Ancrum Moor. The Council in the North was told of all the impending dangers and ordered to increase the standing army to thirty thousand men. The castles of Berwick, Wark, and Carlisle, which lay along the frontier almost from coast to coast, were to be heavily fortified, garrisoned and provisioned. Sir Ralph was in charge of this important work, and at once set off on a tour of inspection accompanied by engineers, bombardment experts, and siege consultants.[9] His report disclosed that much work was needed to be done: this was put in hand at once. The castles of Berwick and Carlisle still stand to this day, but Wark, twelve miles north of Hexham, has virtually disappeared.

The Earl of Hertford was put in command of the whole army

of which Sir Ralph was natural choice for Treasurer.

In the south of England, Henry was equally alert. He increased his standing army to some hundred thousand men, formidable by any standards. Castles along the south coast were furbished up, garrisoned and put on an emergency footing. Lord Lisle, still Lord High Admiral, was given a free rein with the navy he had been building up over the years. Flying his flag in the thousand-ton *Harry Grace-à-Dieu,* with a crew of seven hundred, he brought every available ship down to Spithead, where they lay at the alert twenty-four hours a day.[10]

Little secrecy by then surrounded the ponderous preparations of the French. On a squally morning, 18th July, the massive threat materialised in the form of a French armada of over two hundred ships laden, it is said, with sixty thousand heavily armed troops.[11] Astonished but undaunted by the apparent strength of the invader, Lord Lisle set sail direct for the enemy. He caught them in the act of trying a landing on the Isle of Wight, from which they were duly repulsed.[12] Apart from that, he either was unable to bring them to battle, or skilfully kept them in constant manœuvre. After three weeks, disease and seasickness overwhelmed the French, who thankfully withdrew to their home ports.[13] The Papist invasion had proved a fiasco, much to the disappointment of Henry's adversaries. The Scots, too, were crestfallen at the outcome. Had there been some measure of success, French troops would doubtless have been poured into Scotland to complete the invasion through the Borders into the North Country. This would have been most satisfactory for Scotland, and would have averted any possibility of Henry avenging the ignominious rout of Ancrum Moor. The Scots knew that Henry could not easily be harried with impunity; news of the mustering of troops in the north had tinged the afterglow of Ancrum with shades of gloomy foreboding.

Meanwhile, various plots had been hatching in Scotland, the most interesting of which was one to kidnap or assassinate Cardinal Beaton.

This novel idea had first been brought to the headquarters of the Council in the North the previous year by George Wishart, an outspoken preacher who had fallen foul of Beaton. Associated with this was the Laird of Grange, who had been ousted by the Cardinal from his profitable office of State Treasurer. From Newcastle, Wishart had been sent down to London where he explained the plan to the King himself. Henry was intrigued with 'the matter which concerneth the killing of the Cardinal', as it is laconically described in the State Papers, but felt he could not openly be associated with it.[14] Political assassination was a game at which two could play and he had enough to worry about already without having to tighten up his personal security arrangements. Wishart was anxious to know exactly what rewards and subsequent protection the King would give to anyone who pulled off this coup. It is not clear what Henry proposed. But either it was thought insufficient or no opportunity presented itself, for Wishart returned to Scotland and the Cardinal remained un-murdered for the time being.

However, whilst engaged at Newcastle with the preparation for Hertford's new army, Sir Ralph received another letter on the subject, this time from the Earl of Cassels. The suggestion was the same as that put forward by Wishart the previous year, and expressly asked what rewards and safeguards could be expected from Henry. Sir Ralph passed the letter on to Henry. The recrudescence of the French party in Scotland, stimulated by the Cardinal's vigorous conduct of affairs to the virtual exclusion of the Governor's waning influence, made the proposal more attractive than when it had been last submitted. Henry was still chary of giving it his personal encouragement. He replied to the Council in the North through his Council at Greenwich on 30th May, keeping it as impersonal as possible.

'His Highness,' declared the instructions, 'reputing the fact not meet to be set forward expressly by his Majesty, will not seem to have to do in it. And yet,' they went on craftily, 'not misliking the offer, [he] thinketh good that Mr Sadleir, to whom the letter was addressed, should write to the Earl of the receipt of his letter, containing such an offer which he thinketh not convenient to be communicated to the King's Majesty.'[15] If the plan had misfired and news of the offer had become public, this disclaimer would have preserved intact the image of a Christian monarch too lofty of principle to descend to such intrigues.

'Marry,' the instructions continued, 'to write to [Sir Ralph] what *he* thinketh of the matter, [Sir Ralph shall say] that if he were in the Earl of Cassel's place, and were able to do his Majesty a good service, he would surely do what he could for the execution of it, believing verily to do thereby not only an acceptable service to the King's Majesty, but also a special benefit to the whole realm of Scotland and would trust verily the King's Majesty would consider his service in the same.'

This was *carte blanche* for Sadleir to arrange for the Cardinal's sudden demise provided the King were not implicated. He accordingly started a clandestine correspondence with the Earl, urging him to go ahead, but as discreetly as possible. Sir Ralph was no more anxious to be embroiled in such a scheme than the King. The Earl possibly thought better of it. He employed the Laird of Brunstoun to protract the correspondence, and nothing came of it that year.

The French invasion of the south of England having been frustrated, Henry was free to launch Hertford's army across the Border. He could thereby justify the stupendous cost of raising and maintaining an army of such magnitude, with its German and Spanish contingents (£20,000 a month in the money of the time), and also avenge the disgrace of Ancrum Moor.[16] For this latter purpose alone he would not have put such a crushing force into commission. He was therefore quite glad of an excuse to use the army upon which so much time and money had already been spent. A suitable pretext for getting it on the move was provided by Monsieur Montgomery de l'Orgue. By producing letters of encouragement from the French King, he had persuaded the ever-reluctant Governor to gather an army, join with the five thousand newly arrived Frenchmen and thrust across into England.[17] Fifteen thousand Scotsmen were levied in the space of a few days. Gathering at Haddington, they all marched off until they came to Bargany Haugh close to freshly fortified Wark Castle.[18] Despite their large numbers they did not feel capable of putting Sir Ralph's reconstruction to the test. They contented themselves with sending out small parties every day to harry the local villagers within a radius of some six miles.[19] They kept this up for ten days until the novelty wore off and no reaction from the English had become apparent. Monsieur Montgomery then pressed the Governor to move across the Tweed and attack Wark. Other English strongholds could also be visited, he suggested. Lord Home, Deputy Commander of the Scottish forces, strongly supported the idea.

But the Governor, in words familiar to the hotheads of Ancrum Moor, protested that they had no heavy artillery or other equipment necessary for besieging castles. They would do much better to turn about and go home; also, he added, the Tweed was about to overflow its banks and they might be trapped the wrong side. Since he was supreme commander, they had no alternative. On the 12th of August the army was disbanded and everyone drifted away. The disconsolate Frenchmen wandered off to Edinburgh and St Andrews. The King of France sent over the noble insignia of the Order of St Michael, with which the Governor and the Earls of Angus, Huntly and Argyll were solemnly decorated to mark such an international occasion.[20] Monsieur Montgomery himself went to Stirling, where they told him about the Earl of Lennox's banishment. These two had been friends in France. Monsieur Montgomery was incensed at the way the Cardinal had behaved in bringing about the downfall of such a splendid young fellow and friend of France. Accusing Beaton of luring Lennox over to Scotland with all manner of promises, Montgomery railed against the Cardinal, who was also in Stirling at the time. In front of the Queen Dowager sharp words ensued between them.

Beaton's temper, always on the slenderest of threads, broke loose, and he slandered the Frenchman in the royal apartments.[21] Montgomery was also a man of spirit: he reacted at once. Stepping up to Beaton, he caught him a smart box on the ears, much to the astonishment of the Queen and the assembled company. Fumbling for his jewelled stiletto, Montgomery would doubtless have run the Cardinal through had they not been parted by horrified courtiers. Calling the Cardinal all manner of names deeply shocking to those who heard them, Montgomery eventually stamped out of the building. The Queen Dowager, checking Beaton's loud protestations, tried hard to reconcile the two. But Montgomery never spoke to him again and refused to stay even in the same town. Beaton doubtless realised that some of his evil treatment of Lennox was in danger of being publicly exposed. He therefore tried to patch up the quarrel by currying favour with Montgomery's officers and aides, putting them up at St Andrews in great luxury, and supplying them with horses and hawks, as well as other things for their amusement.[22] But Montgomery remained inflexible, eventually sailing angrily off to France with all his men and equipment.

The next month it was Hertford's turn. Sir Ralph and the rest of them surged forward across the Border into Scotland along the well-worn paths. The country was laid waste yet again : being the richest agricultural land, the losses to the important harvest were heavy. In one day alone, the unlucky 13th of September, Dryburgh Abbey and both town and abbey of Melrose were burnt, thirteen or fourteen towns and villages were sacked, and large quantities of stored grain set on fire. After wreaking the utmost destruction unopposed, Hertford's army returned to Newcastle and was disbanded.

It only remained for Lord Hertford and Sir Ralph to tidy up and put the accounts and reports in order before returning home themselves. They completed it all in three weeks and arrived back in London about 20th October 1545.

Sir Ralph had been away for so long that all his domestic affairs, including those of his Mastership of the Great Wardrobe, were very behindhand. To these he applied himself vigorously. With equal vigour he set about building himself the splendid house of Standon Lordship on the lands granted him in 1540.[23] Standon was in the centre of his eight-thousand-acre holding in Hertfordshire. The property originally belonged to Anne Boleyn. Sir Ralph had been High Steward there at the time, so knew it well. It was initially given to Sir Ralph for his life, and worth £62 12s 11d. In return for this he surrendered to the Crown two annuities worth £46 13s 4d. But in 1545, as a reward for his Scottish work, it was made into tail male, in other words in remainder to his male heirs. He had, for this reward, to make a payment of £450 4s 9d. This, like many other properties at the time, was bought by instalments. It was eventually only a small part of Sir Ralph's vast holdings of land throughout the Midlands, Home Counties and the West. One deed has an illustration of Sir Ralph kneeling to receive from Henry VIII a gift of all the land on which Bristol now stands.

For a twelvemonth, he was left in comparative peace. But Scotland, from which he was doubtless glad to give his thoughts a rest, was anything but peaceful. By sheer force of personality and the most expert manipulation of bribery and espionage, the Cardinal had made himself a veritable dictator. On all his enterprises he took the Governor with him. This poor man, who must long since have become weary of the burdens of his office, and whose resistance to any form of pressure had crumbled almost to nothing, was probably happy enough to have his every course of action decided for him. His conscience troubled him throughout: he probably knew well enough that many of the things done in his name by Beaton were wrong, even wicked. But he was powerless to protest.

Beaton pushed him forward everywhere like the image on a totem pole. He organised a Royal Progress through the centre of Scotland, taking with him the Queen Dowager, the Governor and several of the more important members of the nobility. At a Convention which they held at Perth, the Earl of Argyll, then Justice General, was obliged by the omnipotent Cardinal to pass sentence of death for all manner of trivial offences brought before him by Beaton. Four young men were hanged for eating roast goose on a Friday. They had also nailed two cow's horns and a tail on to appropriate parts of a public statue of St Francis.[24] A young woman called Helen Stirk and her infant child were ceremoniously drowned because it was reported that she had refused to call upon the Virgin Mary during the birth.

From Perth, after the Convention, the band of tyrants moved on to Dundee. The Cardinal had heard that there was much reading of the New Testament in the old walled harbour town:

this was to be stamped out. Most of the religious excesses were directed against the Lutherans. It was current 'knowledge' at the time, stemming from the ignorant priesthood of the day, that the offending New Testament had in fact been written in its entirety by Martin Luther himself.[25] The Cardinal did not see fit to disabuse his followers of this useful notion.

By the time the Cardinal had returned to Edinburgh with his royal minions and subservient Governor, his astonishing cruelty and inordinate tyranny had earned him many enemies. He narrowly escaped a bid against his life by some of the men of Fife, notably the Master of Rothes and his friends. George Wishart, as we have already seen, was the resident expert on plots to make away with Beaton. The Cardinal got wind of this and caused an assembly of clergy to arraign Wishart on a charge of heresy. The Governor, on being required to send a judge of the Criminal Court to condemn him to death, was about to agree. But after being taken to task in the matter by his cousin, Sir David Hamilton of Preston, he told Beaton to do nothing until he had seen Wishart himself. Wishart's blood would be on the Cardinal's own head if he did not obey, said Arran with quavering defiance, adding inconsequentially that whatever happened now it would not be his own fault.

Beaton's response to this injunction was to condemn Wishart to death himself. A great scaffold was put up before the windows of the Cardinal's apartments in St Andrews Castle on the morning of 1st March. All the surrounding balconies and wall-top seats were hung with tapestries, silks and green cushions.[26] Amongst all these rich stuffs the Cardinal and his men, after jostling for the best positions, ensconced themselves to watch the show.

George Wishart, wearing a long black linen shirt to which were attached little bags of gunpowder at convenient places, was led to the faggotted scaffold.[27] At a signal from Beaton's beringed finger, the fire was lit and the martyred Wishart went off like a rocket. Before he expired, and some time after the flames had caught, Wishart begged the Almighty's forgiveness for his tormentors, but added that within a few days the

Cardinal 'shall lie as shamefully on that same place as he now lies glorious'. This was taken by many present as an utterance of divine prophecy. But there may have been a more mundane explanation: Wishart had been planning the Cardinal's own death for some years.

It is possible to understand that certain religious offences, in the prevailing values of those days, could be thought worthy of the death penalty, although they may now appear to be trivial. But it is difficult to understand how a cultured man such as Beaton, on whom the Pope himself had bestowed the honour in Christ of the office of Cardinal, could justify to his conscience the public torture of a fellow Christian. Even if he thought this violence necessary to expiate the so-called crime and to discourage others, his own exultation in a scene of such bestial savagery is well-nigh incomprehensible. Perhaps the arteries of his conscience had hardened to stone. Perhaps he was himself consumed by flames of megalomania.

As if in support of the cindered hero, a sudden squall blew in from the sea with astonishing suddenness, before the audience had heaved themselves up from their cushioned ease.[28] A torrential cloudburst swept away the foundations of one of the ancient walls in a matter of moments, spilling the grandstand audience of some two hundred people into the courtyard below. Several fell into the well and two were drowned.

It was evidently a day to be remembered.

Beaton himself thought little of it. He set off at once – after a change of clothing – to Arbroath, where he gave away his eldest daughter in marriage to the son of the Earl of Crawford, amid scenes of great jollification and splendour.[29]

But the next month young Norman Leslie, Master of Rothes and a hero of Ancrum Moor, fell out with the Cardinal after a heated argument in which Leslie accused him of defaulting in a private agreement between them.[30] Leslie, a fiery Fifer, was not one to forgive an injury. He determined to put an end to the Cardinal once and for all. With fifteen cronies he came to St Andrews at dead of night. Posting ten of them in the town close to the castle he went with the rest to the castle walls. Beaton had been having repairs done to the castle, and, when the gates creaked open about half-past four on a May morning to admit the early-working tradesmen, two of Leslie's men slipped in with them. They silently stifled the porter and admitted the rest of the band. Each going swiftly to his appointed places, they had seized the castle before half the guards were awake.

One of them, Peter Carmichael, went swiftly and noiselessly up the winding stairs to the East Blockhouse chamber where snored the naked and unsuspecting Beaton. A rapid knock obtained admittance. Lightning stabs of a dagger then ended the life of the Cardinal.

'You cannot kill a priest!' he shrieked. But, finding himself mistaken, he died croaking, 'Fie, fie, all is gone', according to John Knox.

By this time the alarm was raised, the courtyard thronged and townspeople running to the castle walls. Beaton's servants set ladders against the East Blockhouse wall, like firemen, thinking to assist their master out of his room. Only when his gory corpse was hung upon the main rampart could they believe what had happened. When a man called Guthrie went so far as to relieve himself into the Cardinal's gaping mouth, George Wishart's grim prophecy from the scaffold was forcibly brought to mind.[31]

Norman Leslie rapidly brought order to the chaos. Many who approved of his action flocked to the castle with their goods, arms and munitions. The great gates were slammed and defiance proclaimed.

The Governor and the Queen Dowager were appalled at the cataclysmic news. The murderers were given six days in which to appear to account for their action. Disdainfully making no response, they were outlawed. Leslie sent a messenger to England for help.

The Governor himself was in a difficult position, and had a better excuse than usual for doing nothing: his eldest son had been given to the Cardinal as a pledge of his adherence to Beaton's cause, and was still inside the castle. He thereby managed to remain inactive for six months.

Eventually giving way to the clamour of the priesthood, and exhausted by the Queen Dowager's daily questioning about what he proposed to do, the Governor at last collected a small army, and laid siege to the castle. To help in the bombardment two monster cannon were brought from Edinburgh. One was called Crook Mouth, the other Deaf Meg.[32] But after three months, despite the earthquaking exertions of Deaf Meg and Crook Mouth, the castle remained intact. Various epidemics swept the town and threatened the troops. The Governor then gave up and dispersed the army, returning to Edinburgh in time for the next sitting of Parliament.

The castle was finally overwhelmed the following year by forces from France, who carried the occupants away with them, together with all the Cardinal's great treasure. John Knox, the preacher, was one of the captives and served a period in the French galleys, as readers of his works are not allowed to forget.

Meanwhile in England the year of 1546 progressed uneventfully. The Protestant party had grown almost equal to the Catholic in numbers and influence.

Sir Ralph, a moderate Catholic with adequate enthusiasm for the Reformation, made peaceful headway in the construction of Standon. He managed to keep free from political entanglements of every sort. But, at the Court, the health of the monarch was giving cause for alarm. Into his fifty-six years he had crammed the life of several average men. He had ruled with unchallenged authority for thirty-eight years.

But his massive body had not been able to stand the pace set by his whirlwind mind and searing will. His legs had long since capitulated: he could only reach the upper floor of palace or council chamber by means of an elaborate mechanical chair, modelled on the engineering devices used for building the Pyramids.[33]. His skin could no longer hide – and scarce contain – the now curious composition of the flesh within. By December 1546, it was clear that the end was near.

Two rival factions for control of the State on his anticipated death started their unseemly and jealous lobbying. Henry's son

Edward would become King, but who could make himself Regent during the minority?

The Duke of Norfolk championed the Catholic cause, together with his poet son, the Earl of Surrey. They both overstepped the mark, declaring their plans while the King was still alive. Sonnet-writer and blank-verse inventor, the Earl of Surrey would have done better to have kept to his poetry. Convicted of treason through meddling with politics, he was beheaded on 13th January 1547.

Champion of the Protestant faction was the Earl of Hertford, well-known general and uncle of the nine-year-old Edward, Prince of Wales. Sir Ralph wisely adhered at this stage to neither side, but naturally inclined to Lord Hertford, especially after serving with him on the Council for the North, and accompanying him in battle. He knew the Earl well, without being a bosom friend.

At last, at midnight on Thursday, 27th January 1547, a monumental era came to an end. The King with a smile to Archbishop Cranmer, whose hand he was holding, and a last draught of white wine from a goblet, died peacefully in his reinforced bed.

As in life, so in death, drama was his constant companion. For on the way from London to its burial at Windsor, the coffin lay the first night in the chapel of the monastery at Syon, by the river.[34]

And, through some imperfection, the great leaden casket split at the seams with unfortunate results. Early next morning, as reported by a man called William Consett who went with an emergency team of plumbers, dressers, embalmers and others performing secret offices about the persons of the dead, a little dog appeared in the chapel. With busy tongue and wagging tail he brought to fulfilment the strange prophecy of a friar called Peto of the Order of the Observants, who had been an outspoken critic of Henry's marriage to Anne Boleyn. Henry had singled out the monasteries of the Observants when starting his campaign of suppression.

In a sermon before the King, Friar Peto had told him: 'Your preachers resemble the four hundred preachers of Ahab, in whose mouths God had put a lying spirit. But I beseech your Grace to take good heed lest, if you will needs follow Ahab in his doings, you incur his unhappy end also and the dogs lick your blood as they did his, which God forbid.'

12

The Battle of Pinkie, 10th September 1547

THE REMAINING CONTESTANTS for power had clustered like vultures round the dying King. The instant his body was seen to be lifeless, each person's plan was set in motion. The Earl of Hertford had the initial advantage: he commenced operations in the corridor outside the King's room. Catching hold of Sir William Paget, Secretary of State, as they left the bedside, he persuaded the Secretary to take his side. It is possible that cautious advances had already been made to the influential Paget as soon as the King had taken to his bed. Whatever means Hertford actually used – and his resources were ample – Paget declared strongly in favour of Hertford being proclaimed Protector and Regent.

Henry had appointed in his will sixteen executors to run the affairs of State equally until Edward was eighteen years old, with an inner Council of Twelve as their advisers. Sir Ralph was named as one of the Twelve. Henry had always had a high opinion of him: as a personal gesture, he had left Sir Ralph a legacy of two hundred gold marks. It is alleged that the figure was originally one hundred, but altered by Paget to two. In addition to this, he was designated by the dying King to be one of the important committee responsible for supervising the succession of the throne.

But, in the hurly-burly which ensued, Sir Ralph remained curiously aloof. He neither rushed to join Hertford, nor made any public suggestions about what should be done to direct the affairs of State. He had got on well enough with Hertford during their campaigns. But the slight suggestion of restraint discernible in his reluctance to commit himself at this crucial point may indicate a latent mistrust or disapproval of Hertford which he was too prudent to express.

Hertford rushed ahead with his plans. Aided by Paget, he persuaded the other Executors to approve his appointment as Protector and Regent, with full powers for the conduct of the country's business. The only dissentient voice was that of Sir Ralph's friend Thomas Wriothesley, the Lord Chancellor, who was, to begin with, most outspoken in opposition. But getting no active support, perhaps especially lacking that of Sir Ralph, Wriothesley thought better of it. Sir William Paget then, to everyone's astonishment and some people's approval, announced that shortly before his death King Henry had wished to distribute various lucrative honours. Hertford for instance was to become Duke of Somerset and Wriothesley Earl of Southampton. Useful grants of Church lands were to accompany these distinctions. Possibly a hint of Paget's (or Hertford's) brainwave had reached Wriothesley to account for the complete withdrawal of his opposition. But, whatever the reason, the Executors and Council settled down with Hertford, now the omnipotent Duke of Somerset, as their acknowledged leader. Surprisingly, there was no mention of Sir Ralph during the distribution of favours. Yet there is no suggestion anywhere that he expected or wished for preferment, or was in any way disgruntled. No fit of pique or bout of intrigue withdrew him from public life.

From his general attitude, one of calm acceptance of events, it can reasonably be inferred that he was satisfied. He certainly received official confirmation of many of his extensive grants of Church land which were either in his possession already, or being negotiated with the King. It is possible that in preference to a high-sounding name and irrevocable commitment to a particular policy or faction, he was well content with the accumulation and securing of enormous wealth. His estates were prodigous even at the time of Henry's death. Many of them were enumerated in a closely written document of twenty-five sheets dated 30th June 1547. Centred on Standon, they ranged from Selby Abbey in Yorkshire to Woolwich and Plumstead Manors in Kent, from the rectory, church and living of St Martin's in London to lands in Gloucestershire, from Clifton near Bristol to Haslengefield in Cambridgeshire. The administration of such a scattered private empire must have called for surpassing skill. It would be diffi-cult enough in modern times, with all the aids to travelling, accounting and checking.

He retained his royal appointment of Clerk of the Hanaper although apparently only in name, since records show that the actual fees began to find their way into the pocket of Lord Hales, one of the Commissioners on Enclosures. He was probably happy enough to keep a foot in the palace door through merely holding the appointment, and could well afford not to bother about the fees.

As soon as Somerset felt himself firmly accepted as Protector of the Realm, he turned his attention to religious affairs. By a process of what was optimistically called the 'Purification of the Church' all manner of desecration was perpetrated on many fine buildings throughout the country. All stained glass, statues, paintings and pictures were to be removed from every church and chapel, every vestigial hint of the existence of the Pope to be erased. Fortunately for posterity, the orders were imperfectly carried out, but much wanton and needless damage was done.

Having established himself as spiritual dictator, Somerset turned his thoughts to the military potentialities of his position. The late King's will had called for the enforcement by his suc-cessors of the contentious marriage treaty between Mary Queen of Scots, now five years old, and the ten-year-old Edward VI. The Executors and Council, themselves appointed by the will, were obliged to be in favour of the enterprise. They gave Somerset full support when he announced his plans for achieving agreement in Scotland by force of arms.

He at once set about collecting an army, in which he appointed Sir Ralph to his customary post of High Treasurer.[1] The Earl of

Warwick was second-in-command. In appearance, this was probably one of the most splendid hosts to issue out to war which England has ever seen. It was certainly the noblest royal army of any pretensions ever to march through England to the Northern Borders.

Even to bystanders, to whom the coming and going of armies was no novelty, the spectacle must have been magnificent. In the main body came the Lord Protector, the Duke of Somerset, before whom fluttered the Royal Standard. Whatever his faults, Somerset was a most handsome man of superlative bearing, a veritable monarch in all but name. Around him trotted a sovereign's escort of warrior nobles, splendidly equipped in costly armour, glinting and flashing in the summer sunshine. Their velvets, silks and jewelled braids shimmered in the breeze as they pounded along the dusty roads. Behind him came the core of the army, four thousand tough, well-disciplined foot soldiers, veterans of many campaigns.

In the vanguard rode the Earl of Warwick with three thousand footguards equally finely equipped. Bringing up the rear came Lord Dacre, hero of many a Border clash, at the head of another three thousand.

The roll of the rest of the army was studded with names which were bywords on the battlefields of Europe, wherever men discussed military skill and valour. Lord Grey de Wilton, High Marshal and Captain General of the Horse; Sir Francis Brian with two thousand light horsemen; Sir Ralph Vane with four thousand demi-lancers in heavy armour, their powerful mounts clad in sheets of burnished steel; Sir Peter Mewtus with six hundred matchlock gunners on foot; the flamboyant Spaniard Sir Pedro Gamboa with two hundred mounted gunners; Sir Francis Fleming, an expert artilleryman and Master of Ordnance, in charge of fifteen massive horse-drawn cannon; that well-known 'deviser of fortifications', Sir Richard Lee. And at the back, no less worthy, Mr John Brown in charge of the Pioneer Corps, fourteen hundred strong. Creaking and rumbling along behind came the supply train of nine hundred wagons of all sizes, and innumerable nondescript carts.[2]

Such a display of panoplied power, over eighteen thousand men, would surely have daunted the proudest aggressor on that August day of 1547.

Lord Clinton, the Lord High Admiral, had a useful fleet in close support, consisting of thirty-four men-of-war and thirty-one supply ships. It was originally intended to take the whole army up by sea but so many ships would have been needed that the plan was dropped. It was also felt that a warmer reception might await such an armada than on the previous occasion when the element of complete surprise had been preserved.

By Saturday the 27th, the host had arrived intact at Newcastle. Six miles out of the town, Sir Ralph, who had gone on three or four days ahead with the Earl of Warwick, came out to meet them, accompanied by his own handsomely appointed personal retinue. About three o'clock in the afternoon Somerset was greeted by the Mayor and city fathers with celebrations and gunshot salutes. Sir Ralph had found him a comfortable lodging at the house of Peter Riddell, a wealthy citizen. To preserve strict discipline among the troops a new set of gallows was set up in the market square and a soldier promptly hanged for brawling.[3] There was no further trouble.

On Sunday morning a mounted parade of the cavalry followed a general inspection. In the afternoon Lord Mangerton arrived with a party of forty Scotsmen bringing local reports and intelligence from the Eastern Borders. The next day Somerset continued northwards, lunching at Morpeth and putting up for the night at Alnwick Castle.

On Tuesday he was entertained at Bamborough Castle by the same Sir John Horsely who had seized the letter carried by Brunstoun, Cardinal Beaton's envoy, the letter Sir Ralph had intended as a trump card in his interview with King James V some years earlier. That afternoon they reached Berwick. Sir Ralph had stayed behind in Newcastle to settle accounts after the departure of the army. Having arranged everything to his meticulous satisfaction, he travelled on to Berwick, where he joined Somerset on Friday, 2nd September. On Sunday the army was set in battle order and prepared for business.

An air of what might be described as cautious optimism prevailed among the directing staff of the operation, although they were aware that everything the Scots could do to oppose them certainly would be done. A man called William Patten was travelling close to Somerset, rather in the manner of a war correspondent, and dressed in military attire. He later became a minor figure in the justiciary, but at the time he was busy making notes for a dispatch to Sir William Paget, whom he described as his 'most benign *fautour* and patron'. Part of his report was certainly of unusual interest, being an interview with Somerset in which the great man told him of a recent dream.[4] They were strolling along the northern walls of Berwick town, and Somerset described it. He dreamed that he had returned to the Court of the King, and although everyone had received him most warmly, he himself 'thought that he had done nothing at all in this voyage, which when he considered the King's Highness's great costs and great travail of the men and soldiers, and all to have been done in vain, the very care and shamefast abashment of the thing did waken him out of his dream'.

Patten was at pains to explain how dreams often went by opposites and quoted innumerable examples from the classics and the scriptures to illustrate this comforting interpretation for the benefit of Somerset on the eve of battle. It was not clear to either of them how much of a dream should be reversed to reach actuality. Such a course might have upset the dreamer if it were taken as a prophecy that he would not return at all to the King's Court.

However, it intrigued Mr Patten. In Somerset's mind it doubtless gave way to more immediate and readily interpreted matters.

Marching six miles out of Berwick, the army camped at the village of Roston. Sir Francis Brian had been sent on to scout a mile or two ahead with four hundred of his light horsemen. The rest of the army had followed at tactical intervals, the baggage train hugging the coast.

After storming one or two strongholds on the way, the army bypassed heavily defended Dunbar and camped on the night of Tuesday, 6th September, near Tantallon Castle, ancient fortress

of the Douglases, which Sir Ralph knew intimately from his uncomfortable stay there on a previous occasion. Another Douglas
castle, that of Dunglass, had been surrendered on the way by Lord
Home's nephew Matthew. Patten was not impressed by the defenders' appearance: 'I never saw such a bunch of beggars come
out of one house together in my life,' he observed.[5] But first notice
of the presence of organised resistance came next morning when
bands of light horsemen were seen cantering about, presumably
spying out the invading force. As a result of a sudden mist which
descended as the English were crossing the little river Lyn, the
Earl of Warwick nearly lost his life. Going back to see that
there were no stragglers who could be picked off by the skirting
enemy, he was lured into an ambush prepared for him by crafty
Scotsmen. They had learned of his presence by the simple method
of shouting across to the English rearguard to ask if there was
anyone of importance there. On being asked why they wanted to
know, they replied plausibly enough that one of their number
well known to the English as a distinguished figure wished to
come across to them if there was an Englishman of rank by
whom he could reasonably be received. Completely taken in, the
lusty pioneers bawled into the mist the news that the great Earl
of Warwick himself was there. Being a man of valour and always
ready to do battle, the Earl had escaped from his staff and bodyguard on the pretext of going back for a short time to see that
all was well behind.

He at once took the opportunity of dashing single-handed at
the knots of Scottish cavalry hovering round the river crossing.
His particular target was 'Dandy' Ker, a Captain of Horse, who
had 'come pricking towards his Lordship apace'. Dandy Ker,
taken aback by this valiant assault, wheeled about and galloped
off, pursued very closely by the Earl of Warwick 'all the way at
spear point, so that if Ker's horse had not been exceedingly good
and wight his Lordship had surely run him through in this race'.[6]

This had upset the ambush arrangements, especially as Henry
Vane, who had suddenly appeared, set off in pursuit of the galloping Earl. The Scots had had no idea such an important figure
was careering about practically unescorted. This was fortunate

for the Earl, otherwise he would certainly have been set upon by every horseman in the vicinity. As it was, the fury of his personal attack swept them all aside. Henry Vane just survived after a desperate encounter. Monsieur Barteuil, a Frenchman, was wounded in the behind, and one soldier was killed. The Scots, although suffering no casualties, lost three men taken prisoner, one of whom was Richard Maxwell. This man had been in England not long before, and had received friendship and hospitality from both Somerset and the Earl of Warwick. In addition to a wound in the thigh, he must have felt particularly uncomfortable about his situation.

The Earl of Warwick eventually turned up again, breathless and battered but undaunted, just as Somerset sat down to dinner. He had discovered useful information about the enemy's disposition of troops, had disrupted their ambush and got the rearguard safely across the misty river.

Somerset was a kind-hearted man, as is shown in several small incidents noted by people present. When Lord Warwick, for instance, told him how splendidly Monsieur Barteuil had come to the rescue, and what an unfortunate wound he had suffered as a result, Somerset sent at once for his own surgeon to dress the wound – and also the injuries of the captured Scots – and insisted that he should travel in the Commander-in-Chief's own battle wagon. This was, by all accounts, 'right sumptuous for cost and easy for carriage'.[7] Whether Monsieur Barteuil was able to take full advantage of the luxurious seating is not recorded.

Before Warwick's arrival, a curious figure had been brought before Somerset under suspicion of being a spy. He aroused much jocular interest among those present, for he was, according to one of them, 'a fellow like a man, but I wot not of what sort, small of stature, red-headed, curled round about and . . . bald in front, forty years old, and called himself Knox. . . . His coat was of the colour of burnt brick – I mean not black – and well worth 20*d* a broad yard. It was prettily fresed and hemmed round about very suitably with pasmain lace of green caddis. . . . However far he had travelled that day, he had not a whit soiled his boots, for he had none on : harmless belike, for he wore no weapon.

He rode on a trotting tyke well worth a couple of shillings,' added the bystander with light sarcasm, noting that 'the loss whereof at his taking he took very heavily, yet did Somerset cause him to be set on a better'. He dribbled rather a lot, which gave the superior onlookers the chance of making many caustic references to it being 'no fault in the man, but the manner of the country' and other patronising observations. Unable to decide whether their loquacious captive was 'a foolish knave or a knavish fool' they sent him on his way, better mounted at least than when he had arrived.[8]

The next day Somerset decided to have a consultation with Admiral Lord Clinton, most of whose vessels could be seen lying at anchor opposite Leith and Edinburgh some ten or twelve miles up the Firth of Forth. The Admiral's party could normally have been left to its own resources to bring him safely ashore. But, as the barge drew near, what was the astonishment of Somerset's staff to see a large St George's banner being waved vigorously up and down further along the coast, well within the lines of the Scottish camp.[9] This was a bold ruse to encourage the Admiral to step ashore as the guest of the Scotsmen. It nearly succeeded. But Somerset sent a party down to the beach with all possible speed and by much shouting and counter-waving the Admiral came safely to land among friends.

After this the army moved on along the coast, eventually taking up a strong position a little east of the town of Musselburgh. Between the two forces ran a large open ditch or 'cleugh' called Pinkie Cleugh, from which the subsequent engagement took its name.

At the sight of an unexpectedly large Scottish force, estimated at some thirty-six thousand, strategically camped between the sea on their left, with an unsurpassable bog on their right and the river Esk to their front, Somerset realised at once that there was no chance of an easy victory. Unless they could come to terms, both sides were bound to do each other terrible injury, and casualties would be heavy. Out of the humanity of his heart, he made a determined effort to avoid a battle.

He sent a message to the Scottish Governor, the Earl of Arran, the substance of which survives in full. He pointed out that the only reason for his appearance with an army was the breaking of a promise solemnly made, through the Governor, by the whole realm of Scotland. He touched briefly upon each item, then made it clear that he did not wish to see a full-scale battle between neighbouring peoples such as themselves. He offered to amend Henry VIII's marriage treaty so that Mary Queen of Scots should stay for ten years in Scotland and be brought up in the Scottish way of life. He urged the making of a peace treaty between Scotland and England for these ten years at least. In return for this he asked the Scots to undertake not to send their little Queen abroad, nor to arrange her marriage with a foreigner.

If they would agree, said Somerset, he would withdraw his army at once, and make full restitution for any damage he had already caused, the amount to be decided by an independent assessor.

This urgent message was brought to the Governor in his headquarters. But instead of holding a general consultation with most of the influential men of Scotland, at that moment all within a few hundred yards of his tent, the Governor showed it only to his half-brother, now Archbishop of St Andrews in place of the murdered Cardinal Beaton, and to one or two other close cronies entirely unqualified to express an opinion in the name of Scotland.[10] These included the Archdeacon of St Andrews, who had been made a Privy Councillor earlier in the year: he had been persuaded to accompany the Governor on to the field of battle only with the greatest difficulty. Another was Alexander Beaton. The fourth was a lawyer called Hugh Riggs of Carberry, a man described at the time as 'noted more for his big body, corpulency and bulky strength, than for any military skill'.

Into the hands of this assorted motley the Governor, abdicating his own sacred trust, placed the decision upon which rested the lives of many thousands of Scotsmen and the political future of the country. Peeping through the tent flaps as they huddled in Governor Arran's headquarters, the undistinguished quartet surveyed the ranks of the Scottish host, and were comforted by the numbers they saw. Beyond the river, glinting dimly in the morning light, they saw the lesser encampment of the enemy. A few cannon, a few horse, a few footmen – this humble letter, they counselled the undecided Governor, was surely dictated from fear of our army. Victory is certain from our great forces, our impregnable position, and, they added with wheedling persuasion, from your great leadership.

Reject the offer out of hand, they said. The Governor at once agreed. Brushing aside protests from one or two of his closest staff, he made no move to consult a single army commander, a single chief, military or political. But worse was to follow. In his name, the four conspirators at once issued their own version of what the letter had contained. The English had announced their intention, they said, of reducing the whole of Scotland to subjection, and of taking away their baby Queen by force to England. No hint of the actual offer. No word of the truth.

Stumbling over their costly braided robes, crucifixes clanking as they hurried along, Archdeacon and Archbishop spread the false news from tent to tent. It went through the camp like the crackle of burning gorse. Indignation kindled anew the half-hearted hostility towards the English. Eager hands snatched up weapons; nearly forty thousand men stood to arms.

Fifteen hundred of the Scottish horse crossed the Esk, which lay along their front, in an unco-ordinated gesture of reconnaissance and defiance. There, according to an eye-witness, they 'pranked up and down' in a highly provocative manner.[11] Fearing a major assault, Somerset ordered Sir Francis Brian to attack with his light cavalry. Surging forward with unexpected suddenness, Sir Francis's men made a lightning charge and fell upon the Scottish horse. After a vigorous encounter, the Scots were overwhelmed and their cavalry annihilated. His action earned Sir Francis the honour of knight banneret.

After this preliminary, Somerset was returning to his headquarters, after setting some artillery on a hill towards the sea further away from the main body. But, before he was halfway back, a Scottish herald with a trumpeter caught up with his party. According to custom, the herald was given free passage on his errand. He announced that he came from the Governor, who wished to know what prisoners had been taken in the clash. He also said he was authorised to offer the Protector 'honest conditions of peace'. A man who described himself as 'one of the riders by', hearing Somerset raise his voice loudly in answer to the herald, drew near out of natural curiosity. He was 'somewhat the bolder to come the nigher, thinking his Grace would have it no secret'.

Whether Governor Arran, once his secret advisers were out of sight, had decided to accept Somerset's terms after all, or, terrified by the unexpected rout of all the cavalry, was trying to make belated amends for not having taken some more reliable military advice, is not recorded. But, whatever the reason, he was too late.

Before Somerset could reply to the herald, the trumpeter piped up with a message too. 'My master, the Earl of Huntly,' he said, 'hath will me to show your Grace that [in order that] this matter may be sooner ended and with less hurt, he will fight with your Grace for the whole quarrel twenty to twenty, ten to ten, or else himself alone with your Grace man to man.'

The audacity of the trumpeter's offer must have caused a gasp of astonishment among those who heard it. There were probably smiles all round.

But from Somerset there came no smiles or gasps. With sure dignity, most moving to those who heard him, he replied to the herald : 'Your Governor may know that the special cause of our coming hither was not to fight, but for the thing that should be the weal of both us and you. For God we take to record, we mind no more hurt to the realm of Scotland than we do to the realm of England and therefore, our quarrel being so good, we trust God will prosper us the better. But as for peace, he hath refused such conditions at our hands as we will never proffer again, and therefore let him look for none till this way we make it.'[12]

Turning then to the doubtless grinning trumpeter he told him shortly that the Earl of Huntly was not of sufficient rank to challenge such a person as himself who was acting on behalf of a sovereign, but that there were others of equal rank to whom he could have addressed himself if he wished. The Earl of War-

wick at once claimed the right to take up the challenge, subject
to Somerset's approval, telling the trumpeter that, if he could
obtain his master's consent, he would give him a hundred
crowns.

But Somerset would not allow Warwick to take up the challenge either. 'The Earl of Huntly is not meet in estate with you,
my lord,' he said firmly. 'But, herald,' he went on, 'say to the
Governor, and him also, that we have been a good season in this
country and are here but a [small] company, and they a great
number, and if they will meet us in the field they will be satisfied with fighting enough. And, herald, bring me word they will
do so and by my honour, I will give you a thousand crowns.'[13]

The Earl of Warwick again tried to get Somerset to allow
him to take up the challenge. But the Protector was adamant and
herald and trumpeter returned to their masters.

While this little group had been gathered together, three or
four stray shots had landed nearby. It was suggested either that
the herald and his companion had been doing no more than spying out the land, their messages a mere pretence, or that they
had been sent to draw Somerset and his chiefs into a readily
recognisable party where they could, with luck, have been picked
off by snipers.

By eight o'clock on the morning of the next day, 'Black Saturday', the 10th of September 1547, some of the English artillery
and most of the attendant auxiliary troops had moved away from
the main body to take up their new commanding position, in
accordance with Somerset's instructions of the previous day.
They went off in the direction of the harbour. This was interpreted by some of the Scotsmen as a withdrawal, either to
leave the scene altogether, or to collect supplies from the ships
at anchor. The whole Scots force therefore suddenly left its unassailable position and raced across the protective Esk. It being
noticed that they had struck all their tents during the hours of
darkness, it was unkindly suggested this had been done 'as well
none of their soldiers should lurk behind them in their camps as
also that none of their captains should be able to flee from their
enterprise'.[14]

Lord Grey de Wilton's cavalry were instantly ordered to attack, for which manœuvre the heavily armed and unwieldy horsemen were not adequately prepared. They did what they could, but the Scottish footmen, armed with eighteen-foot pikes, closed up with exemplary discipline, and stood in solid ranks, the foremost kneeling with pikes pointing breast high to the enemy, those behind standing at their shoulders with pikes straight ahead. It was a formidable barrier.

Plunging across the Pinkie ditch or cleugh, and over the boggy fallow, Lord Grey's heavyweights met their match. 'As easy shall a bare finger pierce through the skin of an angry hedgehog,' noted William Patten.[15] Somerset, clad in splendid armour and accompanied only by Sir Thomas Chaloner, Clerk to the Privy Council, watched from his position among the artillery.

The front ranks of the horsemen fell back upon their fellows and serious confusion resulted. The situation deteriorated very rapidly for the English. Lord Grey himself was wounded in the mouth and neck by one of the long pikes, and his colleague Darcy was struck a glancing blow by a cannon ball. The dent in his armour caused him agony and the forefinger of his right hand was flattened.

The confusion was communicated to the infantry behind, and had not immediate action been taken to restore order out of the mounting chaos, the Scots might well have been victorious. Had they not lost all their cavalry by their riverside 'pranks' the day before, a charge at this moment might have been decisive.

As it was, one figure emerges at this particular stage as the probable saviour of the day for the English. This was Sir Ralph Sadleir. Although High Treasurer, he was by no means the man to take the shelter of a rearward position to which his office legitimately entitled him. He was a warrior more than an accountant. Leaving his books and ledgers in charge of his clerks he had buckled on his well-chased armour, adjusted the visor of his elaborate helmet, and entered the thickest of the fray as soon as he could be certain where that was to be found.

At this crucial moment, it was Sir Ralph who rallied the struggling cavalry, turned them quickly into ordered squadrons, re-formed the disorganised infantry behind and by his fiery example led them once more against the oncoming Scots. It needs little imagination to see why he, together with Sir Ralph Vane and Sir Francis Brian, the cavalry captains, was singled out from the whole army for receipt of the highest battlefield honour that English chivalry had to bestow – that of knight banneret.

Sir Ralph's vigorous action was the turning point of the engagement. It turned in favour of the English. Urged on by their commanders, including the doughty Earl of Warwick, who never ceased to inspire fresh courage wherever he went in the noisy confusion, the English troops braced themselves and fell upon the Scots.

At the first shock of this counter-attack, the Scotsmen began to waver. The Governor, the Earl of Arran, according to an eyewitness, leaped on his horse and galloped from the field long before all doubt as to the result had been dispelled.[16] Sir Ralph captured his personal standard, which he bore home and kept to the end of his life. The standard pole survives to this day, lying against Sir Ralph's tomb in the peaceful shadows of Standon Church.

The sight of the galloping Governor sapped the spirit of the remaining commanders. They wheeled about and were soon out of sight. Abandoned by their leaders, the soldiers gave way once more to chaos. Despair followed quickly. Throwing away their weapons and wrenching off such armour and equipment as they had, they fled. Heavy slaughter followed, which must have weighed sorely upon the Governor's conscience. Apart from the Earl of Huntly, captured by Sir Ralph Vane when inadvertently unhorsed, only a handful of nobles was taken among the fifteen hundred prisoners.

Some fifteen thousand three hundred Scots were slain and two thousand wounded. These huge totals are hardly credible, but from contemporary records they seem to be authentic.[17] They would doubtless have been greater still had not Sir Ralph gone forward, after Somerset had ordered the trumpeters to call a halt at six o'clock, and stopped the onrush of jubilant foot soldiers.

Out of control of their own captains, they might well have exceeded the five-mile limit which Somerset had set to the pursuit. English losses were put at under sixty men. Limitless possibilities for looting had slackened the bonds of discipline. It was left to Sir Ralph to perform the extremely difficult task of returning the scattered companies to some sort of order and military obedience. This in itself was a feat and, according to a soldier there, 'a thing not easily to be done'.[18]

Next day the English marched on to Leith making occasional sallies up either side of the Firth. In the shadow of Blackness Castle they were delighted to discover the great ships *Mary Willoughby* and *Antony of Newcastle* which had been captured in English ports by the Scots before any of the troubles has started, together with another big ship, which the Scots had called the *Boss*. These were seized after a battle with the castle garrison.[19]

Meanwhile the Queen Dowager had removed her little daughter, Mary Queen of Scots, to Stirling, twenty miles beyond Edinburgh, for safety. She now decided to send her away to France. Accordingly an ambassador went to acquaint the French with the decision and to report the precarious state of affairs in Scotland.

Later in the week the Earl of Bothwell, father of James the fourth Earl, newly released from his Edinburgh prison by Governor Arran, came to visit Somerset and was handsomely entertained to dinner.

Before withdrawing his army, Somerset sent Norroy King of Arms over to the Scottish Council at Stirling to discuss arrangements for peace. He later returned with the Scottish Rothesay Herald and a guarantee that envoys would meet the English Commissioner at Berwick within a fortnight.

On Michaelmas Day, Thursday, 29th September, the English army was disbanded south of the Border. Somerset made tracks for London, while the Earl of Warwick, Lord Grey de Wilton and Sir Ralph Sadleir went to Berwick to await the arrival of the Scottish envoys. But as no one had arrived by 4th October, the end of the agreed time, they started home the next day. While at Berwick the Earl of Warwick took the opportunity of knighting Monsieur Barteuil, who had been wounded during the Earl's foray in the mist at the crossing of the Lyn.

Meanwhile at the western end of the Border the Lord Warden of the West Marches had conducted a small invasion of his own with five thousand men. Storming north as far as Lockerbie, he assaulted, garrisoned and victualled Castle Milk, and then withdrew.

The season of 1547 had therefore been a fiery one for Scotland. England had won battles, but little else. The coveted Marriage Treaty was no nearer being honoured. The young Queen of Scots, so far from setting out for Hampton Court, had one foot on the boat for France. The next summer she actually sailed, later marrying the French King's son. Apart from death, destruction, and vengeance, no more useful result had been achieved by the Duke of Somerset's heroics. Sir Ralph had had the fork tail of his personal pennant clipped in the name of the King, elevating him to the pinnacle of chivalry as knight banneret. Apart from one creation by Charles I at Edgehill, and another by George II at Dettingen, the roll of bannerets was closed for ever.

Sir Ralph had not forgotten his accounting. Sword was soon exchanged for pen, and a fair copy of his meticulous accounts was presented to the Auditors on the 20th of December. From the 1st of August to the 20th of November, a lengthy addition of innumerable items reveals a total cost to the Crown of £44,912 8s for the whole expedition.[20] His own expense account, allowing for such necessary items as parchment, books, quills, carthorses, dust for blotting, sand boxes, counters, canvas bags, four yards of green cloth, trussing coffers and a telling table, came to £570 9s 5½d.

13
'. . . like a King . . .'

THE DUKE OF Somerset, Lord Protector, was a popular figure with the man in the street. Unaware of political intrigues behind the scenes and without vigilant daily papers to throw sudden light in dark corners, the ordinary citizen saw him as a valiant glamorous national leader. He was given a rapturous welcome on his return to London after the Pinkie campaign. Reports of his overwhelming victory had gone before him: London was jammed with a cheering waving crowd.

Somerset himself fully appreciated the warmth of these sentiments. He had no compunction about arranging to receive handsome additions to his already extensive holdings of Church property as a reward from a grateful people. The neat signature of the eleven-year-old King completed the authenticity and spontaneity of the gift. Somerset's personal estate was now bringing him over £10,000 a year, a figure which, if it could be accurately represented in modern terms, would be considered astronomical.[1]

Feeling himself thoroughly secure on the military fronts, Somerset now turned his attention to religion. His ardour for the Reformation outstripped the speed at which it could be established throughout the country. His first obstacle was Dr Gardiner, Bishop of Winchester, a staunch old Papist. Somerset was determined to eliminate him, and sent Sir Ralph, together with Sir Anthony Wingfield, down to the Bishop's Palace at Southwark. Duly carrying out his instructions, Sir Ralph solemnly sealed up the doors of cabinets and studies to preserve the contents for any subsequent investigations.[2] He then conducted the learned Bishop to a cell in the Tower of London. This was a distasteful commission for Sir Ralph. He not only was a personal friend of Gardiner's, but had never shown himself in favour of violent religious persecution. However, if he was to maintain his own position, he had no option but to carry out Somerset's instructions.

At this stage, life began to run away with Protector Somerset. 'I am like a King,' he said. Although this was partially true, he had not the solid constitutional and executive backing needed for carrying out schemes of princely aggrandisement. To complete the building of Somerset House in London – the site of the present repository of wills and other records – he swept away a parish church and blew up a new and exceedingly beautiful chapel. Part of St Paul's Churchyard was levelled, and excavated bones flung into the surrounding fields.[3]

In January 1549, the Act of Uniformity swept away all Latin services and established the Book of Common Prayer throughout the country. By such precipitate action, Somerset rekindled the Papist fervour which he had stifled by the imprisonment of Bishop Gardiner. Taking advantage of what appeared to be a rising tide of difficulties, Lord Thomas Seymour, Somerset's scheming brother, began to fancy himself as a better Protector. He had started well by marrying Queen Catherine within two months of Henry VIII's death. When she inconveniently died, Seymour set his cap at sixteen-year-old Elizabeth, the young princess being nurtured at Hatfield. When he should have been sailing the seas in command of the Navy as Lord High Admiral, he was romping round Hertfordshire with the titian-haired embryo Queen. Her subsequent lack of enthusiasm for marriage has been attributed to her experiences in his jolly company.

Trading on his relationship with his all-powerful brother, Seymour established a 'trencher-fed' army of ten thousand ruffians, available on call.[4] With two cannon foundries, an armament works of his own, and a useful highly paid pirate navy, he was becoming a formidable figure. He even bought the Scilly Isles as a lair for his brigands.

Sir Ralph was a law abiding man, and disapproved of plots and commotions against established authority. He was probably quite glad to put his signature to the death warrant which was eventually served on that enterprising buccaneer. 'He was a wicked man,' added Latimer, 'and the realm is well rid of him.'[5]

Throughout the country the chief sign of some malaise at the head of government was the abysmal state of poverty and distress into which the peasantry had fallen. Enclosures and the discontinuing of unprofitable cropping had put out of cultivation almost two-thirds of all the arable land. Food therefore became scarce and expensive. But those with the money indulged in an astonishing bout of luxurious living, concentrating their attentions on making their clothing and general way of life more and more exotic.

'To behold the vain and foolish fashions of apparel used among us,' wrote Becon, a disapproving contemporary,[6] 'is much too wonderful: I think no realm in the world – no, not among the Turks and Saracens – doeth so much in the vanity of their apparel as the Englishmen do at this present. Their coat must be made after the Italian fashion, their cloak after the use of the Spaniards, their gown after the manner of the Turks, their cap must be French, their dagger must be Scottish, with a Venetian tassel of silk. I speak nothing of their doublets and hoses,' he goes on with mounting indignation, 'which for the most part are so minced, cut and jagged that shortly after, they become torn and ragged. . . . What a monster and a beast of many heads is the Englishman now become!'

In a few years' time it had got so out of hand as to require government action to restore a sense of proportion and semblance of dignity. An order was drawn up to restrict the quantity of clothing a woman should possess, with government inspectors appointed to examine all ladies' wardrobes at regular intervals.

Nor did the menfolk escape these ponderous enactments.[7] 'Provided also for these monstrous breeches commonly used' – they were evidently the talk of the town – 'no one under the degree of a lord or baron shall wear any under pain of £3 a day: none to have any stuffing of hair, wool, flock, or other ways : and no man of little stature to have a bow [a sort of crinoline support] more than a yard and a half in the outersize, and the bigger men and the guards two yards, upon pain of 20s a day the wearer and 40s the maker of the hose'.

By the summer of the next year, 1549, there was such dissatisfaction with the Protector's religious stipulations and enactments that much of the country was bordering on revolt. On Dartmoor, outraged Cornishmen – 'many of us speak no English' – and doughty Devonians gathered in a nondescript army several thousand strong. They issued a fifteen-point memorandum demanding the return of all the disused religious services including the celebration of mass in Latin. 'We will not receive the new service, because it is but like a Christmas game. We will have our old service of Matins, Mass, Evensong and Processions, as before.'[8] Incorporated in their challenging charter were clauses demanding the reduction of staff in gentlemen's households. 'We will that no gentleman shall have any more servants than one [per hundred mark income] to wait on him.' This army gathered round the walls of Exeter, but the Mayor refused to let them in.

A man called Raleigh, a shipowner in a small way, was chased round his parish of Budleigh Salterton for having told an old woman by the wayside to give up such an outmoded pastime as telling her beads. He was eventually caught and severely manhandled by the mob.[9] The experience probably made an amusing bedtime story for his little son, better known later as Sir Walter Raleigh.

While the West Country men were laying uncertain siege to Exeter, and making tentative plans to march on London, other parts of the country were also led to take up arms by the strength of their religious convictions.

The most notable insurrection occurred in Norfolk, where some sixteen thousand country folk gathered in a great armed encampment on Mousehold Heath, just to the north of Norwich. Under their leader, Robert Ket, a silver-tongued tanner from Wymondham, they maintained themselves in orderly fashion as an insurgent force. The oak under which he sat in judgment each day on offending local landlords and transgressors of his own strict discipline stands to this day beside the busy main road, marked by railings and a metal plaque. They had no idea of marching on London, nor indeed of marching anywhere. They issued no proclamation challenging the King or the Protector. They merely stated their religious grievances, to which they added protests about the rising cost of living and the confiscatory activities of local landlords.

There were the seeds of serious revolt throughout the entire country. Decisive action by Somerset would have quelled the insurrections before they reached such proportions. But Somerset had lost all grip of government affairs. He had no idea what to do, and consequently did nothing but issue a steady and often conflicting stream of orders, proclamations, announcements and bulletins of all descriptions. They came pouring out in such profusion that after a very short time few people knew what was supposed to be happening. Regiments of heralds, town criers and government spokesmen queued up all over the country to read out innumerable circulars. There is no evidence that anyone listened to them. Even the Privy Council were bemused by the turn of events.

Like a majestic ostrich, Somerset buried his handsome head in the sands of England's domestic disintegration and started thinking up plans for another invasion of Scotland.

Meanwhile, the French King thought it a good moment to assault Boulogne, which was still in English hands where it had lain for three hundred years. Francis of France himself rode triumphant along the battered boulevards adjoining the actual town. In the Borders, the Scots themselves overran some of the outposts established by the English troops after the Pinkie campaign of two years earlier.

Somerset actually dispatched the Earl of Warwick, his Pinkie second-in-command, with a small army to carry out a vaguely defined invasion of Scotland. But, before he had got further than Warwick itself, the Earl – on 10th August – received an urgent countermand instructing him to go at once to Norwich.

He was certainly needed there. Somerset, whose private sympathies lay with Ket and his peasant army, had reluctantly agreed that the Marquis of Northampton, brother of Catherine Parr, should go down to Norwich and restore order. With him rode Sir Ralph Sadleir, accompanied by a well-mounted and handsomely appointed company of retainers and tenants from Standon and his other properties. With the Marquis and Sir Ralph went some other members of the Privy Council with their own little private armies equipped at their own expense,[10] since Somerset was still disinclined to do anything positive. Somerset's offer to go to Norfolk himself to chat with the rebels was hurriedly declined.[11] He did, however, provide a company of Italian sharpshooters to accompany the force as a government gesture.

Being thankfully admitted to Norwich by the city fathers, who were somewhat embarrassed by the immediate presence of such a host of encamped insurgents, the Marquis and Sir Ralph set about putting things in order.

But nothing went according to plan. The Italian company was pushed to the front to do battle with Ket and his men, who had armed themselves from the surrounding country towns and houses, belligerently refusing to go home peacefully with a general pardon – 'We have done nothing wrong, we need no pardoning.' The Italians were promptly routed, their captain captured, stripped of his Mediterranean finery and hanged naked on misty Mousehold Heath.[12]

This was an unpromising start. But worse was to follow. Ket's men violently attacked the town, ignoring their heavy losses and making fine use of several cannon they had found. Eventually breaching the walls they came flooding into the narrow streets of the ancient town. Sadleir and the Marquis scampered out through the suburbs, leapt on horses and made off across country to join the Earl of Warwick, who was known to be coming to the rescue. They left behind, considerably the worse for wear, their depleted force and many dead, including other less nimble Privy Councillors.

This was a new role for Sir Ralph, who had never before been obliged to flee from a battle. However, the two of them got safely away to Cambridge, where they met the daring and impulsive Earl of Warwick. He had travelled south at great speed, outstripping the main part of his force which consisted of stolid German mercenaries and dainty Italian conscripts. Clumping through the Midlands, the Germans were taking their time. The Earl of Warwick, after conferring with Sadleir and the Marquis, decided to get on to Norwich and let the remainder of his force come on in their own time.

Taking new heart from the enthusiasm of the Earl of Warwick, they all turned round and hurried back to Norfolk. They went so eagerly and so fast that they omitted to keep their columns properly closed up and in tactical formation. For, after blowing open the city gates in fine style, hacking their way into the centre of the town and hanging the first sixty prisoners in the market place, they looked round for their ammunition and baggage train. Too late they discovered that these had been neatly abducted by Ket and taken away into Mousehold Camp.[13] The Marquis of Northampton, having recovered some of his lost prestige, placed his powderless artillery so as to command the northern gates of the city. Ket returned, briskly attacked the gun positions themselves, and carried off every piece of artillery. Mousehold was now a place of some military consequence.

Warwick's action appeared to have been more enthusiastic than strategic. If Ket had attacked, supported by his newly acquired heavy artillery, it looked as if there would have been yet another suburban escape, this time featuring the Earl of Warwick as well. Sir Ralph and the Marquis would at least have known the way. But, declining advice from all sides, Warwick decided to fight it out. A solemn little scene occurred according to an eye-witness, when the Marquis, the Earl, Sir Ralph and some others gathered round to kiss swords in a 'do-or-die' pact.[14] Fortunately the strength of these bonds of chivalry never came to the test, for the next morning Warwick's German mercenaries arrived – there was no sign of the Italians – and Ket's army was routed with heavy loss of life. Ket himself was later captured and hanged from his own oak tree.

The rebellions were over – but at a cost of some ten thousand lives at the hands of foreign troops. Even the least perceptive observer at the time could see that the ship of State was drifting rudderless with sails flapping. The Earl of Warwick had gained what little glory was obtainable from suppressing the Norfolk rising, and Somerset the Protector was increasingly blamed for every misfortune, whether individual or collective. Sir Ralph eventually joined up with Warwick and other members of the Privy Council in an attempt to pull things together.

As soon as Somerset heard that so many influential people were meeting from time to time to discuss affairs of State, he gave way to panic. The Privy Council originally wished to do no more than persuade him to adhere to his original charter of appointment and to remember that by Henry's will he had no authority to turn himself into such a potentate. All the Council were supposed to have been equal in authority, and Somerset merely the chairman. But Somerset did not hold that view. He issued yet another proclamation, declaring that the Earl of Warwick and his adherents were traitors planning the overthrow of the State and the capture of the King.[15] All loyal supporters were to arm and gather at once at Hampton Court in defence of King and country. This inflammatory bulletin caused a sensation: hundreds of people flocked to Hampton Court, expecting to hear of invasion, revolution and all manner of danger. Instead they found the Protector standing in the courtyard of the Palace shouting hysterical threats against the lords and urging all the people to rise against such dangerous tyrants as Warwick and his friends. The King himself was brought out into the torchlit yard and persuaded to say a few words in support of Somerset, 'our loving Uncle'.

But no one seems to have been very impressed. Many concluded that Somerset had gone off his head. Much of his sense of judgment had certainly departed from him. For Sir Ralph openly to ally himself at last with direct opposition, it was clear that Protector Somerset was no longer in effective control.

Towards the end of the year Somerset, in a welter of remorse and despondency, surrendered himself to the Lords of the Council and went off to the Tower in ecstasies of self-pity. The

'London Lords', as they were called, promptly handed round noble titles among themselves. They also, with some justification, reimbursed themselves from the Royal Mint to cover their costs of suppressing the various rebellions and usurping the Protector – all of which had been done at their own expense. They gave themselves silver bullion with authority to the Mint to turn it into coinage. Sir William Herbert, who had brought a party from Wales, was allotted almost a ton of silver.[16] The monumental piles of coins into which all their shares were quickly converted swamped the already enfeebled economy of the country. It was years before a series of drastic devaluations of the pound restored some fiscal stability.

Meanwhile the French possessions were surrendered and the Scottish outposts abandoned. A not very honourable peace was concluded on all fronts, and the Earl of Warwick took it upon himself to restore order in the country.

Before long Somerset had recovered some of his lost favour and position, emerging from the Tower as a chastened and ostensibly reformed member of the Privy Council. His daughter married the Earl of Warwick's son at Richmond in June 1550, and his spirits generally improved. Sir Ralph kept clear of him, however, and worked away at his own affairs in company with the 'London Lords'. Somerset soon started plotting to regain his lost Protectorship. This time he was given no quarter by the rest of the Privy Council and was beheaded for treason on 22nd February 1552. The indignation and sorrow of the London mob, to whom he had remained a popular hero, caused the authorities no little concern for a day or two.

Shortly before Somerset's downfall, there had been yet another distribution of honours among Warwick's associates. Dukedoms, marquessates and earldoms were handed round with fine abandon. Curiously, Sir Ralph neither applied for nor received anything. His close friends all did well, but he remained plain Sir Ralph, knight banneret. Possibly he considered the rare honour of banneret, won in the very dust of battle, sufficient in itself. Perhaps he had no wish to emulate some of his acquaintances who, in racing up the ladder of nobility, had occasionally

found a rung missing. The consequences were usually ignominious.

The Earl of Warwick, who had now made himself Duke of
Northumberland, soon fell victim to the over-grand ideas which
had brought Somerset to ruin. He rapidly and deservedly earned
the hatred and distrust of most of his associates and nearly all of
the people. In the summer of 1553, the King, still no more than
a lad of sixteen, fell seriously ill with consumption and other
more obscure ailments. His last days were clouded by the new
Northumberland's tawdry deathbed schemes to alter the constitutional succession of Henry VIII's daughters to the throne.
Whether or not Mary and Elizabeth were technically illegitimate,
a view widely held at the time, it was to be made a pretext for
Northumberland to arrange hasty marriages for his son and
daughter to secure the succession in preference to the King's
half-sisters.

He drew up a document at Greenwich, where he was hovering round the dying King like a bejewelled vampire, and coerced
the principal lords, judges and men of state to assemble and
sign it. Sir Ralph's tidy signature appears among those of the
Privy Councillors. He probably signed more to keep out of immediate trouble, like most of the others, than through any
conviction of the validity of the document.[17] As the King lay
increasingly feeble in the royal apartments the clamour and protests of Northumberland's unwilling signatories will have
reached his ears. Every now and again the door burst open and
Northumberland's imperious hand impelled a particularly reluctant witness to the bedside to be convinced by the whispering
King himself that – despite the existence of Parliamentary Acts
to the contrary – it was the royal wish that the document should
be signed.

In charge of the patient was a mysterious woman from
Norfolk over whose name the passage of years has drawn an
impenetrable veil.[18] Of no nursing qualifications, she was undoubtedly a quack. Laden with bottles, unguents, ointments and
pills, she claimed to be able to cure the King. She was left in sole
charge, a circumstance which laid the deepest suspicion on those

by whom the death of the King was impatiently awaited.

At length, exhausted by the domestic uproar, the young King's wasted body was pronounced lifeless a little before nine o'clock on Thursday evening, 7th July 1553. The last few threads which bound him to life had been snapped by the Norfolk witch. His hair, his nails, his toes had dropped off; for the last fortnight he neither ate nor drank. Northumberland was at considerable pains to keep the death secret. Some days afterwards, the pale corpse of the King was carried to the Palace window and pressed against the panes to reassure the doubting fearful crowd, to whom a rumour of his death had filtered through.

Northumberland's desperate efforts to have his daughter-in-law, Lady Jane Grey, recognised as Queen, and his son, seventeen-year-old Guildford Dudley, consequently made King, ended in fiasco.

Mary, Henry VIII's daughter by Catherine of Aragon, clambered on to the throne to the relief of most people. The prospect of any perpetuation of the Northumberland dynasty was too horrible to contemplate. While the headsmen were busy on Tower Hill, Mary wrangled over what sort of burial service should be accorded to her half-brother, the late King Edward VI. What was left of his once lissome body lay unburied in his Greenwich bed for over three weeks. Doctors examining it found traces of poison.[19] Whether these had been deliberately introduced, or were the result of some inadvertence, must remain a matter for conjecture.

Sir Ralph had managed to keep clear of factious recriminations. Apart from his forced signature of Northumberland's 'succession' document, he had done little more than side with the 'London Lords' as soon as Somerset's downfall seemed certain.

When Mary sent a letter to the Council claiming the throne, she received a reply signed by nearly all the members dismissing her claim because of her alleged illegitimacy. Sir Ralph astutely did not add his signature. He doubtless foresaw the eventual outcome and looked to the future.

Once she was established, Sir Ralph resigned his position

from the Council, and was probably deprived of his office of Master of the Grand Wardrobe. But, not being forcibly put out of favour and managing to keep friends with many of the new régime, he retained his appointment of Clerk of the Hanaper for the time being.

For Queen Mary he had little admiration and no love. She was an ardent Papist, while he remained a moderate Catholic. He kept out of harm's way at Standon, devoting himself to the improvement of his great house which was still building and the management of his extensive private affairs.

During the whole of her reign, he seems only to have received two letters from her, both at the beginning when the country was still in a state of unrest. The first, to 'our trustie and well-beloved Sir Rauff Sadleyr' commanded him 'to put forthwith in a readiness of your own servants, tenants and others your friends about you, as many hable [*sic*] men as well on horseback as on foot ye are able . . . to repress any . . . tumult that may fortune to spring or arise in any . . . part of our country where you dwell'.[20]

Whether this was to force him into the open as a downright supporter of the new Queen, any hesitancy about which would immediately make his loyalty suspect, or whether it was a normal circular to all men of substance in the Home Counties at that time, is not clear.

It seems likely that it was more in the nature of a mildly punitive gesture to an influential man who had resigned from the Council and was known to have consorted with factions opposed to the present Queen. The letter closed with the conventional phrases: '. . . whereof fail you not . . . as you will answer to the contrary.' Perhaps on this occasion there was a hint of menace. It was hardly the tone to be adopted by a gracious Queen asking a loyal subject to come to her help if occasion arose. But she was not thought to be a gracious Queen by many people, and she may not have known how loyal a subject Sir Ralph would prove to be.

To make sure he could not deny having received the letter, special instructions were scribbled on the outside of the letter:

'Post of Ware, see this letter delivered.' We may suppose that the Postmaster himself, officer of the efficient public service inaugurated by Thomas Cromwell, hurried at once along the six miles of dusty road to the great new house and thrust the royal command directly into the hands of the eminent house-builder.

Next year she wrote again, after she had launched her campaign of vicious religious persecution. She may by this time have realised that her previous peremptory instructions were a little out of place. Her letter, addressed this time to 'Sir Raffe Sadler' – showing of what little consequence was the spelling of names – came from 'Philipp and Marye the Quene'. It required him to have forces ready, 'at an hour's warning, to be employed for suppression of any sudden tumult, stir or rebellion within our realm, and for resisting any foreign invasion'. The menacing tone had been dropped, and the letter ended: '. . . whereof we pray you not to fail, as we specially trust you.'

Nicholas Heath, who had emerged from prison at Mary's accession and been made Archbishop of York as well as Chancellor of England, also wrote to Sir Ralph, in February 1556: 'Our loving freeinde Syr Raffe Sadler . . . touching the office of Clerkship of the Hamper . . .' It was a request to Sir Ralph to relinquish this official appointment in favour of a protégé of Heath's called Francis Hemp. Hemp himself brought the letter to Sir Ralph, and doubtless watched triumphantly as he read the thinly veiled threats by which the Clerkship was to be extracted from the holder.

Sir Ralph gave up the appointment without demur; any protest would only have jeopardised the quiet life he had determinedly been leading.

But it was about this time he began to turn his thoughts towards the heir to the throne. This was Elizabeth, an idol of the public whose popularity grew with each savage excess practised upon a smoulderingly indignant people by Mary and her associates. By the end of her vengeful reign, Mary had been responsible for the public torture by fire of nearly three hundred people, and for the misery and destitution of countless others. Edmund Bonner, Bishop of London, was chief ogre. However much convinced of the necessity for capital punishment in dealing with non-conformists, there could be no excuse for a man clothed in the vestments of Christian service to revel in scenes of human torture. On one occasion, thwarted of burning to death a batch of eighteen simple people – some of whom had no understanding of what they were supposed or supposed not to believe – by the turbulent anger of a London crowd, Bonner carried off the remaining six to his private house at Fulham. After a mock trial in one of the rooms, the Bishop took his victims into a garden and burnt them secretly after dark.[21] It was small wonder that a published broadsheet of the day denounced him as 'the common cut-throat and slaughter-slave to all the Bishops in England'.[22]

Mary herself was much devoted to her scheming husband Philip of Castile, son of the Emperor Charles V, whom she had married despite protests of people and Parliament. Although not assailed himself, his retinue was constantly provoked, insulted, robbed and hated.[23] His only aim in the marriage was to secure the succession of the English throne upon himself or upon a child of the marriage. He was frequently ill through eating large quantities of bacon fat, like a bullock at a tub of swedes. He got most of Mary's money out of her, and treated her with disdainful mockery. Her pathetic false pregnancy made her the laughing stock of Europe. No one seemed to have diagnosed the advanced stage of dropsy which was obliging her, according to secret dispatches of the French Ambassador, de Noailles, to the King of France, 'to wear her clothes very straight'.

The combination of all these events, in addition perhaps to a conscience tortured by the hatred she was attracting, brought her to the verge of insanity. Unbounded jealousy of her sparkling-eyed half-sister Elizabeth, whom she knew to be so popular, served further to unhinge her. She had never a vestige of good looks, grace or charm. The only time her gritty features had been seen to crease into reasonable pleasantness was on her triumphant ride into London at her accession: 'La beauté de visage plus que médiocre,' admitted Renard, the Emperor Charles V's Ambassador in London.[24] Her face was no fault of her own.

It was certainly not her fortune. As she rolled about the bare floor of her room clutching her knees for hours on end, or pattered along the corridors of Hampton Court, grasping crumpled tear-stained letters addressed to her indifferent husband, courtiers must have wondered how long she was to be spared.

The same thoughts must have frequently crossed Sir Ralph's keen mind. Hatfield House, where Princess Elizabeth, the young heiress, spent many days under a mild form of house arrest as a potential rival, was only fifteen miles from Standon. It was no coincidence that led Sir Ralph in that direction on so many of his days out hawking. Nor was it any less of a coincidence that the Princess was very fond of falconry. What more natural than regular meetings at which the sport could be taught by the experienced statesman to the budding Queen? There is reason to believe that much of her grounding in the ways of diplomacy was learnt from her well-informed sporting neighbour. They became firm friends. As Sir Ralph well knew, his return to the public life to which he was so admirably suited was being soundly prepared.

An hour before daylight on the morning of Thursday, 17th November 1558, Queen Mary died. No time was lost in declaring her successor. Parliament met at eight o'clock the same morning and proclaimed Elizabeth Queen.

Another influential man who had been astute enough to cultivate the friendship of Elizabeth was William Cecil, later Lord Burghley. Of nimble conscience as far as religion was concerned, he had offered his services as a devout Papist to Queen Mary, quoting as a testimonial his secretaryship to the Protector Somerset. Having acted rather ineffectually on the Queen's behalf, and seeing no considerable opening awaiting him in public affairs, he had, like Sadleir, retired to the country and started to build an enormous house. But unlike Sadleir's, his house, Burghley, survives in its entirety to this day, a monument of splendid architectural achievement and crammed with great treasures.

Cecil declared to Elizabeth that he was no longer a Papist, and felt that he could be of great help to her. Elizabeth was inclined to agree.

As soon as Cecil heard of Mary's death he rushed to Hatfield to be first with the news. But within minutes of the death, and before leaving London, he had considered himself the Queen's appointed agent. In this capacity he issued all manner of instructions and proclamations in her name, changed the guard at the Tower of London, dispatched envoys to all the European courts, put the coastal garrisons and Northern fortresses on an emergency footing – even arranged for an approving sermon to be preached at Paul's Cross, 'in order', he wrote in his eager, well-formed handwriting, 'that no occasion might be given to stir any dispute touching the governance of the realm'.

He had made himself a founder member of the new regime: Elizabeth duly appointed him her Secretary. He at once made arrangements for a grand levée at Hatfield to which everyone of importance was invited. Old allegiances were cast aside as the country's dignitaries jostled and lobbied in the Great Hall on Sunday, 20th November, eager in their protestations of loyalty and anxious at all cost to preserve or acquire some lucrative office.

The lightning speed of his well-prepared *coup* set Cecil firmly in the saddle as director of the Queen's affairs.

When this tide of clamouring would-be courtiers receded from the Great Hall at Hatfield, Sir Ralph and Cecil were among the three or four who remained behind with the new Queen to plan for the future. Sir Ralph was there officially as representative of the 'London Lords'.

The next day, Monday, 21st November, Sir Ralph was authorised to issue various proclamations, including a general summons to all the lords in and around London to come to Hatfield on the 23rd and accompany the Queen on her triumphal progress and entry into London. This was duly accomplished with great celebration, and she was fêted all the way to the capital.

When Elizabeth formed her new Privy Council, thirteen of the old members were reappointed to preserve continuity in the direction of affairs. Eight new ones were added, forming a balance between the Papists and the more Protestant-inclined favourites of the new Queen. She had always been more Protestant than Catholic herself, although to prevent trouble while

Mary, the arch-Catholic, was on the throne, she gave an outward show of being a true Catholic.

Although he was busy with her affairs of state, in company with the more inexperienced Cecil, Sir Ralph was not reinstated as a Privy Councillor until several months had gone by. This was curious. It may have been because Cecil did not want any initial competition from such a formidable figure as Sir Ralph, or that the Queen herself felt she could get more of her own way through the yielding Cecil than the less malleable Sir Ralph. The Queen was twenty-five years old, and Cecil thirty-eight, whereas Sir Ralph was fifty-one. Or possibly Sir Ralph declined to accept such a prominent position until he had seen that the new régime was beyond likelihood of sudden overthrow.

14
Warden of the Borders

IN JULY 1559, King Henry II of France was toppled off his horse at a jousting tournament being held to celebrate the marriage of his daughter with Philip of Spain, former husband of Elizabeth of England's predecessor, Queen Mary.

The resounding clang as the heavily armoured monarch crashed to the ground had more than immediate repercussions. Prising up the royal but dented visor, Monsieur Montgomery de l'Orgue, his opponent, discovered to his dismay that he had inadvertently killed the King with a splinter from his well-couched tilting lance.[1] Henry's heir to the throne was the Dauphin Francis, whose wife was Mary Queen of Scots. Not only Queen of Scotland, she laid claim to Elizabeth's throne of England. Now Queen of France as well, she was in a better position to press her claim. To show that she was in earnest she quartered the arms of France, Scotland, England and Ireland on her Great Seal.

Elizabeth and her Council were rightly alarmed at this development. In Scotland, Mary of Lorraine – Mary Queen of Scots' mother – had ousted the Governor, the Earl of Arran, and had become Regent of Scotland in his place. She was known as the Queen Regent. Her supremacy gave renewed vitality to the Catholic party in Scotland, where the Reformation had been making considerable headway, actively assisted by the Protestant nobles. These nobles were determined to sweep away the Catholic Queen Regent and her following of Frenchmen whom she imported in a steady stream, placing them in the best offices of State.

The lords banded together and became known as the Lords of the Congregation. Ill provided with funds and other supplies, they were steadily losing ground in the face of new support for the Queen Regent which flowed from France. Now that her daughter was Queen of France she could expect even more formidable help.

The whole situation was fraught with anxiety for Elizabeth. Somebody would have to go up at once to the Borders and stiffen the Congregation party. The impending danger of Scotland becoming a province of France could not be ignored.

There was only one choice for this awkward assignment – Sir Ralph. In order to give his mission some form of disguise, the Earl of Northumberland and Sir James Croft, Governor of Berwick, went with him, ostensibly to investigate the state of the Border defences. Sir Ralph had therefore an acceptable reason for staying some months at Berwick, where they foregathered in August 1559. The Earl of Northumberland, thirty-one-year-old Thomas Percy, was an ardent Catholic. Sir Ralph rarely took him into confidence about his own secret mission, declaring to Cecil in a dispatch that the Earl was 'very unmeet for his charge here'.[2]

Sir Ralph's entourage consisted of fifteen gentlemen with all their servants, followers and equipment. He also took his eldest son Thomas and another person called Richard Sadleir, whose identity is not clear. Sir Ralph took his favourite horses with him: Grey Cross, Grey Somerset (perhaps a veteran of Pinkie), Bay Reynold, Bay Markham, The Bald Nag and The Heriot, as well as many others.[3]

Once more he plunged into the drama of political intrigue. There is no evidence to show that he did not relish the prospect as soon as the situation began to grow tense. Two or three days after Sir Ralph had left London for the North, the Earl of Arran slipped into Cecil's London house. This was not the indecisive and now usurped Governor of Scotland, with whom Sir Ralph had had so many exasperating dealings in Henry VIII's time. It was his son, a slack-limbed man of twenty-nine, Huguenot by conviction, but showing disconcerting signs of being unable to marshal what few thoughts he had in his head. His father, on being ousted from the Regency of Scotland five years previously by Mary of Lorraine, had been created, rather incongruously, Duke of Châtelherault by the French as some sort of compensation. He still cherished the hope that his son would marry Mary Queen of Scots. But during Mary's four-year marriage to Francis of France he had fancied Elizabeth of England as a daughter-in-law. This suggestion had originated as a bribe by Henry VIII.

Mary Queen of Scots was anxious to lay hands on young Arran, who was in France at the time. His name had been put forward as her rival to the throne of Scotland. If, as had been suggested, he were to marry Queen Elizabeth, his claim would be strongly backed by power, all of which would be most inconvenient to Mary. She therefore decided to eliminate him. But Arran got word of the hunt for him and escaped to London.

It is not clear whether he was combining business with pleasure, and diplomacy with courtship, but during his secret stay in London – ostensibly to discuss Scottish affairs with Cecil on behalf of the Protestant Lords of the Congregation – Queen Elizabeth paid him a visit. Although she scurried secretly into Cecil's house, she had not been quite so secret as she thought. Vigilant spies of the Spanish Ambassador, de Quadra, discreetly posted and all-seeing, immediately recorded her arrival. Just as quickly they discovered the identity of the mysterious guest who had remained in the back rooms the whole time. De Quadra duly reported to King Philip of Spain, guessing that Arran's role was that of suitor for the hand of the Queen. Before leaving, Arran took the opportunity of borrowing two hundred crowns from Cecil.[4] But that was his only success. Elizabeth was not amused by him.

The French Ambassador was also taking an intense interest in Arran's activities, as well as in those of the Lords of the Congregation in general. He sent round a complaint, in the name of the Queen Regent, that Elizabeth's agents and officers on the Scottish Border were intriguing with the Queen's enemies.

The news that Sir Ralph was going north again will have confirmed his fears that mischief was brewing. Elizabeth herself wrote in answer to the Queen Regent[5] ('Très haute et très puissante Princesse, notre chère sœur et alliée . . .') saying that it was too extraordinary that any of her officers should intrigue with the Queen Regent's enemies of their own accord – and, of course, it must have been of their own accord, since she herself knew nothing about it. Please would the Queen Regent give exact details so that all those concerned could be caught and punished.

Elizabeth's conscience was elastic to a degree: her letter was dated the very day before Sir Ralph departed with instructions to inject new courage into as many of the Queen Regent's enemies as he could find.

To strengthen his hand, Sir Ralph took with him £3,000 in French coin, the first of a series of similar infusions of welcome aid for the Congregational party. Had it been in English coin its source would have been more readily guessed. As an additional but rather unconvincing disguise for Sir Ralph's real mission, the Queen Regent was told that he was going up as part of a commission to improve the general standard of administration of the Borders, a commission to which she was invited to send representatives for joint discussions. Such special mention of Sir Ralph must of itself have confirmed any latent suspicions about him in Scottish minds.

Sir Ralph was in regular correspondence with Cecil, the tone of which provides evidence of the close friendship between them. Personal notes are found in many of the official letters: 'I am here [at Burghley] like a bird out of a cage,' Cecil confided to Sir Ralph on one occasion when he was able to take a weekend off.[6] He told Sir Ralph of the difficulties about the builders who were at work in Burghley House, and of the business of paying them. 'I have been a builder in my day,' replied Sir Ralph, referring to his own palatial Standon, 'and never lacked money, so I think builders should not.'

At Berwick, Sir Ralph set to work with his customary briskness. He reported at once on the work of Sir Richard Lee, the fortifications engineer, who had excelled himself at Berwick. He wrote specially to the Queen to bring this to her notice, suggesting some important figure be sent up to admire it all, 'for surely the works be worthy the seeing,' he enthused, 'being both fair and likely to be made very strong'. The fact that Sir Richard Lee was father-in-law of Sir Ralph's second son, Edward, perhaps lent additional inspiration to the glowing testimonial. The Duke of Norfolk was duly sent up and reported well on the defences.

The most effective agent of the Congregation party was the well-known Reformation preacher, beak-nosed Mr John Knox. A letter from him awaited Sir Ralph at Berwick, seeking material aid for the anti-French Congregation party if they were to survive at all in the face of the Queen Regent's influx of Frenchmen. Sir Ralph at once replied – in his colleague Sir James Croft's name, to avoid his own machinations being revealed if the letter went astray – suggesting Knox should send someone, such as 'Mr Henry Balnaves, or some other discreet and trusty man secretly [to] repair to Berwick to confer on this great and weighty business with Sir Ralph Sadleir, who is specially come for the purpose'.[7]

Sir Ralph soon realised that the cause would be well served by the presence of the Earl of Arran in Scotland. He wrote at once to Cecil to tell him so. Arran was accordingly sent out of London and up to Berwick, all under conditions of great secrecy. It was not, of course, secret from de Quadra, the Spanish Ambassador, who always seemed to know about the most private and confidential affairs almost before they occurred. But his colleague, the French Ambassador de Noailles, did not discover what had been going on until the following month, when he wrote an angry dispatch to the Queen Regent's French Director of Operations, d'Oysel.

On 1st September, Arran with one travelling companion, a man called Randolph, arrived incognito at Berwick. There they awaited completion of Sir Ralph's arrangements to introduce him quietly into the heart of the Congregation party. The next week, de Noailles, suspecting that Arran might have come to London, officially informed Elizabeth that Arran was a 'wanted man' in France, and that if he were to turn up in England it was her duty – by an extradition clause in the Treaty of Cambrai – to arrest and return him to Paris.

Elizabeth laughingly looked the worried Ambassador straight in the face. She denied that she had heard anything about Arran, and had certainly never seen him. She would, of course, be only too glad to do as the King wished: Arran would be arrested at once if he should turn up. De Noailles was doubtful whether she was telling the truth: she had already won a great reputation for cunning. He saw on her face, he reported, 'plus de dissimulation que de certitude et bonne volonté'.[8]

* * *

In Scotland, the Congregation party was making no headway, either with religious reformation – despite the fulminations of John Knox – or with loosening the grip of the Queen Regent's French forces on the country. They had no money or equipment worth speaking of. They could not even obtain whole-hearted support from the ordinary country people. Although disliking French control, few of these relished the prospect of committing their slender livelihood to such hazardous adventures.

Sir Ralph, ensconced at Berwick, was the nerve centre of Elizabeth's half-hearted efforts to support them openly with troops for fear of precipitating a war between England and France. With the national defences practically non-existent after Queen Mary's incompetent reign, England could not have withstood a French invasion. Sir Ralph's mission was therefore one of double importance. He had to prevent the French from gaining an even stronger grip on Scotland by spurring on the Congregation party, who were supposed to be bitterly opposed to the Queen Regent. Yet all his activities must be deadly secret. As we have seen, he was ostensibly at Berwick to discuss improvements in Border administration.

Henry Balnaves, messenger from the penniless Congregation, sculled ashore at Berwick as the old church clock clanged midnight on 6th September 1559.[9] Slinking through the misty streets he came to Sir Ralph's lodgings. A quick tap on a side door and he was admitted, and given a bed. Not three hours later came more stealthy footsteps on the cobbles and into the house slid the Earl of Arran with his companion, Mr Randolph, at the end of their incognito journey from London.

Early next morning Balnaves gave Sir Ralph a detailed account of the state of affairs in Scotland, the best first-hand report he had received so far. Balnaves was delighted when Arran then walked into the room. He had had no idea Arran was on the way to Scotland, much less that he was actually under the same roof. Arran was looked to for leadership, to bring new spirit into the flagging Congregation. Sir Ralph confirmed the birth of this new spirit by giving Balnaves two leather portmanteaux containing £3,000.

After a long talk with Arran, Balnaves went quietly out again at nightfall. Rowing across to Holy Island, where Captain Reid was harbouring the boat which had brought him down from the coast of Fife, he went aboard. After waiting six days for a suitable wind, Balnaves set sail in the morning for Fife and a great welcome from Congregation headquarters.

Arran then lost no time. Sir Ralph had by now set up his customary network of contact men and was able to get Arran secretly into Scotland through Teviotdale and then up to Hamilton Castle. There, his father, the Duke of Châtelherault, was thumbing through muddle-headed plans for usurping the Queen Regent and her Frenchmen.

There was much enthusiasm over the arrival of the £3,000 among the depleted forces of the Congregation, who mustered at once, hoping for a share-out. A cavalry division was finally got together. This description must have been unduly flattering, for when the Queen Regent had been met by a cohort of Scottish cavalry on her return from France, she had wept at the sight of them. The cavalcade of ponies of all shapes and colours, bestrode by men with many individual idears on what a cavalryman's outfit should be, had brought tears to her eyes. It will have borne little resemblance to the French dragoons which she had so often seen pass before her in thunderous jingling parade. But the Congregation were only too glad to get anyone to come and join them. In addition to the horsemen they managed to form a whole section of men with arquebuses, and to buy a little ammunition to go with some of them. Thus re-equipped, both morally and materially, they set out once more against the Francophile Regent. They surged through Edinburgh, sweeping the slight French opposition aside. They were obliged for the second time to ignore the actual Castle. Heavily entrenched in this craggy fortress every door barred and bolted, every portcullis well down, the Lord Erskine, Keeper of the castle, continued to deny entry to anyone.[10] He claimed that he was responsible to Parliament alone, and that neither the Queen Regent nor the Lords of the Congregation had parliamentary authority. Parliament itself had not met for some time, there being too much internal dissension to provide a quorum. Lord Erskine therefore continued in command. Whenever threatened with attack from either side, he declared he would turn his guns on Holyrood Palace, which lay in the valley below. Since no one wished to be the cause of destroying the Palace, he remained unmolested. But he was doubtless an inconvenience to whomever happened to be occupying the rest of Edinburgh.

The refreshed Congregation force now assailed the town and fortress of Leith, two miles from Edinburgh. This harbour town had been made the Queen Regent's operational and administrative headquarters. Garrisoned by a formidable force of Frenchmen and newly supplied with fresh troops and equipment direct from France, Leith had become a symbol of the French occupation of Scotland. The Duke of Châtelherault, in the name of the Congregation, had called upon the Queen Regent to clear it of French troops and to stop fortifying it. She had replied that she would do as she pleased, and that she had as much right to build at Leith as the Duke had to build at Hamilton.[11]

Leith was accordingly the objective for the Congregation army and they duly rushed against it. But since nearly all the brass cannon in the country were in Edinburgh Castle, under the fierce command of Lord Erskine, and they had no other siege equipment, they made no impression against Leith.

They camped bravely in front of the walls, but that was all they could do. There was not much left of the £3,000, and the soldiers began to drift away unpaid and unfed. The only hope was to get more money. It was therefore decided in the greatest secrecy that John Cockburn of Ormiston should go down to Sir Ralph and see if he could get some more money out of him. Balnaves had been very successful, and Ormiston would surely do even better, especially now that Queen Elizabeth's agents could see that the Congregation army was at last on the move against the Papist Queen Regent.

Ormiston duly arrived at Berwick. After hearing an account of the situation, Sir Ralph handed him £1,000 in a leather sack and Ormiston set off delighted. But he had not got away from Edinburgh unobserved. The Queen Regent's intelligence service was highly developed. One of her best agents was James, fourth Earl of Bothwell.

He soon got to hear of Ormiston's mission and reported at once to the Queen, offering to get hold of the money for her. She accordingly directed him to intercept Ormiston on his return from Berwick. She also arranged for advance notice of Ormiston's departure from Sadleir's lodgings to be sent to Bothwell by a man called Home who lived at Blackadder, ten miles from Berwick. This was an excellent spot from which to gather information about the comings and goings at Sir Ralph's headquarters.

As Ormiston trotted through the night from Berwick back to Edinburgh, his leather sack strapped firmly over his saddle, a shadowy figure rose up suddenly from the tree-lined route and struck the messenger down.[12] Battered and made prisoner, his precious leather sack torn away, Ormiston had failed in his mission, and Bothwell had succeeded. Triumphantly the resourceful Bothwell hurried back to his nearby castle of Crichton.

In no time, word of the disaster reached Arran, who guessed the culprit at once. Appalled at the thought of the captured Ormiston being made to tell all the details of the support which the Congregation was getting from Elizabeth, he was doubly dismayed at the loss of the money. Within a few hours he was cantering out of Edinburgh with two hundred men: two of the precious cannon bumped along behind. With luck he could retrieve the stolen money and rescue Ormiston before word of the mission reached the Queen Regent: he fondly imagined she still knew nothing about it.

He moved fast, but Bothwell moved faster. Breathless word being brought to him that Arran was on the way, Bothwell dashed out of the house without waiting to pull on his boots or saddle his horse.[18] Leaping on its bare back and clutching the precious leather pouch, he galloped down the grassy banks of the Tyne, which flows below the castle walls. Fifteen minutes later the first of Arran's horsemen struck sparks from Crichton's cobbled yard. Helter-skelter down the dales, through the wynds and closes of old Haddington town, they pursued the scampering Bothwell. Abandoning his horse he dived down a passage called the Goul and through an open doorway into the midst of the astonished family of Sandybed. Quickly they hid him in a dark corner until the hue and cry had faded. When he emerged he promised the householder a substantial annual reward to him and his successors for having undoubtedly saved his life. The reward, several bags of corn, was duly paid for over two hundred years.

Arran vented his annoyance by scourging Crichton Castle with fire. Bothwell's goods were spoiled, and his treasure and charter chest carted off to Edinburgh. But the English money had gone and so had Ormiston. Before he was finally felled, the faithful Ormiston had torn to shreds the letter he was carrying from Sir Ralph to the Lords. But the purpose of his mission was now laid bare. Bothwell later proclaimed Arran a traitor, and challenged him to a duel. Arran wisely declined.

In addition to these complications Sir Ralph was trying to bring some order into the general administration of the Borders. Warden of the East and Middle Marches, the most important sector, was the Earl of Northumberland. Never in all his experience of this part of the country, Sir Ralph reported, had he seen such inefficient and lax government, for which the Earl was entirely to blame.

'I never knew it in such disorder . . . all of which proceedeth [from] the lack of stout and wise officers,' he declared.[14]

Affairs in the West Marches were little better. The Warden there was Lord Dacre, who was no friend of Sir William Cecil.

'I would gladly have some good matter against the Warden of the West Marches,' wrote Cecil to Sir Ralph.[15] Cecil was determined to bring about the downfall of Dacre. His request, which was little more than an invitation to produce some trumped-up charge against the Warden, was disguised in code. Northumberland and Dacre were both ardent Catholics – perhaps over-ardent for Cecil's peace of mind. He suspected the loyalty of both of them.

As a result of his adverse report on these two, Sir Ralph found himself appointed Warden in place of Northumberland, who was recalled to the Court. Sir Ralph tried in vain to escape the consequences of his meddlesome dispatches on the state of the Borders. Having complained so much about the bad local administration, he was now to see if he could do any better. He flung himself into the task with brisk efficiency. By the end of the six months of his appointment he had thoroughly justified his reputation : civilian affairs had begun to run more smoothly.

He did not enjoy his time at Berwick. Even the two couple of hounds sent over to him from Ripley in Yorkshire by Sir William Ingleby, Treasurer of the Berwick garrison, did little to relieve the bleakness of life in the northern city.

'I trust you will not forget me when my service can be spared,' he wrote to Cecil, 'for this is an ill place to winter in.'

He would doubtless have preferred to have taken a more active part in the Scottish escapades, and to have left the district altogether. He found it most irksome and frequently asked Cecil to obtain his release. But there was no one who could have replaced him adequately and he had to stay there.

He had concluded a small Border treaty in September with Bothwell and Richard Maitland, a poet and lawyer, both of whom signed for Scotland. It was no more than an attempt to discourage the general lawlessness on both sides of the Border and was of little significance. But it did give some authenticity to the published reason for Sir Ralph being at Berwick.

In Scotland, the Lords of the Congregation were still making no headway. They were in fact doing the opposite. The people of Edinburgh and the surrounding country were weary of being under permanent siege and in endless turmoil as a result of Congregation activities. They were exasperated by their commercial port of Leith being maintained as a fortress in their midst, bristling with guns and garrisoned by battling Frenchmen. They blamed the Lords for the unsatisfactory state of affairs and resented the wheedling exhortations of that self-appointed messiah, John Knox.

Some slight encouragement was given, both to the citizens and to the Congregation, by the action of the independently-minded Lord Erskine, still entrenched in Edinburgh Castle. One day, without any warning, he suddenly discharged all the great guns of his armoury in two mighty volleys in the direction of Leith and 'declared himself open enemy unto the Dowager [the Queen Regent], which hath greatly comforted the people of this town and grieveth the Dowager very sore'.[16] This splendid news reached Sir Ralph in a letter from Thomas Randolph, spy and general intelligence agent employed by Queen Elizabeth herself. It was he who had accompanied the young Earl of Arran from London to Berwick the previous August, and had – at the Earl's request – been seconded to him in Scotland as a personal agent acting through Sir Ralph.

According to John Knox, Lord Erskine 'suddenly repented' of his brave gesture, so that the value of it to either side remained in some doubt.

But early on the morning of 5th November 1559 the gates of Leith flew open; with Gallic shouts and shrill huzzas two thousand of the Queen Regent's loyal Frenchmen, leavened by the presence of Lord Seton, surged out and attacked the lethargic Scotsmen encamped round the walls.[17] Entirely unprepared for such bravado, the Congregation force was heavily defeated and over thirty of their number killed, as well as forty taken prisoner.

Their morale, already low, was now as scarce as their means of support. Their tented army looked more like a tinker's camp than a mighty instrument of the Reformation and mirror of Scottish valour. As they slouched about the streets of Edinburgh, wincing at the hoots and rotten apples bestowed upon them by their fellow countrymen, and trying to ignore the slammed doors and output tongues, the rank and file lost the will to continue the struggle. At midnight on 6th November, the whole ragged outfit stole away as silently as their rusty harness and creaking wagons would allow. Daybreak found them all back in the safety of Stirling, and the French sentries gazing out in astonishment on the litter of the abandoned camp.

On their arrival at Stirling they were treated by John Knox to the concluding part of a lengthy sermon on the Eightieth Psalm, 'Our enemies laugh among themselves', the first part of which he had delivered in Edinburgh.[18]

The retreat was a serious setback to Sir Ralph's efforts. But, although he received more money from Cecil for the encouragement of the Lords of the Congregation, the Lords were beyond encouragement at the moment. Their troops were becoming mutinous because, as was reported at the time, 'they had not their pay down upon the nail'.[19]

They were almost at the end of their tether. The French, on the other hand, were in triumphant mood. Powerful reinforcements had come to them from France, including the warrior Bishop of Amiens. There were also three philosophers from the Sorbonne equipped with a dialectical armoury to confound the arguments of the defecting Protestant Congregationalists. In charge of the French troops, virtual director of the Queen Regent's affairs, was the crafty politician and skilled military man, Monsieur d'Oysel.

The Lords at this stage sent a special messenger direct to Queen Elizabeth asking for immediate aid. Without this, they said, they could not remain in existence as an effective opposition to the Queen Regent and her French faction. The messenger chosen was a well-known figure at the time, thirty-one-year-old William Maitland of Lethington. Up to a few days previously he had been the Queen Regent's secretary and confidant. On hearing a rumour that she was thinking of doing away with him, he had suddenly abandoned her and thrown in his lot with the Lords of the Congregation. Supported by Sir Ralph's recommendations, he obtained a promise of substantial support. Randolph, who had remained on the Earl of Arran's staff, accompanied Maitland on his journey to England.

About the same time, the Queen Regent's health began to fail. Sir Ralph reported this at once to Cecil. 'The bruit goeth about that the Queen Dowager is departed this life,' he wrote, adding disappointedly, 'but we think the news too good to be true.'[20] As a result of her increasing inactivity, Monsieur d'Oysel took an even greater part in running affairs, and assumed most of the powers of the Queen. She could do little more than smile wan approval of whatever he proposed.

For Sir Ralph, life became increasingly hectic with his enforced assumption of the office of Warden of the East and Middle Marches. He found time to deal with all the trivial details of local jurisdiction which came before him, including such matters as disputes over stolen cows. His personal comforts and pleasures suffered as a result. He could rarely get a drinkable glass of wine, a trouble which he had frequently experienced when billeted in Edinburgh.[21] Here at Berwick he had hoped to arrange things more satisfactorily and had asked Sir John Foster, a colleague, to send him over a hogshead from Alnwick. But even in this he was thwarted, for the vile weather that winter made the rough roads practically impassable for sizeable wagons.

'For your wine,' wrote Sir John, 'unless the weather mend, there is no carriage can pass: so that for want thereof you must be content to drink beer.'[22] There seems to be a note of satisfaction in the message about beer. None of your fancy London tastes, Sir John perhaps was thinking; what is wrong with our good Northumberland ale that you must go sending out for hogsheads of claret?

Sir Ralph got on well with the Border landowners and dignitaries with whom he had to deal. In view of his personable character and diplomatic training, this was only to be expected. Relations were obviously cordial. The Earl of Home wrote to thank him for a gift of two couple of hounds. If these were the same two couple Sir Ralph had recently received from Sir William Ingleby, the shortness of their stay with Sir Ralph seems to suggest that the present was not as handsome as it sounds. There is no record of Lord Home's opinion of the hounds.

In London the Scottish situation was the subject of many long discussions by the Privy Council. It was finally decided, chiefly on Sir Ralph's advice, that the only solution was to send a large force up to assault Leith and drive the French out once and for all, irrespective of the illusory Congregation army. It was decided to wait for the better conditions expected in early spring. The impossible weather which had so delayed Sir Ralph's supplies of wine to Berwick also caused dismay in London. A harmless water spaniel, going about his lawful occasions alongside the wall of St Hallows' Church in Broad Street, was killed outright by a fearful thunderclap.[23] The same phenomenon knocked the sexton senseless to the ground and cracked the church's fine stone steeple, which had to be demolished.

Queen Elizabeth's Court had become firmly established as the undisputed hub of the country's affairs. Cecil was the lynchpin. The Palace was daily thronged with a brilliant cosmopolitan gathering. But the occasions arranged for their entertainment were not always a complete success. On New Year's Eve 1559, a chronicler recounts that 'a play was performed at Court before the Queen, but they acted something so distasteful that they were commanded to leave off, and immediately the masque came in, and the dancing'.[24]

In January 1560, word reached London that a French fleet, under the Marquis d'Elboeuf, was ready at Dieppe to sail for Leith with a strong relief force for Monsieur d'Oysel and the Queen Regent's Frenchmen. Elizabeth was anxious not to provoke the French into open war, yet was equally anxious to remove them from Scotland. D'Elboeuf had to be stopped somehow. The solution devised was the sending of Admiral Winter up to

Scotland with fourteen men-of-war. His instructions were to disrupt the French fleet and blockade Leith, yet on no account to let it be thought he was acting on direct orders from Queen Elizabeth. These ludicrous orders were cheerfully accepted by the resourceful young Admiral. What explanation he could possibly have given if asked on whose behalf he was acting cannot be imagined. His written instructions commanded him to say, if challenged, that he was 'acting on his own responsibility'.

He duly arrived in the Firth of Forth and captured the French ammunition and supply ships based on Leith. The Marquis d'Elboeuf had set out from Dieppe but was blown away by a violent storm. His vessels were dashed ashore all along the North Sea coast, he himself struggling back to Dieppe. Only one ship reached Leith with a hundred weary men on board. The sizeable, well equipped army which the fleet was transporting had ceased to exist. Had they all reached Scotland safely, matters would have gone very differently north – and perhaps south – of the Border. By the end of the episode some nine hundred French reinforcements eventually arrived in Scotland out of the several thousand who had embarked at Dieppe.

Queen Elizabeth, having finally decided that an army should be sent to Scotland to clear out the French even at risk of open war with France, suddenly had second thoughts. What guarantee did she have that the Scots would not turn again on England once the French had gone? Could she be sure that the French faction would not gain the upper hand once more and all the Frenchmen be invited back again? It was all going to be very expensive – there were already over £5,000 owing to the troops at Berwick for arrears of pay. Could she not come to some arrangement with the Queen Regent and avoid the tremendous expedition which her councillors were advising her to undertake? She was in an agony of indecision, giving and cancelling orders in the same breath.

'Her acts are of one kind, her words are of another,' reported de Noailles, the French Ambassador, to the King of France. The fact was that she did not know what to do and could not make up her mind.

Her retractions and vacillations alarmed the Lords of the Congregation to the verge of despair. Old Châtelherault abandoned himself completely to panic, writing desperate letters to the Queen Regent and to the King of France offering to do anything they liked and making a frenzied effort to win their approval. He even offered to send his son Arran and all his other children into France as hostages, to save himself from what looked like the impending eclipse of the Congregation party. His ignoble cringing was treated on all sides with the disdain it deserved.

The French party exulted in the chaos among their opponents. Monsieur d'Oysel entered the field again and marched about the country scattering the feeble Congregation levies like chaff. One person alone refused to be scattered : this was Lord Erskine, still entrenched in Edinburgh Castle. He had withdrawn his earlier expression of partisanship with the Lords of the Congregation, and had reaffirmed his allegiance to the non-existent Parliament. He accordingly continued to deny entry to the Castle to all comers, threatening again to bombard Holyrood if anyone attacked him. D'Oysel was undeterred by his threat and launched a full-scale offensive against him. The French had found it extremely inconvenient to have the Castle occupied by such a belligerent neutral when they themselves were in occupation of the rest of the city. But Lord Erskine turned the gleaming rows of his bell-mouthed cannon upon the haughty Frenchmen and blasted them off the streets. D'Oysel was obliged to abandon his assault, leaving the citadel as securely held as ever by the sabre-rattling Erskine.

The news that Queen Elizabeth was thinking of treating with the Queen Regent and consequently of postponing or even abandoning the invasion, completed the despondency of Arran and his Lords. The whole Congregation force was now reduced to barely two hundred men, entirely unable to act effectively against d'Oysel and hardly in cohesive existence at all. Arran wrote to Cecil telling him of their plight and saying they would try to keep going as long as they still had twenty horses among them.

Had it not been for Admiral Winter's morale-raising *coup* in the Firth of Forth, whereby d'Oysel was seriously inconvenienced through the loss of his stores for Leith, it is doubtful whether Arran could even have kept the twenty horses together.

15
'Yet it burns, yet ... yet ... !'

ENGLAND WAS IN serious danger from the concerted efforts
of France and Spain. This made the presence of French forces
in Scotland an additionally severe menace. Sir Ralph was appalled at the thought of the Queen abandoning her project for
invading Scotland in conjunction with the Lords of the Congregation. By many vigorous messages he was able to persuade
her and Cecil to go through with the plan and risk the consequences. A force of six thousand foot soldiers and two thousand
horsemen was accordingly raised in the North under the osten-
sible command of the Duke of Norfolk. The effective commander was actually Lord Grey de Wilton, the seasoned cam-
paigner. The honour of titular command was only given to Norfolk to cement his loyalty which the Queen had a suspicion was
beginning to crumble.

The army lay in restive idleness until the final order to march
was received from the Queen. During this time, on 25th February, Sir Ralph arranged a conference at Berwick attended by
Scottish envoys. As a result the representatives of the Lords of
the Congregation gave all the assurances which Elizabeth demanded before letting her army forward. They also surrendered
hostages as a guarantee of their good faith. The Duke of Norfolk signed on behalf of the Queen: 25th March was agreed
as the date upon which the English forces would cross the Border. The Scottish envoys returned with their heartening news
which encouraged the Lords to see about raising a respectable

army to join up with the English when they came to the assault of Leith.

D'Oysel soon learnt of the impending invasion and hastened to put Leith into a state of siege. The Queen Regent herself had given up any effort at directing affairs. The dropsical condition to which she was gradually succumbing denied her the will or ability to take any active part. Uncertain where to go, she was admitted to Edinburgh Castle by the magnanimous Lord Erskine. He made it clear that she was to come as his guest and with only a small retinue of servants. He remained in full control of the destiny of the Castle, and emphasised that the receiving of his guest implied no allegiance to her faction.

Orders were at last received for the northern force to cross the Scottish Border. With Lord Grey at their head they crossed the Tweed on Thursday, 28th March, and marched leisurely up the coast. Sir Ralph and the Duke of Norfolk remained at Berwick with the reserves.

Back in London, Queen Elizabeth was still hoping to find some way out of being committed to the Scottish enterprise. At one moment it looked as if she might have found a pretext: the French Ambassador had hurried into her presence waving in his hand the actual letter of craven submission which the Duke of Châtelherault had written to the French King in his moment of panic the month before.[1] Monsieur de Sèvre, who had succeeded de Noailles as Ambassador, made much of the apparent double dealing of the Scottish leader, but the Queen paid little attention. Châtelherault himself declared the letter a forgery and challenged de Sèvre to a duel, either with him or with one of the Hamiltons. Needless to say, neither side took further action.

But Elizabeth sent an urgent message to the Duke of Norfolk – whom she now positively suspected of disloyalty and regretted having appointed to such a command – to settle the whole affair with the French without any bloodshed if he possibly could. If a battle were inevitable, she said, then it must be finished with at once, since the ships then lying in the Forth under Admiral Winter could no longer be spared away from their home waters. The Duke was much disturbed and dubious about the whole enterprise.

'The matter is confused,' he wrote to Cecil, 'to proceed in this manner with force *and* treaty, and if the navy go, it had been better the army had never come to Scotland.'

He was very short of supplies of every description as well as money for the troops' pay. Sir Ralph, Treasurer of the army as usual, was particularly vexed by the lack of funds and joined with Norfolk in a steady stream of complaints to headquarters.

'What is £20,000 more or less in a prince's purse?' snorted Sir Ralph to Cecil. 'Consider what dishonour it would be, besides the danger that might follow, if our army should be forced to return through lack of money!'[2]

Cecil did his best to meet their complaints, promising money and supplies which the Queen was most loath to authorise. Everyone longed for the whole episode to be finished.

'For God's sake now, good Mr Sadler,' wrote Cecil, 'bestow all your labour and promote this matter with all the speed that ye can : let no time be lost.'[3]

Lord Grey at any rate was losing little time. On 4th April he joined the Congregation forces in a historic meeting at Prestonpans, a small place some nine miles east of Leith. This was probably the first time a Scottish and English army had come together for a common purpose. Lord Grey's pleasure was somewhat diminished by finding that the Scottish soldiers had only been engaged for a period of twenty days, twelve of which had already elapsed by the time of meeting. In eight days' time, his allies would have departed for their homes, leaving the full burden of the operations on his own shoulders.

This was an inauspicious start, but Grey determined to make use of them while he had them. He arranged for them to storm Edinburgh Castle and try to capture the Queen Regent, who was still a guest there at the invitation of Lord Erskine. Greater preparations would have to be made before the heavily fortified town of Leith could be attacked : his heavy siege equipment had not yet arrived by sea, and the Edinburgh Castle exploit would be a useful way of filling in time. The Duke of Norfolk was doubtful about the idea and referred it back to Cecil. He reported that the Queen would on no account allow such a step, and reiterated her wish that the whole affair should be concluded without loss of life or open battle.

On 15th April, Norfolk received a letter from Cecil, instructing him to send Sir Ralph up to Edinburgh to discuss terms for a treaty with the Queen Regent. There was fresh dismay at this news of yet further parleying by the English Queen. Not only the Congregation party but Lord Grey – essentially a man of the battlefield rather than the conference table – felt let down by the lack of clear battle orders.

Sir Ralph, however, had already left for Leith at the head of three thousand men, doubtless glad to end his lengthy session of administration and letter writing so many miles behind the scene of action – or inaction, as it had been hitherto. On Tuesday, 16th April, he arrived at the joint camp a mile from Leith.

'He is best esteemed by the Scots of any Englishman,' said Norfolk in his reply to Cecil.[4] He had sent Sir Ralph across to the Lords of the Congregation 'to content them meanwhile with gentle and fair words'. The Scots, like the English, were becoming extremely restive through such prolonged inactivity. Discipline among the English had become lax to a degree: the streets of Edinburgh resounded to the blasphemous shouts of card-playing, dice-throwing soldiery who lounged about the town with tunics unbuttoned, beer mugs in their hands and weapons left behind in camp. It had needed a sudden sally by the French garrison – after a preliminary reconnaissance by spies dressed as women sauntering through the English lines – and the loss of a hundred and sixty English soldiers, before the atmosphere became more military and businesslike.[5]

As this supposedly female party had picked their way daintily through the English fortifications, hoisting their petticoats and patting their hair, they had suddenly laid hands on a lounging sentry and cut off his head. The fact that such unfeminine behaviour caused no comment or reaction among the rest of the camp shows how slack Lord Grey's security arrangements had become. The 'Ladies of Leith', after further inspection of the defences, tripped back across no man's land carrying their grisly trophy which they stuck upon the top of Leith church.

The Lords were especially pleased by Sir Ralph's presence in their midst: 'The noblemen received new minds and courage,' reported Norfolk. The noblemen had become extremely downhearted at the lack of any English action against Leith, and began to suspect some underhand treaty. If Elizabeth had made peace direct with the Queen Regent, they would have received little mercy at her hands, as they well knew.

By the end of April it had been decided definitely to try to capture Leith. All day long the heavy guns lobbed their shot into the beleaguered town, which eventually caught fire, a third of it being destroyed. During the huge conflagration Lord Grey sat penning a report in his tent. The flames which blazed across the night sky doubtless played on his triumphantly grinning face as he peered eagerly round the tent flaps in between sentences. Here was action at last. He scratched an excited postscript to the Duke of Norfolk: 'Yet it burns – yet – yet!'⁶

But his gunners could not rightly claim the credit, since the fire had been started by mistake by two members of the garrison itself.

A breach was eventually battered in the walls and it was decided to make an amphibious attack. Sir Ralph, who was a recognised expert in fortifications in addition to his other talents, went forward at dusk with Sir James Croft, one of the other commanders, and Kirkcaldy of Grange, representing the Lords of the Congregation, to make a closer reconnaissance.

They discovered that the bombardment had not been as effective as had been thought. The breach in the main defences, which had led them to decide upon an assault the next morning, was by no means extensive enough to give a reasonable chance of success: the town's fortifications had not suffered severely. Sir Ralph therefore suggested that the attack should be postponed until more damage could be done by the siege guns. Sir James Croft and Kirkcaldy of Grange agreed, and they decided between them not to attack as arranged. Sir Ralph and Kirkcaldy strolled off together to their tents, bidding goodnight to Sir James Croft, whom they understood was to go at once and advise Lord Grey to put off the assault.

But Sir James Croft either never told Lord Grey or put it in such a way that Lord Grey saw no point in postponing the attack, and did not accept their advice. If the latter was the case it is curious that Lord Grey never told Sir Ralph or Kirkcaldy. For, to their amazement, the original order to attack was never cancelled. Between two and three o'clock next morning, trumpets called the men to arms: shock troops rushed forward against the walls of Leith. As Sir Ralph had known would be the case, the defences were well able to resist them. The scaling ladders set up all round the breach proved too short by six feet. This Sir Ralph could not have known: it only made the whole mistake more grievous. Scrambling helplessly round the foot of the walls, exposed to withering fire from strongly prepared positions as they desperately and courageously sought for non-existent openings, the English and Scottish troops were mown down by the score.

The French soldiers were aided by the womenfolk of the town who made busy chains of kettles of scalding water and bowls of boiling tar to spray down on the gallant attackers, toppling from their too-short ladders. They carried powder, bandaged the wounded and helped load the guns; it was a concerted effort which thoroughly repulsed the attack. These ladies were even more anxious than the soldiers that the assault should not succeed. By their willing attention to all the needs of the French 'invaders' in the town they had earned a most unflattering reputation throughout Scotland. They would have received short shrift had the town fallen.

Sir James Croft himself did not arrive with his division until it was all over. He either thought the assault had been postponed, and was therefore unprepared in the early morning, or knew well enough the battle was on and kept discreetly out of the way, knowing of the extremely slim chances of success. He came in for much justifiable criticism: his action only adds mystery to the Curious Case of the Uncancelled Orders.

By breakfast time, the abortive assault had come to an end: so had the lives of nearly a thousand Englishmen and Scotsmen. Most of the latter were part of a division brought up the day before by the Earl of Argyll: Lord Grey had been anxious to make some use of them before they all slipped away.

For the English the whole event had been a most unfortunate disaster. If the French in Leith had not been so weakened by lack of food and military supplies owing to Admiral Winter's relentless blockade, they could undoubtedly have put Lord Grey and Sir Ralph to rout with the whole army, Scotsmen included.

The bad news soon got back to the Duke of Norfolk, who reported at once to the Queen. It threw her into paroxysms of wrath and apprehension. The faithful Cecil had a terrible time with the Queen: 'I have had such a torment herein with the Queen's Majesty', he wrote in code to the Ambassador in France, 'as an ague hath not in five fits so much abated me.'[7]

The setback entirely deflated Lord Grey's army. 'Daily and nightly our men steal off and run away,' Sir Ralph reported to Norfolk. As Treasurer, he made an immediate advance of ten days' pay to keep the army together. Had not Norfolk sent up two thousand of his reserves straightaway and offered to come up himself from Newcastle, the camp would doubtless have disintegrated.

The citizens of Edinburgh had not risen to the occasion after this fiasco. They slammed their doors on the Scottish wounded, leaving them to die in the streets of the capital. In evident fear that the French would soon be complete masters of the situation once more, they refused to raise a finger to help their stricken compatriots. They doubtless thought the English would withdraw at once and that the last had been heard of the Congregation forces.

The Queen Regent herself, in the final stages of her wretched disease, had been dragged out on to the battlements of Edinburgh Castle to witness the attack. The sight of the joint repulse of the Scots and English by her Frenchmen brought a smile to her swollen face. For a few weeks longer, she kept cheerfully alive. At length, abandoned to her incurable dropsy, she died in the second week of June, noting with interest that 'a finger will sink into my leg like butter'.[8]

Her struggle to maintain the status of Catholicism in Scotland was doomed to failure. Even in death the Catholic rites were severely abbreviated. She lay in the castle chapel until her body could be taken back to her native land and rest for ever in the tomb of the Dukes of Guise, her illustrious forbears. 'I saw the Dowager's corpse in a bed,' reported Randolph the erstwhile spy, as he went padding round the castle, 'covered with a fair white sheet, the tester of black satin, and the bed hanged to the ground with the same.'[9]

Both sides were anxious to make an honourable conclusion to the whole wearisome business of the Siege of Leith. One of the last acts of the Queen Regent had been to write a message in invisible ink on a handkerchief to d'Oysel, the French commander in Leith, asking him how long he thought he could hold out.[10] The handkerchief was to be smuggled into Leith by an agent. Unfortunately the agent was caught and the handkerchief – either declared by the agent under torture, or exposed by its own singular appearance – brought to Lord Grey. He astutely held it before a brazier and the tell-tale writing appeared in black letters. From this, as well as from inside information, the English knew that the garrison were in considerable difficulties. Sixteen ounces of bread and a slice of salt salmon was the daily ration in the town. Starvation and disease stalked the streets in grim company.

Queen Elizabeth was now determined to make peace. To Cecil's unspeakable dismay she told him to go up to Edinburgh himself and conclude a satisfactory treaty. He accordingly arrived in Edinburgh on 16th June 1560. Elizabeth never had a more loyal or selfless servant, and yet she refused to pay his fare or any of his expenses while he was in Scotland on her behalf.

A week's armistice was declared while the treaty was discussed. The way for this had been prepared by Sir Ralph, who acted as conference secretary and adviser to Cecil throughout the proceedings. While this was going on, wrote Randolph to his friend Henry Killigrew, a former MP for Launceston, the

French and English officers held a picnic on Leith sands, 'each bringing with him victuals as he had in store'. Lord Grey's men unpacked great hampers of hams, capons and chickens, and crate upon crate of beer and wine. The starvation-level Frenchmen produced with a flourish one emaciated chicken, pieces of horse cooked in thirty-two different ways, and 'six delicately roasted rats'. These last, they declared, were 'the best fresh meat in the town, of which they had abundance'.[11]

On 6th July, a pact was finally signed, known as the Treaty of Leith. Sir Ralph had done much diplomatic work behind the scenes to ensure the success of the talks. His satisfaction at this happy conclusion was only equalled by Cecil's. Failure would undoubtedly have cost the Secretary his place at Queen Elizabeth's side and probably his life as well.

The Treaty provided that Mary Queen of Scots, still in France, should abandon all open claim to the throne of England and should stop quartering English arms on her seal; that the French, as well as the English, should leave Scotland for good; and that none but Scotsmen should hold high office of state.

In addition to this, a general pardon and amnesty was declared for all political offences in Scotland. Parliament was summoned at Edinburgh for the following month. This Parliament declared the Protestant faith to be the national religion.

The Lords of the Congregation had won after all. Sir Ralph's unremitting efforts under months of most exacting conditions had at last borne fruit. With relief and satisfaction he returned with the rest of the leaders to England and went at once to Standon. Finishing touches were still being put to his splendid house; he must have felt he deserved a respite from the country's affairs in its stately comfort.

16
'Is there room for Mary there?'

FOR THE NEXT eight years Sir Ralph was able to devote time to his own massive private concerns untroubled by commissions from the restless Queen. He attended the infrequent meetings of Parliament, spending many hours in the preparation of his speeches which evidently were heard with interest and respect. To judge from the laborious notes for many of them which survive to this day, the good sense and unbiassed observations for which he could be counted on were of considerable value to those in charge of public affairs.

He saw much of his friend and neighbour William Cecil, helping him all he could during the ups and downs of that statesman's relations with Elizabeth. It is very probable that the Queen herself consulted him on many occasions. Although she was usually disinclined to accept advice from anyone, however worthy, Sir Ralph's opinions on current affairs were always worth having.

In 1568, he emerged voluntarily from, or was prised out of, his semi-retirement to accept appointment as Chancellor of the Duchy of Lancaster. During his quiet and comfortable years at Standon the English political scene had been mercifully preserved from momentous upheaval. The force of the Queen's electric character, and the agility of her mind, had maintained her at the vortex of government. Schemes and plots revolved round her like particles in a whirlpool to be flung out by centrifugal force after a brief spin.

In Scotland, the customary craggy events of internal strife had broken loose again. The fleeting promise of peace and quiet brought about by Sir Ralph's Treaty of Leith in 1560 lasted little longer than it took the signatures to dry.

Five months later, at eleven o'clock in the evening, Francis II of France had died 'of a rotten ear', an event not so remote from the Scottish scene as might be supposed. For his widow was eighteen-year-old Mary Queen of Scots. Her subsequent fortunes had an important bearing on Sir Ralph's later life. Many must have been the times when he wished their paths had never crossed.

Mary's mother-in-law was Catherine de Medici, one of the most militant on record. This formidable woman was making extensive plans for the future of her younger son Charles, the new King of France, even before his elder brother – Mary's husband – was buried. These plans did not include Mary. Childless, ambitious and luxury-loving, the glamorous teenage widow saw that the French Court was no longer the place for her.

She decided to return to Scotland, from which she had been smuggled away at the age of five in 1547, and to establish herself on her Scottish throne. She also decided she was Queen Elizabeth's rightful successor to the English throne. Some of her friends even thought she had a better claim to it. Sir Ralph was not one of those. When the matter of succession was debated in Parliament, it was Sir Ralph's forthright opposition which prevented her name being put forward. Mary, the ardent Catholic, was thought by non-Catholics to be a menace to Elizabeth's Protestant throne. Elizabeth was determined not to name any successor for fear of a rival party growing up round the nominee.

When Mary therefore asked permission to land in England and journey through the country up to Scotland to save the long and hazardous sea voyage, permission was declined. Elizabeth, with crow's feet puckering her too-close eyes despite long hours of work at the boudoir glass, and her teeth turning black, was not prepared to risk the consequences of her charming Parisian cousin making a 'Progress' from Dover to Berwick. The more she thought about it, the more she saw young Mary as a potential threat.

A coded message went out to the English Admiral at Spithead. Mary's ship was not directly to be intercepted, and no orders about her would be issued from the Admiralty, but 'she might be met withal, and if anything happened . . . being done unknown, [whoever did it] would have found it afterwards well done'.[1] Suggestions that this possibility had been put about by Sir Ralph cannot be supported by evidence. But he was not beyond seeing the advantages to England which might result from Mary's ship being lost at sea. He had been party to Cardinal Beaton's assassination arrangements some years before, although his particular scheme was never put into effect.

Accordingly, as Mary's ship left Calais on 14th August 1561, bound for the Scottish port of Leith, English men-of-war shadowed its passage. The captains were surprised to notice some French ships also acting in a peculiar way, keeping her in sight but not sailing as escort. It turned out that their orders were much the same as those given to the English ships. They had been told that, if anything happened to Mary on the way over, Catherine de Medici and various others would not be at all displeased.

This was a poor start for any young Queen returning after years of exile to her native shore. All the way over, the horizon was never empty of sail, now English, now French. It was an anxious journey. No one can tell what might have happened had a gentle mist not shrouded the ship of the widowed Queen for most of her voyage. This caused one of her attendant vessels to wander off course, whereupon it was promptly seized and taken to London. On board was the protesting Earl of Eglinton. He was eventually released, and allowed to continue his journey.[2]

No further attempts were made to molest the Queen's party, and the sea remained kind. The Scots eagerly awaited her arrival, seeing in her the reinvigoration of the monarchy and a settled future for Scotland. Perhaps by design, no word had gone ahead when exactly to expect her. Leith pier on the drizzly morning of 19th August was therefore quite deserted when she set foot on Scottish soil again. No cheering crowds, no beflagged buildings greeted her. The outlook was sombre.

Mary soon changed that. She brought to unsmiling Holyrood Palace more than a breath of continental gaiety. The place was swept by a positive whirlwind as shipload after shipload of splendidly dressed courtiers streamed ashore from France. Gay furnishings went up all over Holyrood. Balls, banquets, dinners and dances became the order of the day – and night. 'The court', observed George Buchanan, one-time tutor to James VI, 'was drowned in vice and loosed the reins to all luxury.'[3]

The cosmopolitan way of life, including the re-establishment of mass in the Chapel Royal, dismayed many of the nobles and others who had gathered in Edinburgh to greet their six-foot Queen. Most people hoped for an era of peace and quiet, but mutterings began to be heard at once. Mary, unversed and uninterested in Scottish ways, abandoned herself to jollifications. Her half-brother, James Stuart, managed the affairs of state.

John Knox tried to bridle her extravagant way of life by sermons and private interviews. 'In communication with her,' he said, 'I espied such craft as I have not found in such age.' Her half-brother did his utmost to moderate her general behaviour, but achieved little more success than Knox. A web of personal scandals and intrigues of all sorts soon enveloped her Court.

Arran, sullen and vacuous, was fast losing hold of what senses he had, lying in bed for a week at a time wondering how he could persuade her to marry him.[4] Mary was prepared to marry again, but had taken an immediate fancy to Lord Darnley, the lanky son of Lennox and Margaret Douglas, who had been sent up on approval by Elizabeth. They had met for the first time at Wemyss Castle on the coast of Fife. Poised on the rocky shore above the Firth of Forth, this craggy home of the Wemyss family was the perfect setting for such a romantic occasion. Today the Castle with its lawns and brilliant flowers is still the home of the Wemyss family, as it has been since the twelfth century.

Mary had cunningly invited Queen Elizabeth's assistance in the choice of a husband, thereby hoping to get the nomination as her successor. But relations between the two Queens were now distinctly cool. They had not been improved by Elizabeth's discovery of Mary's participation in a grand plot to restore Catholicism to England, Scotland and Protestant Europe in general.

The old divisions between the Papist faction and the original Lords of the Congregation began to appear again. Mary's marriage to Darnley soon ended in grisly fashion at the explosion of Kirk o' Fields House, Edinburgh. But not before she had produced a son on 19th June 1566. Contemporary speculation about his probable father included Mary's music-maker, confidant and secretary, Signor 'Davie' Rizzio, and various others. Her husband was also suggested, rather as an afterthought.

Godparents to the child who became King James VI of Scotland and James I of England were Charles, King of France, Philibert, Duke of Savoy, and Mary's 'dear cousin', Queen Elizabeth. She sent up a handsome gilt-and-enamel font as a christening present, worth £1,403 19s before it was melted down for coinage, which was quite soon. It then yielded three hundred and thirty-three ounces of fine gold.[5]

Darnley did not attend the christening itself, which gave rise to much comment at the time. The mother was a twenty-four-year-old woman of beauty; the father an athletic twenty-one of distinctive looks. The child was a staring-eyed, hunched-up creature, unable to walk until seven years old, his tongue too big for his mouth.[6] Portraits of him are few since he could hardly sit still for more than a few minutes. But the Scots were glad of his arrival, since, if he survived, the succession of the monarchy was assured.

In England, the same question lay still unanswered. Parliament met on 17th October 1566, the first time for three years, to consider the Queen's application for funds. An effort was made to make the granting of money conditional upon Elizabeth naming a successor. The party in favour of Mary Queen of Scots was stronger now, but Sir Ralph, Cecil and a few others again persuaded Parliament against her. Elizabeth had once more got her way without declaring who was to succeed her.

But Mary lost popularity in England and Scotland through her supposed complicity in Darnley's murder on 9th February 1567.

James Bothwell, deeply involved in the matter, ran off with her to Dunbar two months later. The following month the two were married. Such was the scandal that some of the Lords ranged forces against the eloping pair. But Bothwell's men deserted them both; the gay and gallant Earl, the truest friend she ever had, galloped from the unfought battle of Carberry Hill, out of her life and into oblivion. Eventually he died in a Swedish prison in 1578, 'after ten years' nasty imprisonment'.[7] Mary hoped to save her cause by marrying the Duke of Norfolk when she was herself later imprisoned, but this never came to pass.

After Bothwell's departure, Mary was brought back to Edinburgh by the Lords, more as a captive than as a sovereign returned to the fold. Any idea of her resuming government was soon dispelled. The people of Edinburgh and of most of the rest of Scotland were so incensed at the part Mary had apparently played in the crude murder of her husband Darnley, and at the licentious example she had set by her conduct after the crime, that the city was in uproar as soon as she arrived. A huge banner had been prepared, showing the murdered King with his little son at his side calling on God for vengeance.[8] This was paraded in front of her as she made her way to Edinburgh clad only in 'a tunicle, and that a mean and threadbare one too, reaching but a little below her knees'. She fainted at the first sight of the banner.

She had reached Edinburgh just before nightfall, dirty and tear-stained and covered in dust, where mud had been thrown at her on the way. The outraged citizens thronged the narrow streets even at that late hour to jeer and hoot at her. Eventually the dense throng watched her in absolute silence, which must have been worse, leaving her a passageway through them 'so narrow that scarce one could go abreast'. Mounting the steps of where she was staying she turned on the silent throng and shouted back at them.

'She told them,' reported a bystander, 'that she would burn the city and quench the fire with the blood of the perfidious citizens.'[9] A howl went up from the perfidious citizens, and as she appeared at an upper window the gruesome banner was displayed to her again. 'Whereupon,' said the same spectator, 'she shut the window and flung in.'

Her own people had no doubt about her guilt in the murder. With her supposed complicity in crime died all hope of upsetting the Reformation and of restoring the Catholic faith to Scotland.

After two days in her lodgings, public indignation against her rose to such a pitch that the Lords attempting to carry on the government feared a complete revolution. She would have to be removed if orderly government were to continue.

They proposed to lodge her in Edinburgh Castle. But they had reckoned without Lord Erskine, who had been made Earl of Mar in 1565. He still held the Castle against all comers. He declined to admit her. The Lords therefore decided upon the island castle in Loch Leven, where she was accordingly locked up. Her little son was then proclaimed James VI. James Stuart, her half-brother, who had been helping her since her return from France, and whom she had created Earl of Moray in 1564, was appointed Regent during his minority. Loch Leven Castle belonged to his mother, a Douglas. Bitterly jealous of Mary, and believing that her son had a better claim to the throne, she was likely to prove a vigilant gaoler.

In England any goodwill towards Queen Mary had evaporated as news of her outrageous goings-on and complicity in crime became known. Support for her cause faded, prompted by the righteous outcries of Sir Ralph, Cecil and others of Queen Elizabeth's advisers.

Paradoxically enough, Elizabeth took the opposite view. While admitting that Mary's reputation had suffered severely she could not condone the imprisonment of a constitutional monarch by her subjects. It was an uncomfortable example of what could be done by a determined people. Elizabeth did not wish any of her own subjects to get any similar ideas. She therefore sent an Ambassador to Scotland against Sir Ralph's strongest advice to try and arrange for Mary's restoration to the throne. This was Sir Nicholas Throckmorton. But there was little he could do.

'It is public speech among all the people,' he reported back at once to Elizabeth, 'that their Queen hath no more liberty nor privilege to commit murder nor adultery than any other private person, either by God's law or the laws of the realm.'[10]

Rising in the North

ONE OF THE party of people appointed to occupy romantic Loch Leven Castle and have charge of the banished Mary was George Douglas, the Regent's youngest brother. An impressionable youth, he soon caught the eye of the captured Queen. As they sat together on the battlements with the moonlight rippling on the reedy lake, or strolled to the water's edge in the lee of the Lomond Hills, she allowed her charms full play. His resistance as a warder was slight. Dreams of riches and grandeur danced before his eyes as she told him in her soft French accents what she would do for him if only she were free.

Plans were laid at once, and on 3rd May 1568, the creaking of oars roused the island guard too late. Jumping up from their dinner, they rushed to their boats to pursue the royal fugitive. But the plan had been thoroughly laid. Their boats were breached, the oar holes blocked, the oars themselves adrift.[1]

The Queen was free. A few thousand dissenters rallied to her banner. But the Regent's troops, although outnumbered, had routed her sizeable army at Langside, near Glasgow, within a fortnight.

Deserted and forced to flee, she crossed the Border and sought sanctuary in Carlisle Castle. From here she appealed to Elizabeth for help.

Sir Ralph was yet again most outspoken against Mary, branding her in a speech before the Queen in Council as 'a murderess and adulteress'.[2] He advocated keeping her under detention, and giving full recognition to the new regime of the little King James VI under the Regent Moray.

Queen Elizabeth was uncertain what to do. She eventually appointed a commission, consisting of Sir Ralph, the Duke of Norfolk and the Earl of Sussex, to meet representatives both of Queen Mary's side and of the Regent's to decide what should be done. Sir Ralph did all he could to excuse himself from what promised to be a most difficult and contentious occasion. All manner of questions would arise, he complained to Cecil, in which he had no desire to act as arbiter. Such questions as: 'Who was a tyrant?' and 'Who might depose a tyrant?' He continued: 'It is a matter which toucheth not Scotland and England only, but all Kingdoms. I had liefer serve her Majesty where I might adventure my life for her than among subjects so difficult as these,' he ended up querulously.[3]

But despite his protests he had to go off with the rest of the commissioners. Having been newly appointed Chancellor of the Duchy of Lancaster, he was doubtless able to make additional use of his enforced journey north, but his reluctance to leave Standon was well known at the time. In a letter to Sir Ralph, Cecil notes that the Queen herself 'sometimes says you like it at home'. Sir Ralph told Cecil: 'I have no great desire to be a courtier, but prefer to live quietly at home.' He left Standon as seldom as he could, apart from the times of Council meetings, at which he was a regular attender and frequent speaker.

The Duke of Norfolk, as Sir Ralph suspected, was involved in an elaborate but as yet embryonic plot to marry Queen Mary and restore not only her fortunes but those of the whole Catholic party in England and Scotland. He had already paid her a secret visit in Bolton Castle, to which she had been removed during the sitting of the commission.

But, before the commission could get down to business, a whisper of the Duke of Norfolk's budding plot and plan to marry Mary reached the ears of Queen Elizabeth. She instantly cancelled the whole commission and ordered Sir Ralph to come back to London at once and give her a full report of all the rumours. She also ordered the witnesses who were to have been examined by the commission to appear in London. The chief obstacle in the way of the Catholic schemers was Cecil's anticipation of events, and Sir Ralph's constant suspicion of Queen Mary's motives. While professing friendship and devotion to Elizabeth, Mary was busy trying to gain allies from France and Spain for her overthrow.

Cecil's remedy for the whole situation was quite simple. In October of that year, 1569, he wrote a note to Sir Ralph: '[The Queen] might do that which in other times Kings and Princes have done by justice – take the Queen of Scots' life from her.' He was continually irked by what he described as 'her flexible wit and sugared eloquence'.

Elizabeth was reluctant to believe Sir Ralph. But the interception of letters from Mary to foreign powers eventually convinced her of the soundness of his views. Elizabeth had also been reluctant to consider Mary guilty of Darnley's murder. All grounds for doubt on this score were swept away by the production of a series of love letters supposedly written by Mary to Bothwell before the murder. After Bothwell had escaped to Dunbar, he had sent a messenger to fetch these letters, which he had kept in a casket. But his messenger was intercepted and the letters seized by the followers of the Regent, the Earl of Moray. The Regent appeared himself at Elizabeth's renewed court of inquiry in London, and produced the by then notorious Casket Letters. All who saw them were finally convinced of Mary's guilt, despite the patent forgery of some of the letters.

Mary herself managed to arrange a plot by which the Regent was to be assassinated at Northallerton on his return to Scotland, and the Casket Letters to be destroyed. She evidently set great store by them, in spite of denying having written them. The plot went astray and the letters survived for the time being. They eventually disappeared, and remain only as copies of doubtful accuracy.

Meanwhile the insurrection of which the Duke of Norfolk was to be leader rapidly took shape. All plans were ready, needing only the word to be given by the Duke. Had he done so, there is a possibility that a pro-Catholic rising would have gripped the country, sweeping Queen Elizabeth, Cecil, Sir Ralph and the rest of her advisers into the dungeons.

As it turned out the Duke could not bring himself to give the word. Fearful, hesitant and dissolved by cowardice, he went lamely to Elizabeth. He was clapped in the Tower, where he divulged most of the secret plans.

As a result, the ringleaders, the Earls of Westmorland and Northumberland, were summoned to London to give an account of themselves. They refused, and called their men to arms. Their first act in the whole insurrection, which was aimed not specifically at overthrowing Elizabeth, but at restoring the Catholic religion, was to march in a body sixty strong into Durham Cathedral at four o'clock in the afternoon of Sunday, 4th November 1569. There they tore up the English Bible and prayer books, replaced the altar which was lying outside in the long grass, and celebrated mass.

The next day they marched to York, gathering support from most of the district. At York was the Earl of Sussex with a garrison of three thousand men. Hurriedly slamming the city gates, he denounced the rebels and sent an urgent message to Elizabeth for help. By 23rd November, a rebel army of nearly fifteen thousand men lay between Wetherby and Tadcaster. Their advanced cavalry was preparing to gallop ahead and rescue Mary from dismal Tutbury Castle, on the Trent, not far from Burton, in Staffordshire, to which she had been removed.

News of the insurrection did not alarm Elizabeth. She refused to take it very seriously. But Sir Ralph, Cecil and the others were well aware of the danger. They had no illusions about the volume of support which such a rising might readily obtain, especially if Mary were rescued.

Elizabeth, almost too late, was suddenly convinced of the peril. Her mind once made up, she acted with a rapidity of decision that astonished her advisers. One of her chief difficulties was to find enough influential men upon whose loyalty she could depend without question. The Earl of Sussex, peering over the ramparts of York, was himself highly suspect. He was known to be a close friend of the Duke of Norfolk. His brother, Sir

Egremont Radcliffe, was even a captain in the rebel army.

Elizabeth chose two of her most loyal servants to go at once to York and get matters set in order. These were her cousin Lord Hunsdon, forty-five-year-old son of Anne Boleyn's sister, and Sir Ralph, Treasurer and general adviser. The Earl of Warwick and Sir Ralph's friend, Admiral Lord Clinton, were instructed to collect their respective forces and set off for York as soon as they could. Into Sir Ralph's care the Queen entrusted the thirteen-year-old Earl of Rutland, who had declared his intention of mustering forces and doing battle at once with anyone whom he could persuade to fight.[4]

Elizabeth felt responsible for the lad since he was a ward of the Crown at the time; Sir Ralph was to 'nourish his courage . . . [but] admonish him if found negligent of resort to common prayer'. 'I have delivered him some money in his purse,' wrote Cecil in a note with the Queen's instructions, adding that he had sent his own son, twenty-seven-year-old Thomas, to accompany the young Earl. Thomas Cecil was not, by all accounts, likely to exert much of a steadying influence, being rather wild and unpredictable himself.

Sir Ralph set off with forty of his own mounted servants, together with other clerks and orderlies. When he got to Stamford a messenger, called Mr Binks, brought him news that rebel horsemen were blocking the northern route not far ahead. He ventured on to Gainsborough where he arrived at nine o'clock in the morning. The news was confirmed to him, and he accordingly branched off to Hull in the steps of Lord Hunsdon, whom he met there about midnight.

He kept Cecil regularly in touch as he went north, sending letters whenever possible. Little reliability could be placed on them being safely delivered. The countryside was full of people trying to act as spies for one side or the other, and sometimes for both. The Earl of Sussex had difficulty in getting any of his letters through from beleaguered York. 'We doubt his letters have been intercepted, because we have not heard from him for a good while,' Cecil told Sir Ralph.[5]

Lord Hunsdon was quick to realise the danger of a striking

force reaching the prisoner Queen; she would have been of inestimable value to their cause, and he insisted on her being moved again immediately. She was accordingly taken off by the Earls of Shrewsbury and Huntingdon to the Castle of Ashby de la Zouch, in Leicestershire. Her departure was precipitate and attended by scant ceremony: her complaints were strenuous but unheeded.[6] The next night she was moved yet again to Coventry, well out of reach of the advancing rebels.

The youthful Earl of Rutland was now a source of constant anxiety, both for Sir Ralph and Cecil. Nobody knew what he would be up to once he found himself on a fine horse, with a new suit of damascened armour and hundreds of his tenants clattering along behind his freshly embroidered personal banner. 'I pray you suffer [him] not to venture his person in any vain enterprise,' begged Cecil of Sir Ralph, 'for the special purpose of sending him down was [rather] that his name and estimation might be used to allure his tenants and others to service, than to be employed in any corporal service himself, although I know he will spare none to show his duty.'[7]

On 24th November 1569, Sir Ralph and Lord Hunsdon journeyed on to York. Eight miles out they met by two hundred horsemen, sent by the Earl of Sussex to convoy them safely into the city. Sussex was especially delighted to see Sir Ralph. The Earl had been uncertain of how he stood with Elizabeth, his brother being an active rebel and he a known friend of Norfolk: he was much reassured to receive such an influential representative of the Queen's. Sir Ralph was very gratified at his reception. He wrote to the Queen to say that Sussex had told him, 'that of all the benefits whichever he [Sussex] did, or shall receive at your highness's hands, he doth account this for one of the greatest, in that it pleased your majesty to send me to him in this sort and in this time'.[8]

On 26th November, Sir Ralph received a message from Lord Clinton, the Admiral. He had got as far as Lincoln, and 'this county is in readiness under my charge, with 12,000 men well appointed'.[9]

Sir Ralph was surprised to hear that the Admiral, resourceful though he was known to be, had suddenly acquired such a large and apparently well-equipped army all of his own. Three days later came the explanation. 'I have sent you two letters before this time, whereof I received no answer,' he told Sir Ralph, 'and in one of the letters I made great boast of the numbers of men in this county because the rebels being then next between this and York, I doubted the interception of them.' It was merely one of the Admiral's ruses to confound the enemy: it turned out that his 'army' was no more than two or three hundred strong.

Sir Ralph spent the next week in helping the Earl of Sussex to marshal a sizeable force in York, and in collecting money, munitions and supplies to enable them to take the offensive. So busy was he that his letters home became very infrequent. For on 8th December, writing at ten o'clock at night from Windsor, Cecil sends a message to Sir Ralph: 'You forget to write to my Lady Sadleir, who lately sent hither to know how you did, and I answered her very well. But you yourself shall be better believed.'[10]

By 2nd December the rebels had reached Raby Castle, the Earl of Westmorland's home. They had not received the massive support they were expecting from the South, nor other effective support from any quarter. Had they been able to capture Mary, a large Spanish force at Antwerp had orders to land at once and join up with them. But, with their leader in prison and their royal mascot beyond rescue, no help would come from abroad. They knew their cause was lost almost as soon as it started, but they struggled on to make the best of it. Rather than follow up their initial advantage of surprise and mobility, they turned back to assault Sir George Bowes, who was defying them from the recesses of Barnard Castle. They wasted much valuable time before the desertion of most of his eight hundred followers obliged Sir George to surrender.

Elizabeth herself, having sent a meagre force northwards, although in the charge of the finest men she had, persisted in considering the whole affair now as good as settled. Sir Ralph was at pains to explain that it was much more than a little local difficulty, and that substantial supplies and munitions were needed if the rebellion were to be put down at all quickly. 'I do perceive,' he wrote anxiously to Cecil, '. . . that her majesty will hardly believe that the force and power of her good subjects of this country should not increase and be able to match with the power of the rebels. But surely, sir . . . there be not in all this country ten gentlemen that do . . . favour her majesty's proceedings in the cause of religion.' The Reformation had not yet grown deep roots in the North, but although the country people looked back wistfully to the days of Catholic worship, they were not prepared to rush to arms in wild insurrection.

Elizabeth took Sir Ralph's warnings seriously and made arrangements to augment the northern army. She also wrote to the Regent of Scotland, the Earl of Moray, inviting him to take some action in suppressing the rebels or at least to catch them should they cross into Scotland. Moray at once collected an army and bestrode the Border. He had no wish to see Queen Mary restored and the Reformation in eclipse.

By 15th December, the Earl of Sussex had completed preparations for making his force fully mobile. Accordingly, he issued out of York with Lord Hunsdon and Sir Ralph in the advance guard, and marched up to Ripon, where they waited for the Earl of Warwick and Admiral Lord Clinton to bring up the main body. Sussex had intended to go on without waiting for the rest of the army from York, but, as Sir Ralph explained to Cecil, 'Because my Lord of Warwick and my Lord Admiral are so desirous to be at this service, we do stay for them, of intent to join all our forces together, whereby we may proceed with surety.'[11] Warwick and Clinton were professional soldiers: they had no desire to trail along behind while the others got all the excitement and glory.

The rebels by this time had lost heart and purpose. The majority of their force, apart from the hard core of the two earls' own retainers, were not equipped to do more than stand and shout in the streets.

The Earl of Westmorland was a courageous figure, ready to do battle for the cause whatever the consequences. But the Earl of Northumberland proved an irresolute partner. As soon as the chances of success had faded he was in favour of surrendering. Several times he tried to steal away, but was prevented by the scornful example of his wife, who, as Lord Hunsdon reported to Cecil, 'being the stouter of the two, doth harden and encourage him to persevere, and rideth up and down with the army, so as the grey mare is the better horse'.[12]

There was hardly a piece of armour amongst them. Weapons taken down off walls of cottage and manor were more fitted for a poaching foray than for challenging the might of Queen and Government. As soon as word came through that some twelve hundred royal troops were at their heels, the whole enterprise broke up. A rumour went round that the two earls were abandoning their troops.[13] Individuals then hurried away to their homes, hoping not to be noticed. Groups of the insurgents scattered as best they could, going into hiding in the wild uplands of Westmorland and Cumberland.

The two earls themselves had no option but to flee with the rest. 'The rebels do lurk and hide themselves in the woods and deserts of Liddisdale,' reported Sir Ralph to Cecil from Hexham the day before Christmas. 'The Earls have changed their name and apparel and ride like the outlaws of Liddisdale.'

Before the final rout a most unsavoury character made himself known to Sir Ralph. This was a certain Robert Constable, who claimed to be in the employ of the Earl of Leicester. He wrote a long letter from Ferrybridge, near Pontefract, offering his services as a spy.[14] If adequately paid, he said, he would find out all manner of information about the rebel army. Sir Ralph 'need not doubt nor fear to hazard a portion of money with me : it shall not be wasted nor converted to the payment of my debts or my use, but bestowed as it ought to be. If I escape with my life, I will render a true account thereof,' he added handsomely. 'If I die, the Queen's Majesty may think it a cast lost at dice.'

Sir Ralph's action was cautious in the absence of any corroboration of Constable's claims of loyalty to the right side. Four days afterwards the persistent would-be agent wrote again. This time he enclosed a safe conduct pass which he had treacherously obtained from the rebel Earl of Westmorland himself. This was a fine weapon of espionage: he was sure Sir Ralph would now be only too glad to employ someone who had ready entrance into the enemy camp. His treachery was the more despicable since the Earl of Westmorland was his cousin.

'Cousin Robert,' wrote Westmorland from Brancepeth on 14th December, 'I thank you with all my heart for your gentle offer.' Had Constable offered to bring valuable information about the government forces into the rebel camp? 'I find my fortune is now to have need of friends: I pray you show yourself now such a friend as nature [should] bring you to be, and here I promise you of mine honour to come safe, and go safe, and this letter shall be your warrant. Your assured friend and cousin, C Westmorland.'[15]

Sir Ralph still gave him no money to speak of. But the spy considered himself duly on the strength and lost no time in getting after the rebels. He sent his first dispatch from Catterick Bridge, with specimen information. The mantle of cloak and dagger fell easily on to his shoulders, and he at once indulged in simple melodrama: 'The first letter of my name here written,' he added at the end of his dispatch to Sir Ralph, 'shall, from henceforth, serve for my name.'[16]

By the end of the first week of January 1670, the North Country was quiet again, although unhappy. Vengeance and punishment were dealt out universally by government agents: many people were summarily hanged. The two rebel earls had crossed into Scotland with their few remaining partisans. There the Earl of Northumberland was promptly betrayed by a traitor called Hector Armstrong. The Countess had got left behind in the confusion of the last dash across the Border: the wretch Armstrong offered to guide the Earl to where she lay in Liddesdale, at the dwelling of a Border ruffian called John o' the Side. It was little more than a hovel, and according to an account in a contemporary manuscript 'not to be compared to an English dog kennel'. Armstrong had arranged for a party of the Scottish Regent's horsemen to set an ambush: he then led Northumberland straight into it. The name of Armstrong has been treated with some reserve in the staunchest retreats of the Border country ever since.

The Earl of Westmorland was more fortunate, although he also had a potential Armstrong in his 'loving cousin' Robert Constable. He was received, with the whole of the rest of the rebel gathering, by Sir Thomas Kerr, the warrior Laird of impregnable Ferniehurst. Remains of this defiant fortress, perched above the waters of the Jed, can be seen to this day. The present building is a later reconstruction. The left-handed family of Kerrs were among the most militant along the whole of the Borders, the laird of the day being almost an uncrowned king.

Imbued with the centuries-old tradition of offering asylum to those seeking refuge from another country, Sir Thomas Kerr threw open the gates of his castle and welcomed in the Earl and his party. It was an act to be expected of the family of Kerr: most of Scotland looked on with approval, whether given to the cause of Mary Queen of Scots or to that of her son James. The Regent Earl of Moray, by making captive the Earl of Northumberland and hurrying him off to detention in Loch Leven Castle, not long vacated by Queen Mary herself, brought down on his handsome head a torrent of execration from all parties. Scotland was disgraced by his action, declared the Earl of Morton, Moray's right-hand man. Lord Hunsdon told Cecil that 'between Berwick and Edinburgh the Regent could not find one man to stand by him: where he had ten mortal enemies before, he had now a hundred'.

Ferniehurst was nearly three miles from Jedburgh: the bugle calls ringing round the castle courtyard could be heard quite plainly in the market square. They struck a chill through the hearts of assembled strangers: local people knew better than to cross swords with the Laird of Ferniehurst once his blood was up – which it frequently was. The Regent Moray soon arrived at Jedburgh with eight hundred men to remove Westmorland and his friends from Ferniehurst. But the reputation of the Kerrs was not based on fantasy. By the time the Regent had got within two miles of the lion's lair, all his men had vanished except for about a hundred of the most courageous. When the distance narrowed to one mile, he had barely twenty round him. At quarter of a mile from the castle walls, he was alone.

Sir Thomas Kerr had sent a message to say that if the Regent wanted Westmorland he would have to come and fetch him. The Regent had certainly arrived but now being single-handed he felt at a disadvantage. He accordingly trotted back along the river to Jedburgh, declaring that he had anyway only ridden out to 'view the woods'.[17]

Queen Elizabeth was insisting that the Regent Moray hand over the rebels. Sir Ralph, together with Lord Hunsdon and the Earl of Sussex, tried to dissuade her, emphasising how much popularity Moray had already lost, and saying that his life would certainly be in danger if he went so far as to surrender the rebels – supposing he could catch them. But Elizabeth was adamant.

Meanwhile, Robert Constable the spy had been received at Ferniehurst by his 'loving cousin' Westmorland. He wrote a full report to Sir Ralph of all he had heard of their secret plans. He insinuated himself into their private gatherings. He even frequented the local taverns, joining in at cards and other games, only sitting down 'after I had diligently learned and enquired that there was none of any surname that had me in deadly feud, nor none that knew me'.[18] They played, as he said, for rounds of drinks, or for 'blacks and hardheads', which were small coins.

In a pathetic interview with Westmorland himself, reported in detail to Sir Ralph at Durham, the spy reduced the Earl to tears at the contemplation of the misfortunes which had befallen his noble family. Now well versed in the tricks of his trade, Constable screwed up his eyes and managed a few tears himself so that 'neither of us could speak to another for a long time'.[19]

Eventually taking Constable up to his room in the castle tower, Westmorland said: 'Cousin Robert, you are my kinsman come forth out of my house, and one whom I dearly love and trust. I must confess I have as lewdly overshot myself as any man could do: none the less I pray you let me have your counsel what way you think were likeliest for me to obtain my pardon and favour of the Queen's Majesty. . . .'

Constable here saw a chance to make a handsome profit on

the body of his noble cousin. He advised him to cross back to England. Sir Ralph was still an unwilling patron of the scurvy Constable, but had none the less sent his reports straight back to the Queen. Elizabeth was delighted with them and at the prospects of trapping the rebel leaders. Sir Ralph, to his disgust, was instructed to encourage Constable with money and advice to the best of his ability. Constable was consequently equally delighted, permitting himself an unctuous little reflexion on 'this being a treacherous kind of service that I am waded in, to trap them that trust in me, as Judas did Christ'.[20] The jingle of golden coins soon put such thoughts from him.

Westmorland gave him a little ring off his finger to take to Lady Westmorland, asking him to obtain from her 'one of her best jewels for a token to my Lady Kerr of Ferniehurst, and the fairest gelding she could get for the Laird'. The Kerrs, he explained, were being put to great expense on his account and would accept no money.

Constable set off on this mission, riding all night; 'the extremest for wind and snow that ever I rode in . . . and got home all befrozen,' he told the unsympathetic Sir Ralph.

During the course of this arduous ride he discovered something touching his own pocket. 'I have spoiled my best gelding that I have refused £30 for within this half year,' he says. 'I fear he will never do me more service.'[21] He may have derived some comfort from the prospect of getting hold of the 'fairest gelding' that Lady Westmorland could obtain.

Three days later, Constable brought her husband's token and messages to Lady Westmorland. 'I kissed my Lord's ring and gave it to her. She was passing joyful,' he reported to Sir Ralph, and gave him 'a little chain, and a ring with a diamond to be delivered to the Laird of Ferniehurst, a locket for the Lady, and a little ring to my Lord.' She was thoroughly deceived.

Constable triumphantly appropriated the gelding in place of his own, and sent the jewellery and tokens to Sir Ralph, expecting a handsome reward for his miserable trick. Sir Ralph curtly tells him to 'deliver these tokens, which I send you again here enclosed, and . . . do such messages as are committed unto you. . . .'

One may well doubt whether the gifts ever found their way to the Earl.

Constable continued his machinations and succeeded in trapping several of the rebels. But Westmorland at last saw through the base affections of his 'loving cousin'. He escaped to Flanders and was given command of émigré troops in the Spanish army. He died at Nieuwport in 1601 after thirty years of poverty-stricken exile, aged fifty-eight.

Back at the Court, Cecil was conducting the Queen's business with his customary skill, and keeping Sir Ralph regularly informed of what was going on. His fears about the young Earl of Rutland and his own son looked at one stage as if they were going to be realised. 'I have not [for a long time] heard from my Lord of Rutland, nor from my son,' he says in a postscript to Sir Ralph on 13th January, some time after the troubles had died down.[22] Sir Ralph replied on the 18th with reassuring news: 'My Lord of Rutland and Mr Cecil your son I think be with you [before] this time, for they departed hence a good while ago.' On the 22nd, they actually arrived home, much to Cecil's relief, full of gratitude for all that Sir Ralph had done for them during their first experience of active service.

On this same day, the Queen wrote to Sir Ralph instructing him to wind up the affairs in the North and return home. He lost no time in hurrying thankfully back to Standon with Lord Sussex.

He had not been gone a moment too soon. The very next week she sent him another letter cancelling the first one and asking him to go on up to the Borders again since there was new trouble in Scotland. But Sir Ralph was already back home. In the quiet of his great house he made out fair copies of his accounts as Treasurer of the whole enterprise. Suppression of the rebellion had, he found, cost the Queen £22,750 8s 7d. His own expense account was a modest £79.

18

'Now lettest thou thy servant . . .'

EVEN IN HIS declining years Sir Ralph was given no respite. The Queen had asked him to stay on in the North, especially after the assassination of the Regent Moray. The 'Good Regent', as he came to be known, had been the chief instrument of Elizabeth's interests in Scotland, in opposition to Mary Queen of Scots' supporters. His murder in the narrow streets of Linlithgow in January 1570 was a serious blow to Protestantism and the whole Reformation in Scotland. The assassin had crouched behind garments and blankets hung over the balcony railings of the house of the Archbishop of St Andrews. He was James Hamilton, nephew of the Duke of Châtelherault.[1] The Duke lent him his best horse for a getaway: the Abbot of Arbroath lent him his gun for the fatal point-blank shot, which struck just below the navel.[2] Queen Mary was delighted at the success of his aim and granted James Hamilton of Bothwellhaugh a handsome pension for the rest of his life. She denied that she had engineered the murder, or had known anything about it beforehand.

Queen Elizabeth was mad with sorrow and wrath at the deed, shutting herself in her room and giving way to a storm of weeping. Most of Scotland was appalled and dismayed, and rounded on the family of Hamilton with savage execrations. With Moray dead, Queen Mary in prison, and the King no more than a child, the Hamiltons had hoped to get one of their number on the throne of Scotland.

The three thousand mourners who thronged St Giles' Cathedral in Edinburgh for his funeral would, it was said, sooner have torn them all limb from limb than suffer any one of them to mount the throne over the body of the murdered Regent.

Sir Ralph escaped being embroiled in the ensuing tumult by returning to Standon on receipt of the first instructions. 'I . . . prefer to live quietly at home,' he reminded Cecil, not for the first time.

But loyal men of action were at a premium in Elizabeth's Court. Sir Ralph was not allowed to vegetate at Standon. He had just been appointed Lord Lieutenant of his county of Hertfordshire, which at that time included Essex. A few days after his return home, he received the Queen's instructions to muster all the horsemen and other troops within his lieutenancy, and to make a register of them and their equipment, bringing it all up to a higher standard. 'And if you shall find the same difficult by reason of the largeness of the shire, or any other impediment,' then deputies were to be appointed. They were all to be 'seen, mustered and duly registered though in several places, yet in one day for avoiding of deceit and fraud'. It was, the Queen said, 'very necessary that our subjects should throughout our whole realm be otherwise furnished than it seemeth they lately were'. His appointment as 'our Lieutenant General of our County of Hertford' was no sinecure.

It soon appeared that the Queen's instructions were not prompted by any false alarm. Twenty-four hours after the Regent Moray had been mortally struck from his horse in Linlithgow, the Borders were aflame again. The Lairds of Ferniehurst, Buccleugh and other places round about flew to arms and surged over the Border with busy swords and flaming brands. This was the last appearance of the rebel Earl of Westmorland before his hasty departure to the continent, from which he never returned. He went gallantly along with his host of Ferniehurst. He would have needed more courage than the rest of the raider band, since if captured he would certainly have been taken at once to London and not kindly treated in the Tower.

Elizabeth's reaction came quickly. On 10th March 1570, Sir

Ralph was ordered to send up fifty foot-soldiers to York to join the Earl of Sussex, who was gathering together a retaliatory army. 'Twenty of them may serve with corselets and pikes, and the rest, being thirty,' – as the Queen added with impeccable arithmetic – 'as harquebuziers with sword, dagger and murryons.'[3] The 'murryon' was a sort of helmet. Knowing of the civil action which would be needed, the Queen had appointed a body of men mostly from the deep south of the country to ensure that no question of kin or relationship should sap the vigour of their arms.

The very next day Sir Ralph received yet another urgent letter from the Queen enclosing a bundle of circulars addressed to people throughout the county who were reckoned to be able to provide numbers of horsemen. They were all to go quickly up to York. Sir Ralph was to have them inspected to make sure they were serviceable. Any found wanting were to be returned for replacement. They were to be 'armed with an armour having a rest for a lance', if they were demi-lancers of the heavy brigade.

'For the light-horseman, the armour to be at least a corselet, and thereupon a light staff and a pistol. And the coats of either of the horsemen may be cloth and the colour blue.'[4] If some of the addresses on the circulars were wrong, or the people intended to receive them 'be dead or misnamed', the order was either to be returned to the Council Offices with a note of what was in error, or to be altered on the spot. 'And where the Christian names shall be wanting, we authorise you to supply it in the endorsement.'

All this kept Sir Ralph very busy. But the Earl of Sussex's force was eventually assembled, some four thousand strong. Going north over the much ravaged Border from Berwick in company with Lord Hunsdon, the English force wrought worse havoc than had ever been seen. This savagery was partly due to Elizabeth's fear at the sudden reversal of Protestant fortunes in Scotland as a result of the Regent Moray's death, and partly out of spite at the Border lairds having given sanctuary to the rebels of the insurrection.

Hardly a town, village, castle or keep escaped damage or

destruction. Ferniehurst itself, deserted when Sussex reached it, was reduced to rubble. Hume Castle, lair of the Earls of Home, was thought by the Scots to be impregnable. It was heavily garrisoned and filled with all manner of movable property brought in from the surrounding danger zones. Four hours' bombardment by siege guns brought it to the same condition as Ferniehurst.

The Border country, no man's land of the century, was counted out at last. 'Sussex and the Borders' became almost as grim an epithet as 'Cumberland and Culloden' two centuries later. But hardly a man on either side lost his life. The countryside was deserted, and no opposition was offered.

After this episode, Sir Ralph, together with Cecil and one or two others, was subjected to an extraordinarily scurrilous attack. From somewhere in Scotland, a stream of highly defamatory pamphlets and handbills was distributed all over the country.[5] Sir Ralph and the Queen's chief advisers were accused of subversion and charged with being the authors of most of the troubles of both England and Scotland. They were also charged with misleading and deceiving the Queen. But the libellous leaflets only made Elizabeth realise that the people thus denounced were those most valuable to her.

She turned her attention once more to the captive Mary Queen of Scots, still closely confined in Tutbury Castle.

Mary never ceased scheming to secure her release and the confounding of her enemies, chief among whom she placed her 'loving cousin' Queen Elizabeth. Mary never gave up hope of regaining her Scottish throne and of one day joining it to that of England.

Elizabeth had now been excommunicated by the Pope and was trying to placate the Catholic faction, whose strength she was beginning to fear again. Sir Ralph, who had often expressed himself opposed to extremes of religious persecution, was nevertheless obliged to take a hand in the exposing of Catholic plots against the Queen. Where these affected the future of the captive Mary, he was less reluctant. On 13th May 1571, he went with Sussex and Sir Walter Mildmay, Chancellor of the

Exchequer and an ardent Puritan, to interrogate the Bishop of Ross, currently swept up in one of Mary's intrigues.

When the Duke of Norfolk, released from the Tower but again embroiled in yet another Catholic plot (known as the Ridolfi Plot), was to be arrested for the second time, it was Sir Ralph who was woken up in the middle of the night at his London headquarters, Duchy House, Savoy, and ordered down to Howard Place by the Queen to arrest the thirty-five-year-old Duke.[6] For the next three days, Sir Ralph kept him under house arrest, staying at Howard Place himself during the day and returning to Duchy House each evening.

Four days after the midnight arrest, Sir Ralph received a warrant to take Norfolk to the Tower. He accompanied the Duke through the streets with Sir Thomas Smith, Cecil's successor as Secretary of State, their prisoner astride what was described as 'a footcloth nag', or humble pack horse.[7] This seemed a particularly pointless indignity for a man not yet proved guilty.

On 31st October, Sir Ralph made a more lengthy interrogation, as a result of which Norfolk was beheaded in June for treason after an all-day trial on 16th January 1572. Sir Ralph had also helped to interrogate the Duke when he had been imprisoned on the previous occasion; the experience therefore will have been no novelty to him. It will probably have been a relief since Sir Ralph had had to lodge at the Tower himself during the Duke's captivity.

Norfolk's trial brought further discomfort and distasteful duty to Sir Ralph, for the Earl of Shrewsbury had been appointed Lord High Steward of Norfolk's trial. Up to this time, the Earl had been the reluctant guardian of Mary Queen of Scots in his Manor house in the grounds of eight-acre Sheffield Castle, which also belonged to him. And it was Sir Ralph who had to go up and take over guardianship of the captive Queen. A more thankless and unpleasant task Sir Ralph could not imagine.

Mary herself was quite glad to see him. Shrewsbury had become exasperated with his prisoner. To make matters worse his wife, the notorious 'Bess of Hardwick', had charged him with having an affair with Mary. The atmosphere of Sheffield Castle and the Manor was not a very happy one under any conditions. But with the Shrewsburys, who were more host and hostess than gaolers, at bitter loggerheads, it was almost unbearable. Everyone – except Sir Ralph – was glad of a change, even a temporary one. Mary sent a special message of thanks to 'The Queen's Majesty for making so good a choice of a grave and ancient councillor, well known to her, to supply [Lord Shrewsbury's] place in the charge of her in his absence'.[8] Grave he may have been, but whether 'ancient' at sixty-five, is a matter of opinion. Queen Mary herself was then thirty, the Earl of Shrewsbury forty-four and his wife fifty-four. Elizabeth was an unmarried thirty-nine.

Shrewsbury managed to stay away for a month, after which he returned to Sheffield and Sir Ralph went home once more.

For the next twelve years, Sir Ralph observed the passage of events from the majestic shelter of Standon. He had grown old in the service of successive sovereigns, and his judgments and opinions on the happenings of the day were respected by Queen, Court and commoner alike. He was not reticent in the Council Chamber of Parliament. Mountainous notes for speeches on all manner of subjects survive in his still neat script.

Sir Ralph, knight banneret, he remained, while his close friend Cecil took the title of Lord Burghley. He saw the rebel Earl of Northumberland sold by the Scottish Regent of the day to Elizabeth for £2,000, and heard of his subsequent hanging at York.

From all the plots and schemes which darted through the corridors of state like quicksilver, he managed to remain aloof. Help and encouragement to the new Lord Burghley he gave whenever he could: Lord Burghley's unprecedented intelligence and spy service preserved Elizabeth and her throne from all assaults of her enemies.

The office of Clerk of the Hanaper was settled on Sir Ralph, and on his youngest son Henry in succession to him, by Burghley, for which Sir Ralph wrote a charming letter of thanks.[9] It was an old office which he had filled in the days of Henry VIII, and he was doubtless much gratified to come back to a post of such personal service to the Queen.

In 1578, Elizabeth gave him a New Year's present of gilt plate weighing 30¾ ounces.[10] The exchange of presents between the Queen and some of her favourite and most respected courtiers and friends was becoming the fashion. Sir Ralph gallantly returned the compliment: his present to her was rather dull by comparison. It was £15 in cash.

In July that year, Elizabeth stayed at Standon for three days on one of her Progresses through the country. The sumptuous scene at Standon was one of unparalleled grandeur. In the middle of her visit there, on the 24th, a meeting of the Privy Council was held, at which many of the greatest names in the land were present.[11]

Sir Ralph was the perfect host. His wife by this time had become imbued with some of the arts and graces of noble hospitality which Sir Ralph had once so notably professed she lacked.

From Standon the Queen and her glittering retinue went to Audley End in Essex, another great house, inhabited at the time by Pitcairn, the Scottish Ambassador, who was also Abbot of Dunfermline. Elizabeth could never allow the affairs of Scotland to be far from her mind with Mary Queen of Scots still locked up in Lord Shrewsbury's Sheffield Castle.

Young King James VI of Scotland, now twelve years old in 1578, had assumed the powers of government despite the whirlpools of Scottish politics. The Abbot had been sent down to Elizabeth in the hope of making some lasting and friendly alliance. With the Abbot had come a letter to Sir Ralph signed by the King, thanking him for all his good offices in furthering the cause of friendship between the two countries and earnestly asking him to do all he could to help the Abbot in his mission.

Although he had been out of active affairs for some time, Sir Ralph's reputation still stood high in Scotland as in England. The Scottish advisers thought it worth sending him a personal letter from the King.[12]

Nothing much transpired, however, and matters continued as before. In 1581, Elizabeth nearly married the last single son of Catherine de Medici, an unattractive heavily pock-marked youth of twenty, nicknamed Monsieur, in accordance with the French custom for the next youngest brother of the King. A vigorous speech by Sir Ralph helped prevent such an unsuitable marriage. If it had taken place and Elizabeth had predeceased Monsieur without issue, the throne of England would have passed to a Frenchman, an unthinkable state of affairs. Since Elizabeth was twice as old as her French fiancé, both eventualities might well have occurred.

By 1584, Mary Queen of Scots was once more the hub of a hundred Catholic plots. Spies clustered round Sheffield Castle and in the little town at its gates; couriers in disguise carrying coded messages scurried round the Courts of Europe. But Burghley, and Sir Francis Walsingham, now Secretary of State, employed a fine-mesh network of counter espionage through which they all failed to pass. With the collapse of each successive scheme, Mary must have realised that her chances of success were growing progressively fewer.

As a sovereign, her place was with her people and there can be no doubt she should have made every possible effort to escape. Being a lady of few scruples, it is surprising that she did not take the one opportunity of release offered to her by Elizabeth, even if it entailed making a promise which she would have had no intention of keeping. This promise was not to disturb the Reformation, nor seek to usurp Elizabeth herself. The explanation may well be that, after a year or two of captivity, she did not wish to be free. The country house confinement in England was at least security: the maelstrom of Scottish politics held endless possibilities of violence and death for her. The nonchalant way in which she urged each new band of schemers to risk their lives and unmentionable torture on her behalf accords with her cynical outlook. Her Turkey-carpeted suite in the mansion of an English nobleman, protected from assailants by a twenty-four-hour guard and waited upon by nearly fifty personal servants, may well have appeared preferable to the possibility of a draughty cell in the middle of windswept Loch Leven.

By the summer of 1584, matters had reached such a pitch between the Earl of Shrewsbury and his wife that the Earl had insisted on a court of Enquiry before Queen Elizabeth. 'Bess of Hardwick' had so defamed his character both publicly and in private that a regular investigation was the only way he could clear his name.

Sir Ralph was particularly exasperated by this family wrangle, for on 12th August 1584 he received a letter from Elizabeth which must have caused him many a sigh. He was to go again to Sheffield Castle and take over the duties of Queen Mary's gaoler. It was not a complete surprise, since in the previous March a commission had been issued to him and Sir Henry Neville to take over Mary from the Earl of Shrewsbury and remove her to Melbourne Castle in Derbyshire. This had been postponed until matters in Scotland had been clarified, so that Sir Ralph had been reprieved on that occasion.

He was nearly seventy-eight and had surely earned release from such dismal and arduous appointments. Elizabeth was aware of the imposition. 'You may be well assured,' she wrote, 'that in regard as well of your great years, we will for our part have also a care to ease you of that charge as soon as conveniently may be.'[14] The fact was that she had practically no one else she could trust to such an important duty. In Scotland the Catholic cause was in the ascendant again. This naturally gave encouragement to Catholics in England, which made it all the more essential, for Elizabeth's continued security and tenure of the throne, that Mary be kept under constraint. If by any chance she escaped or were rescued civil war might easily ravage Britain. Mary's guardian must therefore be a man of some military experience and of unassailable loyalty. Sir Ralph was the only man of authority who fulfilled these stringent requirements.

But he did not complain. Almost as active as ever, and certainly as quick-thinking as at any time in his long career, he spent the next few days in getting a party together to accompany him to Sheffield.

The Sheriffs of Leicestershire and Nottinghamshire were given orders to stand ready to provide him with any 'assistance and aid [that he might] at any time require'. He was still to have the services of Lord Shrewsbury's men at Sheffield, but he took with him fifty of his own personal servants armed with swords, daggers and pistols. By Tuesday, 18th August, he was ready. Leaving Standon, very regretfully, he reached Sheffield 'by such journeys as I was able to ride' on the following Tuesday. He was probably fairly stiff by the end of it, having travelled thirty miles a day, apart from Sunday, when he rested. His campaigning days, when he would have thought nothing of a week in the saddle, were long over. But he had always been an active man, and had kept his figure well.

Lord Shrewsbury was waiting at Sheffield to hand over to him. The arrangements were most elaborate. Well-armed guards were on duty : those off duty kept their weapons at their bedside. All doors and staircases were constantly watched. At the main gate, a Mr Wombwell was in charge, as 'gentleman porter'. Lord Shrewsbury had been making preparations to remove Mary to Wingfield Castle, yet another of his houses some fifteen miles from Sheffield. The Council had apparently thought that it would be safer to have Mary well away from any town such as Sheffield, where plotters and secret help might collect for a rescue attempt. Sir Ralph had not heard about this plan, and had had no instructions about it. He strongly disapproved.

Strategically, he thought it a mistake. 'In troth, sir,' he wrote at once to Walsingham, now principal Secretary of State in place of Cecil, 'I must tell you plainly that comparing the openness of the country about Wingfield to the straightness of this, and to the [inconvenience] which my lord also confesseth, I would rather take upon me to keep her here with sixty men, than there with three hundred. Besides that, as his Lordship saith, his provisions are much further and harder to be come by there than here.'[15] Sir Ralph did not relish the prospect of a winter on short commons.

In addition to this, the long journey from Standon had been rather much for him, and he had no wish to move off again without a good rest. 'In troth, I find not myself well able to travel again so soon, thanking God that I am so well come hither.'[16]

The additional dangers which might arise from her being in the town of Sheffield were discussed. Sir Ralph finally agreed to take her to Wingfield, out of such a disaffected part of the country which might well be harbouring many of her agents.

On 3rd September 1584, the cavalcade accordingly moved off to Wingfield, the Earl of Shrewsbury accompanying them to see the party settled safely in the new place. Mary's personal entourage consisted of her Secretary for French affairs, Monsieur Nau, who was also her doctor, her Secretary for Scottish affairs called Curle (both 'peevish, lewd and false fellows', according to Sir Ralph), a chaplain, a Master of the Household, 'fifteen servitors, three cooks, four boys, three gentlemen's men, six gentlewomen, two wives, ten wenches and children'.

Once ensconced at Wingfield, Mary reopened negotiations with Elizabeth for her release. Sir Ralph was strongly in favour.

He had now 'of mine own servants forty-three men, every man his sword and dagger, some pistolets and some long shot: and in every chamber where they lodge, all within this house, there is for every man his halberd or partuisans. And here are of my Lord's and mine and at my commandment, good horses and geldings standing in the stables within the base court of this castle, all to be ready upon a very short warning.' Gentleman porter was now a Mr Salter, since Mr Wombwell had been obliged to give up because of gout. Mary herself suffered severely from gout. Lord Shrewsbury wrote to Sir Ralph to say that he was laid up with rheumatism.

These negotiations had been opened and closed intermittently for several years by Elizabeth. It is doubtful whether she ever really meant to release Mary, whatever the outcome of the discussions. The discovery of a new plot or fresh spies was always the pretext upon which talks broke down. Sir Ralph by this time was urging Elizabeth to do something positive about Mary, to make some 'honourable composition' of the matter. 'The death of the lady, of which [I see] no probability, as she appeareth likely to live many years'[17] would, he thought, have been the most satisfactory outcome.

He sent many detailed and lengthy letters to Walsingham,

describing everything that was going on and what progress was being made by the spies on either side. These agents were often being trapped through the interception of their coded letters or by their suspicious behaviour. A Mr Bentall, for instance, by way of being another 'gentleman porter', was observed to go rather more frequently than seemed necessary into the rooms of the Queen's two secretaries, the 'lewd and peevish' Curle and Nau. His excuse, when this drew comment, was that he went 'to see to the safety of their windows and the walls of their chambers'.

Poor Sir Ralph hoped very much to be relieved of his wardenship. He was constantly reminding Walsingham of the Queen's promise to find a substitute, and frequently wrote to Elizabeth. She eventually bestirred herself as a result of an urgent appeal from Henry Sadleir, Sir Ralph's youngest son. 'I have acquainted the Queen,' wrote Walsingham, 'upon the report of Mr Henry Sadleir, with the coldness of the country and of the foulness thereof by situation, whereby you are debarred of your wonted exercise, which hath been the chief and principal preservation of your health, which in respect of the charge now committed unto you, cannot but shorten your days.'[18] A successor was finally chosen. This was Lord St John of Bletso. But Sir Ralph's relief was short-lived. Lord St John refused to accept the office of gaoler, producing so many excuses that by the time he had finally consented under the direst threats, Elizabeth had withdrawn her order to him. Being so unwilling, he would not have been reliable in case of trouble. Sir Ralph lingered on at inhospitable Wingfield.

He recommended yet another move to a place of even greater security. This was Tutbury Castle, a bleak and melancholy place indeed, in which Mary had once been lodged in 1568 before being hustled off to Coventry. Sir Ralph had suggested furnishing it with the confiscated property of Lord Paget, who had recently fled the country from his nearby home of Beaudesert after one of the abortive Catholic plots.

The Council thought this a good plan, although Tutbury was not to be ready before the next January, 1585. Mary thought it a very bad plan. Not only was she aware of Tutbury's almost legendary discomfort, which she had already briefly tasted, but during her fifteen years at Sheffield she had built up a useful chain of communication with the outside world. All this was now to be lost, and she was powerless to prevent the removal.

Sir Ralph was given a questionnaire in which to record all the details about Tutbury and about the domestic arrangements of Mary's household. He noted that she had no serviceable furniture or other 'stuff of her own, neither hangings, bedding, plate, napery, kitchen vessel, nor anything else'.[19] Everything had been borrowed from the Earl of Shrewsbury. Yet she did not go short of food. To Question Number 10, 'What is the Queen of Scots' ordinary diet, both fish days and flesh days?' Sir Ralph replied: 'About sixteen dishes at both courses, dressed after their own manner. Sometimes more or less, as the provision serveth.' Even the 'six gentlewomen, and the two wives and other maids and children have two messes of meat of nine dishes at both courses for the better sort, and five dishes for the meaner sort'. To Question Number 17, 'What proportion of wine is spent by the said Queen and her train yearly?' Sir Ralph filled in the answer: 'About ten ton a year.' Mary was evidently seldom short of a glass of wine.

By December Sir Ralph was well nigh desperate to get home. 'Most gracious Sovereign,' he wrote to Elizabeth, who had urged him to 'use old trust and new diligence' until his release, 'I assure your majesty . . . that I do find myself most unable to endure this life that I lead in this service, trusting that your majesty will the sooner release me of the same according to your most gracious promise, so that now in mine old days, for the short time that I have to live in this world, I may serve God and your majesty at mine own home, with such rest and quietness as mine old years do require. . . .'

The actual date of the move had been left to Sir Ralph's discretion. Mary was now suffering from a swollen arm and hand: Sir Ralph noted that she was 'not yet able to strain her left foot to the ground', being severely attacked by gout. This was 'to her very great grief. Not without tears [she] findeth that being

234

wasted and shrunk of natural measure and shorter than his fellow, [she feareth] that it will hardly return to his natural length without the benefit of a natural hot bath.' The springs of Bolton had been recommended as a cure.

Arrangements at Tutbury had gone on slowly. Sir Ralph had sent a man to mend the windows, but was worried about the beds: 'ten or twelve of these beds . . . are very mean and some lack bolsters, supposed to have been changed.' He concluded a letter to Secretary Walsingham: 'I will worry you with one other unpleasant thing, and not the least important to me. In this country, which yieldeth very little corn, I find none other litter for my horses than fern [bracken] which being spent as fast as they can cut, is brought in moist, which hath almost marred all my horses and geldings, none of them being free from the cough. They should not be so out of this place.' To a man who loved his horses as much as Sir Ralph, this shortage of proper dry bedding was a serious matter.

At last, on 13th January 1585, Sir Ralph was ready to set off for Tutbury, twenty-seven miles away, with his valuable prisoner. The Sheriffs of Derbyshire and Staffordshire had been commanded by the Council to give every help and to accompany the party themselves if required. Sir Ralph had had all the roads regularly patrolled for miles around to prevent any incidents, and he gave 'straight order to the bailiffs and others of Derby', through which they were to pass, 'to provide that there be no assembly of gazing people in the streets, and for all quietness as much as may be done'.

It was his last semi-military operation, but he organised it as efficiently as if it had been his first. On the morning of the departure he wrote to Lord Burghley, who, although away from the Council through 'your old illness', had been doing all he could to speed up arrangements for Sir Ralph's release. 'This day we remove this Queen to Derby, and tomorrow to Tutbury, the ways being so foul and deep, and she so lame, though in good health of body, that we cannot go through on a day, myself also being more unable than she is to travel, for that I have not been well this month and more, nor yet shall, I fear, recover so long as I remain upon this charge, whereof I long to be delivered when it shall please God and her Majesty.'

The removal was achieved without undue incident, Mary being lodged overnight in Derby. Queen Elizabeth complained that it was a rash move even to pass through Derby, much less stay the night there. Sir Ralph replied that the only convenient route lay through the town, 'there being no other possible way for a coach but by the common way, and scant that at that time of the year by reason of hills rocks and woods. And I myself,' he went on, 'making a trial of two or three miles, finding it true, caused bridges to be made to avoid many evil passages.' Mary travelled in a lumbering coach, her sore foot on a pillow. Sir Ralph and Mr Somers rode on either side, and the whole company of about a hundred and fifty on all sides.

There was no convenient country house at which to stay on the way, and the home of 'an ancient widow, named Mrs Beaumont', had been selected in the town.[20] On arrival there, Mary 'so soon as she knew who was her hostess, after she had made a beck to the rest of the women standing next to the door, she went to her and kissed her, and none other, saying that she was come thither to trouble her, and that she was also a widow and therefore trusted that they should agree well enough together, having no husbands to trouble them'.

As a result of this little incident, it was reported to the Earl of Leicester, Queen Elizabeth's former favourite who lived nearby, that Sir Ralph had allowed her 'to salute and kiss a multitude of the townswomen'. Always ready to make trouble, Leicester wrote off at once to the Queen, who naturally asked for an explanation. Sir Ralph indignantly told the whole story to Burghley, and no more was heard of it.

On the way to Derby, Sir Ralph noted that 'Lord Stafford passed speedily through this town with three or four in his company, himself plainly apparelled, and stayed at a village two miles hence called Hilton, in an ale house, whilst this Queen went past, where some of my folk espied him in a window. . . . So soon as we were all a good way past, he rode to Burton that night, as one of the village brought me word, but I knew not where he became after.' He was evidently up to some mischief, but nothing seems to have occurred.

Having arrived uneventfully at Tutbury, Sir Ralph set about putting the house furnishings in order, sending for 'three or four hundredweight of good sweet feathers, none good hereabouts to be bought, good down and fustian for four or five pillows . . . coverlets and blankets we can find hereabouts. . . .'

He wrote to all the Justices of the Peace and neighbours of the district, within ten miles of Tutbury, 'to be themselves and their servants in readiness with their horses upon all occasions, if need shall be'.

He learnt with disappointment of Lord St John's defection, but looked forward – with undue optimism, as it transpired – to the speedy arrival of his substitute Sir Amyas Paulet, who had been Ambassador in France and was now a Privy Councillor. Paulet, who was an unsympathetic warder, was later described by Elizabeth as a 'precise and dainty fellow'. Tutbury was, as Sir Ralph wrote to Burghley, 'parcel of the duchy', in other words lying within the Duchy of Lancaster, of which Sir Ralph was still Chancellor. 'It being therefore within my charge, the woods and game within the forest chase and parks there being greatly wasted and destroyed, I can be well contented for the better service of her Majesty to spend so much time there to put things in better order for the preservation of the said woods and game as much as in me is.' His time was not therefore entirely wasted looking after Mary at Tutbury.

But the beginning of March found him still at Tutbury, where, some busybody informed the Queen, he was allowing Mary more and more freedom from her castle prison, going on hawking expeditions five or six miles away, it was alleged. He was highly indignant at the suggestion he was taking undue risks.

'The truth is,' he wrote to Walsingham, 'that when I came hither, finding this country commodious and meet for the sport I have always delighted in, I sent home for my hawks and falconers wherewith to pass this miserable life I lead here . . . , whereof this Queen hearing, earnestly intreated me that she might go abroad with me to see my hawks fly, a pastime indeed which she hath singular delight in. . . .' She had therefore accompanied him three or four times, 'sometimes a mile, sometimes two miles, but not past three miles, hawking upon the rivers'. She had been well guarded throughout these sporting interludes. Sir Ralph was the outstanding falconry figure of the day and was Grand Falconer to the Queen.

Sir Ralph was near breaking point at still not being relieved from his duty. He was also irked by unwarranted criticism. 'I would to God some other had the charge,' he exploded, 'for I assure you I am so weary of it that if it were not more for that I would do nothing that should offend her Majesty than for fear of any punishment, I would come home, and yield myself to be a prisoner in the Tower all the days of my life, rather than I would attend any longer upon this charge.' With mounting annoyance he went on: 'And if I had known, when I came from home, I should have tarried here so long, contrary unto all promises made unto me, I would have refused, as others do' — this was a reference to Lord St John — 'and have yielded to any punishment, rather than I would have accepted.' The end of the letter is pathetic indeed. 'A greater punishment can not be ministered unto me than to force me to remain here in this sort, being more meet now in mine old and latter days to rest at home to prepare myself to leave and go out of the miseries and afflictions whereunto we are subject in this life. . . . And if [death] were to light on me tomorrow I would think myself most happy, for I assure you I am weary of this life. . . .'

At very long last, on 17th April 1585, the letter of release arrived at Tutbury.

Sir Ralph handed over to stern Sir Amyas Paulet, gathered up his retinue of soldiers, servants, hounds, hawks and falconers, and made his way back to Standon. He was nearly finished with Mary Queen of Scots.

The next year, 1586, she was again removed, this time twelve miles off to Chartley, home of Lord Essex. Scheming as busily as ever, she fell unsuspectingly into one of Walsingham's diabolical traps, dragging many accomplices with her. On the discovery of this, known as the Babington Plot, she was taken to Tixall, nine miles from Chartley. This belonged to Sir Walter Aston. Sir Walter's eldest son, later Lord Aston, married Sir Ralph's grand-daughter Gertrude, child of his eldest son Thomas. Sir Walter's youngest son Edward married another grand-daughter, Anne, child of Sir Ralph's second son Edward.

On 11th October 1586, Sir Ralph was a member of the Commission appointed to try Mary for conspiracy against Elizabeth. Since the end of September she had reached her last lodgings on earth, massive Fotheringay Castle in Northamptonshire. On the morning of 8th February, her grizzled wigless head was held aloft by the axeman.

Sir Ralph did not attend the execution. He would have derived no satisfaction from either pronouncement or carrying out of sentence. He had no wish to see her put to death. Even the trying time when he was her gaoler did not mar his gentle friendship which Queen Mary acknowledged to the end. He must have thought, when he heard the news of her death, of that long ago March morning in Linlithgow, 'as goodly a child as I have seen . . . and as like to live. . . .'

Humanity, kindness and compassion were no strangers to Sir Ralph. In his treatment of the captive Queen, who embodied most of the things against which his life's work had been ranged, he set a noble example of a Christian servant of the State.

For his race, too, was nearly run. As the shortening shadows of an early spring morning played through the lofty windows and polished corridors of Standon, Sir Ralph's life slipped quietly and peacefully away. It was 31st March 1587, not two months after the tragic scene at Fotheringay.

Close by in Standon church his family raised a noble tomb, worthy of his memory. Beside his alabaster effigy kneel in solemn procession Thomas, Edward and Henry, his sons, and Anne, Mary, Jane and Dorothy, his daughters. But of his faithful wife no trace.

Resting against the monument is the great iron-bound standard pole brought back in triumph from the Battle of Pinkie, forty years earlier, the engagement at which he received the chivalrous honour of knight banneret. On the wall itself are fastened his gauntlets of steel and his well-worn spurs. High on a plinth above stands his scarred and pitted helmet. For all the splendour of his tomb, the man himself was a gentle warrior, a worthy friend and a loyal servant to his sovereign.

Notes

CHAPTER 1

1. British Museum: Titus, B1, No 48, p 143.
2. R C Hoare, *Hist of Modern Wiltshire*, Everley, 1826.
3. Sander, *The Anglican Schism 1585*, ed Lewis, p 176.
4. British Museum: Titus, B, p 343.
5. Harleian MSS, 7089, f 453.
6. British Museum: Titus, B, p 343.
7. Hall, p 818.
8. Lindsay, *Hist of Scotland, 1565* (1728 edn), p 159.
9. Contemporary portrait attributed to Marc Geerarts; in private possession.
10. *Sadler State Papers*, pub Clifford, 1809.
11. *State Papers* (Henry VIII), Vol I, pp 526–9.
12. British Museum: Cott MSS, Caligula, B K: 11, p 344.

CHAPTER 2

1. *State Papers*, Vol V, p 103.
2. Ibid, p 63.
3. Ibid, p 70.
4. Ibid, Vol VII, p 669.
5. Lindsay, p 159.
6. Pinkerton, Penman's letter, 1797 edn.
7. *State Papers*, Vol V, pp 63–74.
8. British Museum: Caligula, B1, f 52.
9. Pinkerton, Vol II, p 374.
10. British Museum: Caligula, B1, f 52.
11. Harpisfield MS, Book III, p 7.
12. Reynaldi, *Annal. Eccles*, 1536, n 26.
13. *State Papers*, Vol I, p 573.

CHAPTER 3

1. *State Papers*, Vol I, p 77.
2. Ibid, Vol 5, p 174.
3. British Museum: Caligula, B1, f 52.
4. *Sadler State Papers*, Vol I, p 13.
5. Ibid, p 21.
6. Ibid, p 46.
7. Ibid.

8. Ibid, p 47.
9. Ibid, p 48 et seq.
10. Ibid, p 22.
11. Moncreiffe, *Falkland Palace*, p 18.
12. Pinkerton, p 434.
13. Portrait attributed to Marc Geerarts.
14. *Sadler State Papers*, Vol I, p 23 et seq.
15. Ibid, p 27.
16. Ibid, p 28.
17. Lindsay, Folio edn, p 237.
18. *Sadler State Papers*, Vol I, p 31.
19. Ibid, p 38.
20. Ibid, p 39.
21. Ibid, p 40.
22. Balfour MSS, Adv Lib Coll, No XIV.
23. *Sadler State Papers*, Vol I, p 41.
24. Ibid, p 42.

CHAPTER 4

1. *State Trials*, Vol I.
2. House of Commons Library.
3. Petyt MSS, Inner Temple Library. *Politics and Profit*, p 54.
4. Richard Hilles to Bullingen. London 1541. Letter No 105.
5. Hall.
6. College of Arms. Oxford Grants. MS, Vol I, f 68, also MS f 12, 294 b and R 21, 31.
7. Lindsay (1728 edn), p 170.
8. Leslie, Book IX, p 258.
9. Lindsay, p 176.
10. *Sadler State Papers*, Vol I, p 138. Arran's information to Sadleir.

CHAPTER 5

1. Lindsay, p 179.
2. Holinshed, *Chronicles*.
3. Lindsay, p 180.
4. *State Papers*, Vol V, p 244.
5. Ibid.
6. *Sadler State Papers*, Vol I, p 66.
7. Ibid, p 67.
8. Ibid.
9. Ibid, p 69.
10. Ibid.
11. Ibid, p 70.
12. Ibid, p 72.
13. Ibid, p 75.
14. Ibid, p 76

15. Ibid, p 78.
16. Ibid, p 86.
17. Ibid, p 87.
18. Ibid, p 90.
19. Ibid, p 91.
20. Ibid, p 72.
21. Ibid, p 93.
22. Ibid, p 76.
23. Ibid, p 96.
24. *Dictionary of National Biography*, Vol XXII, p 178.

CHAPTER 6

1. Chauncy, Vol I, p 427.
2. *Sadler State Papers*, Vol I, p 104.
3. Ibid, p 105.
4. Ibid, p 108.
5. Ibid.
6. Ibid, p 110.
7. Ibid, p 111.
8. Ibid.

CHAPTER 7

1. *Sadler State Papers*, Vol I, p 113.
2. Ibid, p 119.
3. *Dictionary of National Biography*, Vol XXIV, p 173.
4. *Sadler State Papers*, Vol I, p 134.
5. Ibid.
6. Ibid, p 135.

CHAPTER 8

1. Sander, Vol I, p 54.
2. *Sadler State Papers*, Vol I, p 168.
3. Ibid, p 232.
4. Chauncy, Vol I, p 527.
5. *Sadler State Papers*, Vol I, p 230.
6. Ibid, p 193.
7. Ibid, p 237.
8. Ibid, p 270.
9. Ibid, p 289.
10. Ibid, p 355.

CHAPTER 9

1. *Sadler State Papers*, Vol I, p 308.
2. Ibid, p 311.

3. Leslie, Book X, p 270. Scottish Text Society: Edinburgh.
4. *Sadler State Papers*, Vol I, p 314.
5. Lindsay, p 182.
6. Records of the Musée de la Marine, Chantilly.
7. *Sadler State Papers*, Vol I, p 321.
8. Ibid, p 324.
9. Leslie, Book X, p 276.
10. Ibid, p 277.
11. *Sadler State Papers*, Vol I, p 327.
12. Ibid, p 332.
13. Ibid, p 335.
14. Ibid, p 333.
15. Ibid, p 337.
16. Ibid, p 338.
17. Ibid, p 345.
18. Ibid, p 345.
19. Ibid, p 349.

CHAPTER 10

1. Buchanan, Book 15, p 82.
2. Lindsay, Chap V, p 24.
3. *State Papers*, Vol V, p 361 et seq.
4. 'Fitted Accompt of the expenses of Somerset's expedition', 1 mo Ed VI, in *Sadler State Papers*, Vol I, p 355.
5. From 'The late Expedition to Scotlande, sent to Lorde Russell by a friend of hys', 1544: *Dalyell's Fragments*, p 111.
6. Ibid.
7. Leslie, Book X, p 279. Knox.
8. Ibid.
9. Ibid.
10. Holinshed, Vol III, p 837.
11. Dalyell, p 9.
12. Ibid.
13. Chauncy's *Hertfordshire*, Vol I, p 427.

CHAPTER 11

1. *Irish Landed Gentry*, 1904 edn: Sadleir.
2. Rymer, *Diary of the Expedition to Boulogne*, Vol VI, Part 3.
3. Du Bellay, *Memoirs*, and *State Papers*, Vol X, p 289.
4. *State Papers*, Vol V, pp 415–18.
5. Buchanan, p 88.
6. Lindsay, p 185.
7. *State Papers*, Vol X, p 354.
8. Ibid, p 186.
9. 17th April 1545. Shrewsbury and Tunstall to the King.
10. Haines, Vol I, p 51.

11. Froude, Vol IV, Chap 22, p 420.
12. Du Bellay, *Memoirs*.
13. *State Papers*, Vol I, p 816.
14. 12th July 1545. *State Papers*, Vol V, p 470.
15. *State Papers*, Vol V, p 450.
16. *Sadler State Papers*, 13th September 1545.
17. *State Papers*, Vol V, p 467.
18. Buchanan, p 91; Lindsay, p 187.
19. Ibid.
20. Leslie, Book X, p 289.
21. Lindsay, p 187.
22. Ibid.
23. Chauncy, Vol I, p 427.
24. Calderwood, *History of the Church of Scotland*, Vol I. Also Knox, *History of the Reformation*, Vol I, p 117. Also Lindsay, Chap XI, p 53.
25. Buchanan, p 91.
26. Lindsay, p 190.
27. Buchanan, p 96.
28. Lindsay, p 190.
29. Buchanan, p 97.
30. Ibid, p 98.
31. Lindsay, p 191.
32. Ibid, Chap XIV, p 86.
33. 'Prevarication of the Holy Churche's liberties', Chap IV, s 31: Eyston MS.
34. Harpisfield, Book II, p 142.

CHAPTER 12

1. Patten's 'Expedition into Scotlande': Dalyell, p 25.
2. Ibid, et seq.
3. Ibid.
4. Ibid.
5. Ibid, p 34.
6. Ibid, p 40.
7. Ibid, p 42.
8. Ibid, p 41.
9. Ibid, p 43.
10. Ibid, p 46.
11. Lindsay, Chap XXV, p 94.
12. Ibid, p 49.
13. Ibid, p 50.
14. Ibid, p 54.
15. Ibid, p 59.
16. Ibid, p 65.
17. Ibid, p 68.
18. Ibid, p 70.

19. Ibid, p 80.
20. *Sadler State Papers*, Vol I, p 363.

CHAPTER 13

1. Froude, Vol V, Chap 25, p 1077 (note).
2. Corbett's *State Trials*, Vol I, p 554.
3. Stowe's *Annals*; *Survey of London*; *Chronicle of the Grey Friars*.
4. Haynes's *Burghleigh Papers*, Vol I.
5. *Latimer's Sermons*, p 162.
6. Becon's *Jewel of Joy*.
7. *State Papers*; Mary Dom MS.
8. Burcher to Bullinger. Letter No 306.
9. Holinshed. Eyewitness account by Hooker of Exeter.
10. Harleian MSS No 660.
11. Cotton MS, Vespasian, f 3.
12. Froude, Vol V, Chap 26, p 207.
13. Ibid, p 221.
14. Holinshed.
15. Tytler, Vol I, p 210.
16. Harleian MSS No 660.
17. Hayward, *Life of Edward VI*.
18. Ibid.
19. Machyn's *Diary*, p. 35.
20. *Sadler State Papers*, Vol I, p 368.
21. Strype's *Ecclesiastical Memorials*, Vol VI.
22. Godly letter addressed to Bonner: Foxe, Vol VII, p 511.
23. Pole to Miranda, 6th October, *Edist Reg Pol*, Vol V.
24. Noailles, Vol IV, p 342.

CHAPTER 14

1. Froude, Vol VII, Chap 11, p 123.
2. *Sadler State Papers*, Vol I, p 410.
3. Ibid, Vol 2, p 21.
4. Ibid, Vol 1, p 437.
5. Teulet, Vol I, p 341.
6. *Sadler State Papers*, Vol 1, p 437.
7. Ibid, Vol 1, p 399.
8. Teulet, Vol 1, p 357.
9. *Sadler State Papers*, Vol 1, p 430.
10. Froude, Vol VII, Chap 11, p 155.
11. Cotton MS, Caligula, B10.
12. Froude, Vol VII, Chap 11, p 155.
13. *Sadler State Papers*, Vol 1, p 570.
14. Ibid, p 444.
15. Ibid, p 537.
16. Ibid, p 444.

17. Lindsay, Book 2, Chap XXI, p 163.
18. Knox, *History of the Church of Scotland*.
19. Ibid.
20. *Sadler State Papers*, Book I, p 592.
21. *State Papers*, Vol 11, p 24.
22. Ibid, p 590.
23. Strype, *Annals of the Reformation*, Vol I, Chap XV, para 195.
24. Ibid.

CHAPTER 15

1. Haines, *Burghleigh Papers*, Vol I.
2. *Sadler State Papers*, Vol I, p 715.
3. Ibid, p 710.
4. Ibid, p 724.
5. Froude, Chap III, p 227 et seq.
6. Buchanan, p 145.
7. Forbes, Vol I, 13th May 1560.
8. Intercepted letter from Queen Regent to d'Oysel.
9. MS Randolph to Killigrew, 20th June 1560.
10. Froude, Vol VII, Chap III, p 240.
11. MS Randolph to Killigrew, 22nd June 1560.

CHAPTER 16

1. Froude, Vol IX, Chap 4, p 361.
2. Buchanan, p 153.
3. Ibid, p 160.
4. Froude, Vol VII, Chap 5, p 406.
5. Lindsay, p 219.
6. Balfour MSS No XIV.
7. Buchanan, p 215.
8. Ibid, p 210.
9. Ibid.
10. Scottish MSS Dept 18th July 1567.

CHAPTER 17

1. Buchanan, p 218.
2. *Sadler State Papers*, Vol II, p 564.
3. Ibid, 29th August 1568.
4. Ibid, Vol II, Chap 33, p 34.
5. Ibid, p 39.
6. Ibid, p 40.
7. Ibid.
8. Ibid, p 42.
9. Ibid, p 44.
10. Ibid, p 57.

11. Ibid, p 46.
12. Border MS, 26th November 1569.
13. Cotton MS, Caligula, B IX, f 488.
14. *Sadler State Papers*, Vol II, p 57.
15. Ibid, p 62.
16. Ibid, p 65.
17. Ibid, p 111.
18. Ibid, p 118.
19. Ibid, p 120.
20. Ibid, p 122.
21. Ibid, p 122.
22. Ibid, p 126.

CHAPTER 18

1. Buchanan, p 246.
2. Labanoff, Vol III, p 341.
3. *Sadler State Papers*, Vol II, p 153.
4. Ibid, p 154.
5. Nares.
6. Sadleir to Cecil: Murdin's *Burghley State Papers*.
7. Ibid.
8. *Sadler State Papers*, Vol II, p 344.
9. British Museum: Lansdown MSS, II, Jan. 7203.
10. Nichol's *Progresses of Queen Elizabeth*.
11. *Register of the Proceedings and Ordinances of the Privy Council*, MS, Privy Council Office.
12. *Sadler State Papers*, Vol II, p 343.
13. Ibid, p 380.
14. Ibid, p 381.
15. Ibid, p 382.
16. Ibid.
17. Ibid.
18. Ibid.
19. Ibid.
20. Ibid, p 505.

Bibliography

The following are some of the sources, published and unpublished, to which reference has been made. It is not by any means a complete list of works dealing with or touching upon the period, which would run into several scores. The credibility of many of these is dubious. Some are downright misleading, even deliberately falsified.

Becon's *Jewel of Joy*.

Berry, William, of the College of Arms. *Hampshire Genealogies* (95). 1833. *Hertfordshire Genealogies* (9). 1843.

Brewer, John Sherren. *The Reign of Henry VIII till the death of Wolsey*. Edited J Gairdner. 1884.

Brown, Professor Hume. *History of Scotland to the accession of Mary Stuart*.

Browne, Robert Gore. *Lord Bothwell*. Collins. 1937.

Buchanan, George. *History of Scotland*. 4th edition. 1751–2.

Burghley State Papers. *A collection of State Papers 1542–1570 from letters and manuscripts left by William Cecil, Lord Burghley, at Hatfield*. Samuel Haynes. 1740.

Burlington Magazine. Vol 83, p 110.

Burton, John Hill. *History of Scotland from Agricola's Invasion to 1688*. 1867–70.

Calendar of State Papers. Calendar of Letters and Papers, foreign and domestic of the Reign of Henry VIII, 1509–47. 1862 etc.
Calendar of Letters and Papers, foreign series of the Reign of Edward VI, 1547–1553. 1861.
Calendar of Letters and Papers, foreign and domestic of the Reign of Elizabeth I, 1558–1603. 1863 etc.

Calendar of State Papers relating to Scotland and Mary Queen of Scots, 1547–1603, in the Public Record Office, British Museum, and elsewhere in England. Scottish Record Office Publication. 1898.

Calthorpe, Charles (1635). *Manorial Society Publication No 10*. 1917.

Camden's *Britannia*. London. 1594.

Chalmer's *Biographical Dictionary*. 1812.

Chalmer's *Life of Mary Queen of Scots*. 2nd edition. 1822.

Chauncy, Sir Henry. *Historical Antiquities of Hertfordshire*. 1826.

Clutterbuck, Robert. *History and Antiquities of the County of Hertford*. 1815.

D'Ewes, Sir Symonds. *Journals of all Parliaments during the reign of Queen Elizabeth*. 1682.

Dickens, A G *Thomas Cromwell and the English Reformation*. English University Press. 1959.

Dictionary of National Biography.

Donaldson, G. *The Scottish Reformation.* 1960.
Dugdale, Sir William. *Antiquities of Warwickshire.* 1656.
Dunn, Lewys. *Heraldic Visitations.* Welsh MSS. Soc 3. Llandovery. 1846.

Edward VI. *Journal of his reign.* Clarendon Hist Soc Reprinted 1884.
Elton, G R. *England under the Tudors.* (History of England, edited by Sir
    C Oman, VH) 1963.
    Henry VIII, an Essay in Revision. Historical Association Publication.
    1962.
    Thomas Cromwell's Decline and Fall. 1951.

Froude, J A. *History of England from Fall of Wolsey to death of Elizabeth.*
    1862.
Fuller Worthies' Library. 1870.

Gentleman's Magazine. 1782. 1835. i. 260.
Godscroft's *History and Collections.*

Hall, Edward, of Gray's Inn. *Chronicle, Henry IV to Henry VIII.* 1809.
Harleian Society Publications. xii 339, xii 481.
Harting, J E. *Bibliotheca Accipitraria.* Bernard Quaritch. 1891.
Haynes, Samuel. *Burghley State Papers.* cf. p. 381.
Hayward, J. *Life of Edward VI.* (Complete History of England, Vol 2.
    1706.)
Hoare, Sir Richard Colt, Bt. *History of Modern Wiltshire.* II. ii. 198. 1822.
Holinshed, Raphael. *Chronicles of England, Scotland and Ireland.* 1577.

Keith, Robert, Bishop of the Scottish Episcopal Church in Fife. *History
    of the affairs of Church and State in Scotland from the beginning of the
    Reformation to 1561.* (Spottiswoode Society. 1844–50.)
Knox, John. *Works.* Edited by D Laing. (Wodrow Society. 1846–64.)

La Mothe-Fenelon. *Correspondence diplomatique, and supplement.* 1838 and
    1868.
    And *Nouvelle Collection des Memoirs.* 1850.
Lang, Andrew. *History of Scotland from the Roman Occupation.* 1900–2.
Lansdowne MSS. British Museum.
Leslie, John, Bishop of Ross. (1527–96). *History of Scotland from the death
    of James I, 1436–1561.* Translated by Dalrymple. 1888–95. Scottish
    Text Society Publication.
Lindsay, Robert, of Pitscottie. *History and Chronicles of Scotland.* Edited by
    J G Mackay. (Scottish Text Society. 1899–1911.)
Lloyd, David. *State Worthies: Statesmen and Favourites of England.* 1st edit-
    ion 1665.

Lodge, Edmund. *Illustrations of British History, Biology, Manners, Henry VIII–James I in papers from the manuscripts of the families of Howard, Talbot, Cecil, containing great part of the correspondence of Elizabeth and her ministers with George, 6th Earl of Shrewsbury during the years in which Mary Queen of Scots remained in his custody with notes etc.* 2nd edition. 1838.

Malet's *Collections of Historical Manuscripts.*
Mattingley, Garrett. *Renaissance Diplomacy.* Jonathan Cape. 1955.
  Catherine of Aragon. Jonathan Cape. 1942.
Merriman, Roger Bigelow. *Rise of the Spanish Empire.* New York. 1934.

Nares, Edward. *Memoirs of Lord Burghley.* 1828–31.
Nichols, John, FSA. *Progresses and Public Processions of Queen Elizabeth with historical notes etc.* New edition. 1823.
Nicholson, Norman. *History of Cumberland and Westmorland.* County Books. 1949.

Patten, William, Judge of the Marshalsea. *The Scottish Expedition into Scotland of Prince Edward Duke of Somerset.* 1548. An English Garner (6). Tudor Tracts 1532–1588. Editions of 1903.
Philipps, Sir T. *Visitatio Comitatus Wiltoniae.* 1623.
Pinkerton, John. *History of Scotland from the accession of the House of Stewart to that of Mary.* 1797.
Pollard, A F. *Henry VIII.* Longmans. 1940.

Royal Commission on Historical Manuscripts Publication. 1876.

Sadleir, Thomas Ulick. *Brief Memoir.*
Salmond, N. *History of Hertfordshire.* 1728.
Sanders, Dr Nicholas. *De Origine et Progressu Schismatis Angliae.* Coloniae Agrippinae. 1585.
Slavin, A J. *Politics and Profit.* Cambridge University Press. 1966.
Sloane, Sir Hans. *Sloane Manuscripts.* Folio 25. British Museum.
Spottiswoode, Archbishop J. *History of the Church of Scotland.* Spottiswoode Society. 1847–51
State Papers and Letters of Sir Ralph Sadleir. Edited by A Clifford with historical notes by Sir Walter Scott. Edinburgh. 1809.
State Trials. *Cobbett's Complete Collection of State Trials.* 1101–1713.
Statutes of the Kingdom. *The Statutes of the Realm.* Record Commission Publication. 1810–22.
Stoney, Major F S. A Memoir. 1877.
Stow, John. *The Chronicles of England from Brute unto this present yeare of Christ,* 1580. (R Newberie at the assignment of H Bynneman. 1580.)
Strype, John. *Annals of the Reformation.* 1824.

Teulet, J B Alex T. *Papiers d'Etat, pièces et documents inedits relatifs à l'histoire d'Ecosse au 16ème siècle.* (Bannatyne Club. 1851.)

Wagner, A R. *Heralds and Heraldry in the Middle Ages.* Oxford. 1956.
Wetherall, Rose. *Standon Church and Monuments.* Pamphlet. Ware. 1900.
Whiteley, Elizabeth. *Plain Mr Knox.* Skeffington. 1960.

Index